I CAN!

I LOVE YOU MORE

CLUB FAME: MEMBERS ONLY

TINKERING W/ THE TIP

FLASH IN THE PANTS

BIG NOSE STAMOS

GOLDEN HANDCUFFS

NEET GIRLS

YOUR BABY'S A PIG

THE ODD COUPLE OF MENTORS

LIFE IS A CABERNET

IF YOU WOULD HAVE TOLD ME

IF YOU WOULD HAVE TOLD ME

A MEMOIR

John Stamos

WITH

DAPHNE YOUNG

HENRY HOLT AND COMPANY

NEW YORK

Henry Holt and Company
Publishers since 1866
120 Broadway
New York, New York 10271
www.henryholt.com

Henry Holt® and 🅷® are registered trademarks of Macmillan Publishing
Group, LLC.

All images are courtesy of John Stamos with the exceptions of these photographs:
Second insert: Page 2, The Beach Boys singing "Kokomo," ABC Photo
Archives / Disney General Entertainment Content via Getty Images; Page 4,
production photos from *How to Succeed* . . . and *Cabaret*, Joan Marcus;
Page 4, Don Rickles with *Bye Bye Birdie* poster, Bruce Glikas; Page 5,
ER still with Linda Cardellini, NBC / NBCUniversal via Getty Images;
Page 7, wedding photographs, Marlies Hartmann.

Library of Congress Control Number: 2023936312

ISBN: 9781250890979

Our books may be purchased in bulk for promotional, educational, or
business use. Please contact your local bookseller or the Macmillan Corporate
and Premium Sales Department at (800) 221-7945, extension 5442, or by
e-mail at MacmillanSpecialMarkets@macmillan.com.

First Edition 2023

Hummingbird art and handwritten titles by John Stamos

Designed by Meryl Sussman Levavi

Printed in the United States of America

1   3   5   7   9   10   8   6   4   2

CONTENTS

Foreword by my friend Jamie Lee Curtis

Before we even met, I knew that if there was ever an actor to play my father, Tony Curtis, in a movie, it would be John Stamos. They have the same comic energy, captivating flair, sharp humor, keen intelligence, childlike passion, and dare I say, deep sadness behind the mask of a ridiculously handsome man. We had known each other in passing and once went to Vegas with others to see Don Rickles perform, but the contact was all pretty surface and performative. I first got to know John—I mean really know him as a person—during our season on the Ryan Murphy TV show *Scream Queens*, and I watched the ease and smoothness of his skill as an actor and his well-honed comedy chops, and off set, we started to peel back the onion of our lives, dreams, and families. At that point, John was newly sober and in a relationship with Caitlin but was not yet engaged, and yes, after she came by for lunch and she and I jointly quoted from the Disney film *Lilo & Stitch*, "Ohana means family and family means no one gets left behind or forgotten," I might have suggested to John that he put a ring on it and seal the deal. Before that I had seen him at a business party in

New York, when he wasn't sober, and looked into his gorgeous eyes, and tried to communicate with mine that there was another way for him. I'm so pleased that he found that path and himself on it and is sharing both with you in this beautiful book.

He pulls the covers on the first page, which is *exactly* who he is. He doesn't play mind games. He doesn't obfuscate. He'll try to charm the heck out of you, that's for sure, and he will succeed, *every time*, but he will also touch you with his deep goodness, born from his exquisite relationship with his mother and his father. It's what we *all* know about him. John is a *good* man, and we're lucky that this good man is a *human*, and therefore filled with love and mercy, pun intended, music and adventures, as well as the contradictions, conflicts, and stumbles that we can all relate to. Despite his exhilarating successes, he still brings such joy to any performance onstage or on-screen.

I immediately texted John when I heard about the passing of his best friend, Bob Saget. John showed great grace not only when wrestling with his grief but also in his continuing commitment to bring Bob's legacy of virtue into everything John Stamos does forevermore. This, again, is a testament to who he is and how he was raised. A good, funny, smart, loving man. He is that way with *everyone*, and especially with Caitlin and his son, Billy.

John Stamos bangs his drums, fueled by his own internal heartbeat of kindness and his desire to simply bring joy and peace to the world.

You really don't need to hear anything else from me, except that I love him, and I respect him, and I need him.

We *all* do.

—Jamie Lee Curtis

NOTE FROM THE AUTHOR

If you would have told me one day I'd be writing my memoir, I would've told you that you're crazy.

Over the years, I've had a fair share of book offers. Made me laugh. Me? Write a book? First of all, I can't spell. I don't really have anything to say. A memoir sounds like history, deep reflection, a narrative spanning a lifetime, kissing and telling, and looking back with profound wisdom. Way too overwhelming.

Then life happened.

When I tell stories, they often begin and end with, "If you would have told me . . ."

If you would have told me that in my mid-fifties I would become a father, filling my life with the greatest joy—I never would have believed it. But here I am, living a reality that was once an absurdity.

If you would have told me that I'd lose one of my best friends in the blink of an eye, I wouldn't have believed that either. But here I am, still processing the confusion, the deep sense of sadness, and the overwhelming loss.

Maybe I do have something to say. I don't even know where to start.

But here I am, starting.

I'm sure you have many "if you would have told me" moments in your life. I'm not saying mine are more interesting, and if you write a book about them, I'm happy to read it. I encourage everyone to put their thoughts on paper, although it's not for the faint of heart. This is hands down the hardest thing I've ever done. Who wants to pull back the curtain and expose your deepest truths not only to the world, but to yourself?

Through it all, I've been humbled more than I've ever felt entitled and surprised more than I've ever been expectant. I'm here for every hurt and heartbreak because I am here for every joy.

Life is both solid and fragile. (Isn't it?) It's amazing how much you can abuse yourself and still live, and how you can die so easily when you least expect it. My gratitude for living this life I've been given is immeasurable.

While writing, I sometimes felt like I was dabbling in fiction. Some stories felt too amplified, slightly exaggerated, and a tad outrageous. Once I got my hands on the facts, they turned out to be exact, often even wilder than imagined.

It used to drive me (and the rest of my family) crazy that my mother saved every picture, poster, piece of press, every contract, piles of teen magazines featuring me, stacks of headshots, and postcards. She had every calendar and schedule of what I did and with whom I did it. She held on to my diaries, scribbles of my thoughts and dreams. I would say, "Why do you keep all this junk, Mom?"

Now I know.

My mother wrote me little notes of encouragement and inspiration, but mostly of pure love. They've been a lifeline, a roadmap to a happy life. I haven't always stayed the course, but they've been there to get me back on track. I read them every day and discover new ones all the time. I've sprinkled them through-out this book in hopes that you make them your own, because everyone deserves to feel special, seen, and supported.

Just as I made a dedication to my parents in my high school yearbook, this autobiography is dedicated to my mother and father. Without them, I wouldn't have a story to tell. Because of them, there's a fairy-tale ending and plenty more magic to believe in.

I honor my beautiful sisters, the cushions on either side of me that break my falls and lift me up. They help make me the man I am without judging the little boy I was.

To my Disney Girl, Caitlin, and my Billy Boy, axis to my world, this is just some of my saga because the biggest part of my life is just beginning with you.

I've changed the name of an asshole or two to protect the guilty, but you know who you are. Read it and weep, dickheads. (That is, if you can read.)

To every friend and fan, I wish that you realize your dreams as you have helped me realize mine. You make my life brighter. I hope to shine a little of that light back at ya.

Everyone has a book in them; this is mine.

John Stamos
Thanks Mom and Dad for everything, I love ya, Without music life
would be a mistake.

IF YOU WOULD HAVE TOLD ME

PROLOGUE: THE MESSENGER

His throat is red, and his heart is fluttering a thousand beats per minute. He's always flying high in flashy iridescent colors, looking for his next hit, his next drink, the nectar of the gods. Like a lot of celebrities, when you see him on-screen or in pictures, he looks huge but in real life he's so small. He's darting this way and that. No attention span. The guy can't sit still, and when he crashes, he crashes hard.

The hummingbird.

Hummingbirds are considered by many to be a lost relative coming back from beyond. It's one of those stories that doesn't seem to have an origin, but it's been part of my family's DNA forever. We don't know who started it.

On the side of our house, my dad built a wooden trellis that showcased his menagerie of hanging plants, potted flowers, and climbing colorful bougainvillea that blossomed all year round. He'd touch them and talk to them. It was his refuge, a sanctuary where he could escape and indulge his passion for agriculture.

If Cyprus in the Mediterranean was famous for its tall, thin trees, juniper shrubs, and bright purple cyclamen, then our house in Cypress, California, would be rich with vibrant flora to rival the isles of his homeland.

He was only sixty-five when we lost him. But we somehow knew he'd come back to check on his plants and make sure me, my sisters, and my mother were taking proper care of them the way he did. We would see a hummingbird hovering over a brilliant blossom in a deliberate way. Hey, Dad.

The past looms large, and losses leave great voids in the heart. It's nice to be reminded of those we've loved in small, spirited ways that don't overwhelm us.

Those who keep my feet on the ground will depart into the unknown.

I have simple dreams I exceed, sometimes crash what I cultivate, and rebuild from rubble.

So much of my life plays out like a film in front of my eyes. I don't understand one frame of the big picture, but still after flickering still, the story starts to make sense.

There's a cinematic term called "persistence of vision." It's an optical illusion where your eye perceives the continued presence of an image even after it disappears from view. If you get pictures flashing in fast enough succession, your brain blends all the still images into motion. Those images make a movie the way memories make a life.

Hummingbirds are the only creatures that move a little faster than all that, traveling from another realm to remind us that our lives depend on the tenacity to keep creating; the persistence of our own vision.

In Asian traditions these furtive little birds are considered good luck. In Native American lore, they're spirits that heal hearts.

Some Christian theologians associate them with death. They are messengers from the other side.

I believe all of it.

Hummingbirds are chaotic and energetic.

Hummingbirds are excessive and pleasure-seeking.

Hummingbirds are self-soothing and addictive.

Hummingbirds have an acute sense of rhythm: fast.

Hummingbirds are generous and beautiful.

Hummingbirds are stupidly instinctual.

Hummingbirds are gracefully wise.

This is a story about Hollywood, fame, fortune, and fuckups.

This is a story about home, heart, healing, and hummingbirds.

1

Mercy

"Hey, Uncle Jesse, pull over, you're fucked-up!"

Tourists. They're not angry, they're just starstruck and sweet, worried about my safety. A car pulls up next to me, the window rolls down, and they start snapping pictures with their phones. I pray to God they delete them.

It's June 12, 2015. I am a fifty-one-year-old man behind the wheel of my silver Mercedes S 550 Coupe. I have no right to be behind any wheel.

The guy they see in the driver's seat is Jesse Katsopolis, the hair-obsessed, bad boy, rocker-with-a-heart-of-gold from *Full House* careening erratically through the 90210.

He also looks a little like Blackie Parrish, the street urchin, bad boy, rebel-with-a-heart-of-gold from *General Hospital* swerving down Rodeo Drive past Tom Ford, Louis Vuitton, Dolce & the other guy.

Or is it Tony Gates, the hotheaded bad boy, doctor-with-a-heart-of-gold from *ER* driving the Golden Triangle of Beverly Hills, over and over?

Those faces are familiar to passengers pleading, "Pull over!" One of these hopped-up lunatics is gonna get someone killed.

It can't be John Stamos. That guy is gone, gone, gone.

Something I took or drank earlier kicks in when I pass the iconic BEVERLY HILLS sign. These one-way streets are confusing enough when you're stone-cold sober, but if you're loaded, they become a maze of mayhem.

The last time I saw myself before sliding into the driver's seat was in my bathroom mirror. Not bad. I've got my dad's rough and rugged features softened up by some of my mom's natural beauty. Right now, I don't want either of them staring back at me. They would want me to be better than this. I'm letting them down tonight.

I'm living in a 1940s Rat Pack bachelor pad in Beverly Hills with Spanish-style architecture, a big stone fireplace, porn star shag carpeting in the bedroom, and a large Lovesac beanbag chair slumped seductively in the corner.

Sinatra had a cool place next to mine in the 1960s. Each wrought iron gate protecting his fortress was emblazoned with a large S. I tried to buy them during his estate sale. Why not? We share last initials, started our careers as teen idols, and both had good taste in music. I look at my wall-size Warholian pop art print featuring a repeating pattern of Frank Sinatra's mug shot and lift my glass in a toast.

The house is full of homages to the Casino Gods: Sinatra, Elvis, and my spirit animal Don Rickles, but there are also innocent tokens from an earlier time: my very first drum set, a Tony the Tiger kit I got for Christmas when I was five. I have a wall of fame, eight-by-tens of me and icons Frank, Sammy, Jimmy Page, and Bette Midler, but what sticks out is a framed note from my mother:

*Don't ever give
the devil a ride
because he will
end up doing
the driving*

Anyone driving on Mulholland from Laurel to Coldwater Canyon could look out their window and see my first piece of Disney memorabilia in the backyard. It's the big D from the original DISNEYLAND sign that had sat on Harbor Boulevard letting you know you had arrived at the HAPPIEST PLACE ON EARTH.

My house hasn't been the happiest place on earth recently. I'm restless, joyless, and the wonderful world of Disney has lost its magic. I'm as free as can be but pacing the place like a prisoner, back and forth, purposeless. I've gotta get out of here.

I'm heading to The Palm to meet one of my closest friends, Bob Saget. This classic surf and turf steakhouse is a Los Angeles landmark. I'm a regular; it's kind of like my personal Cheers where everybody knows my name. After about fifteen minutes of glad-handing agents, managers, and whatever celebs happen to be there, I'll finally get to my booth for a power lunch or dinner.

The walls are covered with caricatures of celebrity customers. When the restaurant moved from West Hollywood to Beverly Hills, all those depicted in the illustrations were invited to take theirs home. I never did. There are only two caricatures that made it into the new Beverly Hills spot: me and Frank Sinatra.

There's something that reminds me of my dad there: old-school, generous portions, no bullshit. My dad, William John Stamos, was the coolest guy in any room he walked into. Although, he never knew it. Most kids get to a point of disillusionment with their fathers, but I never got there. He was always bigger than life to me.

I'm missing my dad, and my marriage has busted up, but it's the loss of my mom, Loretta, who died nine months ago, that has me spiraling. She kept me anchored, solid, and straightened out for most of my life. I'm feeling adrift and alone without her. Empty. She loved me so much that I didn't have to learn how to love myself. Now all that's left of her guidance and grace are little notes in pretty penmanship.

> Dear Son—
> Just to let you know once again how much I love you. I'm the luckiest Mom in the world. Some of my happiest memories are because of you. Enjoy your loves, your laughter and your blessed life!
> Love & Kisses,
> Forever & always,
> Mom
> XOXOXO
> 3-'06

Where are my loves? What laughter? What am I doing with my blessed life?

I'm managing my emotions like a chemist. A little of this to get happy, a little of this to give me confidence, some of this to sleep, and some of that to get back up and do it all over again the next day. For most of my life, I avoided the stuff, but in 2015 I go off the rails. I'm burning my throat with liquor, burning bridges with arrogance, and burning the candle at both ends.

I'm doing a hell of a job processing the five stages of grief:

1. Denial: Gamma-hydroxybutyrate (or GHB) to stay lean and deny time the way Hollywood likes it.
2. Anger: An antidepressant to take the mad away.
3. Bargaining: Please, please, please let me sleep, Ambien.
4. Depression: Women to take the sad away.
5. Acceptance: When all else fails, pour a stiff drink, set sail for nowhere, fall overboard, drown.

Saget will get it. I just need to head to The Palm, have a few drinks, and shoot the shit with my pal. He's the closest thing to the brother I always wanted. He riles me up and evens me out like no one else. He often phones me, tells me he's too busy to talk, and before I can say, "But you called me . . ." he hangs up. I love him so much.

I want to hear one of his rambling stories where he interrupts himself, to make a point about himself, then dives right back into where he left off. I can forget about myself for a while when I'm with Bob.

We plan to have dinner and head out to a big Hollywood party. I was invited and Bob wants to go. He'll be my plus-one. We would often be each other's "date." We're both single. We talk about how we want to find someone good and kind to spend the rest of our lives with.

Back at my pad, I slide into my Benz, fumbling around to turn on the radio. Paul Revere & the Raiders are playing my song, the one about kicks gettin' harder to find. Getting loaded allows me to numb out and be comforted by people I have no business being around. People who don't get me. "Who's Paul Revere? Did he play football for the Raiders?"

My kicks are chasing a combo of dopamine and serotonin. Like any thrill, once you get used to prolonged pleasure hits, it takes more and more to get those neurotransmitters transmittin'. The kind of kicks that would get me excited and happy now need a dose of danger. I'm spinning my record at max rpm with my volume cranked way past eleven. Fast, loud, yes, now; humming. A total hummingbird.

The line I would never cross becomes fainter each time I step over it. It slowly moves further from what's right, honest, and good for my soul. I get involved with things I would never have done a few years back, hell, a few months back. It starts with one thoughtless decision or caving to a desire I used to easily avoid. "See, that wasn't so bad? No one got hurt, and I had fun." What's next? Let's go a little deeper. Let's go a little darker.

Every lost man should be lucky enough to have the grace and goodness of a Brazilian housekeeper to hide his bad habits and store away his secrets for a little while. My housekeeper, Dulce, has been with me over thirty years. She is my nanny. She's used to me, a Peter Pan, playing out fantasies all night and needing to be nursed back to health at daybreak. Dulce lets me be a good guy, a ghost, a piece of shit, and a friend.

I start bullshitting. Secrets covered up by bald-faced lies.

I can sober up at the drop of a hat, just takes me a few days. I meticulously plan it all out on my calendar: *Quit drinking.* On Saturday morning, I'll stop cold turkey, lie in bed and sweat it out over the weekend. Occasionally spilling into Monday, Tuesday at the latest. Cancel a few meetings, work out a bit, and get back to my fighting weight. When the following Monday morning rolls around, I'll show up looking like a million bucks, clean-shaven, bright-eyed, and stone sober until the job is done. Naturally, my reward for heroic self-control is increasing the revelry once the project is completed.

I'm lonely, but never alone. In a sober state, I'd have the pride, morals, and values to avoid the proverbial low-hanging fruit. But what fun is that? Plus, I have an image to uphold. The "bon vivant" character, the cocksman, the ladies' man with a revolving bedroom door. I can't go on my friend Howard Stern's show without him salivating over girls he thinks I slept with. Or Jimmy Kimmel, another pal, who never misses the opportunity to paint me as the ultimate playboy. And who could blame them? I play into it 100 percent. It's flattering. I feel it's my solemn duty to uphold my status as "that guy" keeping the dream alive for all those average joes out there, giving them someone to live vicariously through. Who cares if it's at the expense of my own happiness?

What I don't get is every time I play out the fantasy in real life, I'm giving away a little piece of me.

"Stop trying to charm the world," my shrink, Phil Stutz, says. "You've already done that. Show them you're an actor, that you're the real deal. You must commit to working hard every single day, even if it's not paying off right away. You must practice nonattachment and be willing to lose. You must have self-restraint. Show that you're serious and committed in every microtransaction you have with anyone. Your only reward for success is more work."

He calls my life a "porpoise orgy."

It's time to get serious.

I hate being serious. It's hard to age when everyone is telling you that you don't. I can still slide my ass into skinny jeans as if they were Peter Pan's tights. Almost every interviewer poses some version of the same question: "What's your secret to eternal youth, John?"

"I drink the blood of Rob Lowe."

I've picked up Bob's habit of telling a joke every three minutes to keep everyone entertained; always performing, rarely just being. My shrink says, "You know why you don't have everything you want: a respectable career, a wife, a family? You're confusing the universe."

It's a celebrity cliché to be bored with the four F's: fame, fortune, fans, and fun. But there's an "F" missing. Family. The thing that sustained me for most of my life isn't in the cards. I don't have a family. I don't deserve one. By my age, it probably won't happen anyway. Who cares? Any schmo can have a family. I did things only 1 percent of people do, I justify arrogantly. But, as hard as I might try to believe my own bullshit, no one can see through my facade as well as me.

I don't want to kill myself, but there's a selfishness in death that I flirt with. I'm faded in my car. It's okay if I die. Fine. I've done it all; crossed everything off my list. Got the fame, got the girls, got the sitcom, got to play with The Beach Boys. The end. I'm good to go, in the literal sense. Ready to hit the Pearly Gates. Mom and Dad are waiting for me with open arms and a glass of wine. Drop the mic. Elvis has left the building.

"Uncle Jesse, pull over!"

Things are getting blurry. I don't know where I'm going. Where am I? I keep seeing the same stores, over and over again. Finally, I pull over to the side of the road and park. The cops find me blacked out, slumped in my seat like a scarecrow.

I've seen the TMZ video and pictures from that night. It

makes me sick to my stomach. I'm spinning around the streets, out of my fucking mind. I could have killed a kid, wiped out a family or a grandmother coming home from Bible study. I'm jeopardizing everything in my life: my career, reputation, and worst of all, the kid my parents raised, a guy I kind of like.

"What's your date of birth?" the police officer asks. I get it wrong.

"What did you take?" the EMTs ask as they load me into the ambulance. They're being kind to another pathetic actor who has it all and is throwing it away.

Bob is sitting at The Palm, probably telling dirty jokes to the waiters while anxiously texting me, "Hey handsome, you were supposed to be here thirty minutes ago, where are you?"

I'm passed out in an ambulance with sirens screaming through the streets. I don't get my Frank Sinatra mug shot moment. I should be sitting in a cell, but by the time the Beverly Hills Police get calls from concerned citizens, find me on the side of the road, and cuff me, I'm so dazed and disoriented that they end up rushing me to the hospital. While I'm being treated, I'm being booked for a misdemeanor DUI.

A combo of substances and sadness has me wishing my mom would wrap her arms around me and make everything okay. She's up there somewhere. There's a white light in my eyes calling me to her. I want to be with her now. I want to become a hummingbird, too.

By the time I'm back in my body, I'm waking up in heaven.

"John?"

God?

No, it's not my maker but someone pretty close in my eyes. Bob Saget is by my bedside. No judgment, just concern and love.

The illumination of the surgical lighting in my eyes recedes to reveal my dear friend and the staff at Cedars-Sinai Medical

Center, angels to be sure, but heaven isn't ready for me yet, and I've got the hangover from hell.

There is something humbling about regaining consciousness in front of doctors when you've played one on television for years. I was Dr. Tony Gates, emergency medicine specialist, strutting down the halls of ER's County General in surgical scrubs with a stethoscope casually slung around my neck. I was doing the stuff doctors do: taking out appendixes, saving kidnap victims, performing gallbladder surgery, running into exploding buildings to rescue women, intubating, inhaling weapons-grade ricin after treating a bioterrorist, applying butterfly stitches, and seducing every woman within a one-mile radius, including the hospital chaplain. Tony was a flawed leading man, a risk-taker, sometimes called a "cowboy" by his coworkers. Lately, I've been living that life offscreen with the edge overtaking affability.

When we lose ourselves, it's often about giving in to the perceptions of others. This is how you see me, so this is who I am. This is what you want from me, so this is what I give you. There's no center to a guy like that, no core. There's also no responsibility, no rules. I hate myself for that. If I was depressed before, I'm despondent now.

Bob sits with me for a while. I learn he and my sisters, Alaina and Janeen, have been going crazy all night trying to get ahold of me. They've called every hospital in L.A., but since I'm in the system under my alias, Hair Club for Men founder Sy Sperling, it takes a while to find me. I'm able to talk to them on the phone briefly.

"Are you okay, Johnny?"

"I think so," I say. "This hasn't gotten out, has it?"

They answer through tears, "It's all over the news!"

I want to die.

My sisters will step in for my mom, eventually set up rehab, and follow me out to treatment. I'm the older brother. I'm the one who's supposed to be protecting them, making sure they're okay, not the other way around. They pray that their older brother will be around long enough to assume that role again.

I can't believe I have so many loving people in my life trying to help. I need to get better for them. In the moment, I don't realize that's not how this works. Healing starts with the self.

I slip in and out of sleep. When I'm sober enough to be discharged, my sisters send our good friend Vinny to come sneak me out of the hospital, avoiding the paps, and drive me home. I don't want to hang out. I don't want to talk.

I've been a caricature of my best characters.

Blackie might have acted out a little, but he would have gone home, poured his heart out to his adoptive parents, Rick and Lesley Webber, before heading out to the garage to jam with his band, Blackie and the Riff Raff.

Uncle Jesse would have never doped himself up and sped through Beverly Hills. He would have examined his life and found solace in family as a sappy violin score faded to credits.

Tony Gates could get lost in his ego, but he would have centered his heart in those he loves.

I've made a mockery of the guys I brought to life on-screen; these men taught me about myself as I helped craft their storylines, motives, and vulnerabilities. I've let a bunch of pretty good guys down.

Mostly, I've made a mockery of myself.

I tweet out, "Thanks to everyone for their love & support. I'm home and well. Very appreciative of the BHPD & Cedars for their care." And I mean it. I think about these amazing men and women who wake up every day to save lives. They train for years, endure sleepless nights on the beat, lose weekends and holidays on call, and say goodbye to their families as they go into work not knowing what will be wheeled in on a gurney or, for the cops, if they'll ever come home again. They are heroes. I'm walking through my front door because they care enough to keep a guy like me going. It should inspire me to do better, be better.

I slump into a chair and down a bottle of wine.

My friend and mentor Garry Marshall used to say to me in his heavy Bronx accent, "You need a catchphrase. Each character on TV needs a catchphrase!" On *Happy Days*, Fonzie had "Aaaaay" and Potsie told everyone to "Sit on it!" For my *Full House* character, I was inspired by the purr of Roy Orbison's "Pretty Woman" when he cries out "Mercy."

Whenever a beautiful woman walked by or a child wreaked havoc in the house, Uncle Jesse had a certain way of delivering the line. He'd drag out the first vowel with a slightly pained but resolute facial expression followed by the second word punched up at the end, "Haaaaaaaaave Mer-CEE!"

Redemption is a funny thing. There are infinite ways to get lost and just as many roads to find a path home. We fall back on the wisdom of our earliest teachers and find our innocence in their eyes. We ask more of ourselves and actually live up to it. We open our hearts one more time ready to be screwed over, but hoping for that unconditional acceptance. We quiet the active cynic in our minds and let the biggest dope we know, the dreamer within, start to give directions again. The message becomes clear: take it easy on yourself, have patience, forgive, be merciful . . . have mercy.

2

CLUB FAME: MEMBERS ONLY

Since I can remember, I always wanted to be in the club: Club Fame. There's something about humble beginnings mixed with a backdrop of Disneyland and youthful indignities that gives you this overwhelming sense of wanting to matter or be brightly lit. Here's one of my Mom's notes:

I'm the only person on earth that has shared a heartbeat with you my child.

My mom would always say that in the time between leaving the delivery room and before she got me home is when I decided I wanted to be an actor. She loved to tell me what a homely little guy I was. Said I looked like Dr. Zorba from the TV show *Ben Casey*. She covered my face with a blanket when she brought me home. Didn't want the neighbors to see me until I grew into my looks. Might have been that first game of peek-a-boo that taught me that what we hide, we reveal.

My dad's Greek and my mother's heritage is a delightful mix of British, Irish, and several other ethnicities that she fondly refers to as her "Heinz 57" background, or mutt. She's tall and elegant, like a model, with the sharp wit and sass of a comedic actress, but acting and modeling were never in the cards for her, because she chose to be a stay-at-home mom. She teaches CCD, the Confraternity of Christian Doctrine of the Catholic Church (aka Bible Study for Babies), at Saint Irenaeus once a week, and my sisters and I attend dutifully. She has enough love to fuel a small country.

So, I'm growing up in Orange County, California, in the 1970s. I'm a nerdy kid with a nose slightly too big for my face. I'm obsessed with magic and want to be a puppeteer when I'm older. Saturday mornings I watch Sid and Marty Krofft shows like H.R. Pufnstuf. My dad says if I practice all summer, he'll buy me a real drum set. I do. By junior high school I'm drumming in the marching band and also playing at my church.

Before my life was taken over by all things Disney, there was an old berry farm a mile and a half away from our house. It was called Knott's Berry Farm, and back in the '70s, it was free to enter. My mother would often take me and my sisters there to feed the ducks using stale bread. This was her perfect solution to keep her busy children entertained and exhaust their relentless energy. As time went on, this quaint place morphed into a full-blown amusement park.

Knott's is theatrical. I check out the shows at the Bird Cage Theatre and hang around talking to the actors. They put on melodramas (might be where I pick up a few bad overacting habits).

I'd spend hours and all my allowance at the Magic Shop in the Gypsy Camp area.

Tony Kemeny is a puppeteer I'm mesmerized by. I spend

hours standing by the side of his van waiting for his next show. My mother buys me his book called *A Puppet No More*. The guy has been through the ringer. His brutal past adds something melancholy to his work, but every show ends with kindness and love.

While Tony brings the pathos to puppetry, nothing captures my attention like the park's Wild West Stunt Show. It's a big-scale production with comedy gags and a few stunts easy enough for me to duplicate at home.

There's a high fall, where an unsuspecting volunteer from the audience is dragged into the drama, gets shot, and falls down thirty feet. It only takes me about twenty-seven shows to realize they aren't actually killing innocent tourists.

It's the first real theatrical show I've ever seen. Some actors have stories of sneaking into Broadway shows as children, but the Wild West Stunt Show is where I start dreaming of acting. I memorize every single line, and my friends and I take turns playing different characters at the O.K. Corral on Carob Street.

I borrow my mom's Super 8 camera and spend the summer re-envisioning my suburban, middle-class neighborhood in Cypress, California, as a tumbleweed-infested Wild West wonderland. I form my first production company called Ursula Blairpark Productions. Don't ask me where that name comes from. It just sounds funny.

The mini action films take weeks to develop, and there's no editing. I'm jumping off the roof onto a mattress below.

I'll continue to watch those little films throughout my life. Years later, when there's a stunt on a show I'm doing, I'll knock it out and get props from the stunt performers, never letting on that my taste for danger was born on the Wagon Camp Theater at a berry farm.

My dad owns a restaurant, which is his pride and joy. The Yellow Basket. All windows, perfectly shaped topiary shrubs surrounding the building, 1970s pleather booths, a long counter with an open kitchen, and two gumball machines.

My dad sometimes comes home with a crumpled brown paper bag filled with reject gumballs that don't "make the machine." Punks. Despite what Hollywood will eventually teach me about the golden ratio of symmetry, those faded, lumpy rejects chew and blow just as fine as the perfectly spherical ones. They may even be sweeter.

In our family, the second-generation Greek immigrant dream of owning your own joint is about as good as it gets. There's also an expectation that a father will pass on the family business to his son. At Yellow Basket, I flip burgers, drop fries in molten grease, take out the trash, and clean the grill. I'm fourteen, and I guess child labor laws aren't being enforced on the corner of Western and 182nd Street in Gardena.

Saturday and Sunday mornings are busy. My dad features a $.99 breakfast with two eggs any style, hash browns, regular or wheat toast, bacon or sausage, and coffee. There are lines around the block. I have eight burners roiling with eight styles of eggs: over easy, sunny-side up, over hard, hard-boiled, over medium, soft boiled, broken, and scrambled. An occasional asshole comes in and orders egg whites, throws off my whole game.

I enjoy work. I look forward to it. It's nice having some money each week. It always feels like enough.

My dad passes on a dogged work ethic and a sense of discipline that I try to carry on. His most valuable lesson is a sincerity for treating everyone with equal respect. I watch him treat his busboy the exact same way he treats his best customer. My dad never makes any false moves. No ass-kissing. He doesn't give a shit who you are; if you are a good person, he'll treat you like one.

Like my dad, I connect more to working-class folks than I do with fancy people.

We live on Carob Street. Down the block on Opal lives Mike Owen, a kid who collects war memorabilia. We don't bond over his military trinkets but find truce in our mutual love for Disneyland. We become best friends for life.

Despite a beautiful, loving childhood a few miles down the road with nothing to run away from, I go looking for something more. I feel at home at an amusement park; experience everything I think creators like Walt Disney want people to feel. The outside world becomes nonexistent.

The five bucks I make after a shift covers a general admission ticket to get into Disneyland. Mike's dad often drives us to Diz (that's what we call it) in his green van that has a frog painted on the side with HORNY TOAD written below it.

As we exit the 5 freeway and make our way down Harbor Boulevard, our excitement builds as soon as we catch sight of the big blue DISNEYLAND sign. He drops us off at the front, where rows of cute ticket booths are the only thing between us and the Mickey Mouse flower bed, the train depot with a clock tower, and two tunnels on either side leading to a magical place that celebrates the power of imagination, friendship, and love, and encourages me to believe in the impossible.

We plunk down our five bucks for general admission. No need for tickets because we've saved them from trips in the past. E tickets were the like centurion credit cards of Disneyland. In the '70s, there was a coupon book you'd buy to use for rides. "A" tickets are trash: rides like dumb King Arthur Carrousel, wouldn't be caught dead on there. "E" tickets are golden: the best rides, hands down. We both manage to scrounge up one each. I found mine at the bottom of my mom's junk drawer in our kitchen. We'd need an E ticket for our favorite ride.

We stand in line for the Matterhorn Bobsleds, desperately trying to pick up girls. I'm wearing my dad's Members Only jacket.

It fits him just right but is a little too big on me and sags on my shoulders. The racing sport coat has epaulets and a collar strap that makes me look like a reject from Sgt. Pepper's Lonely Hearts Club Band. There is a single, logoed breast pocket meant to hold secret codes to stolen safes, a femme fatale's phone number, or a Cuban cigar. If my dad has recently worn it, I'll find a broken More cigarette. I like to keep the pockets packed with pretzels.

I round out my look with a bedazzled Harpo Marx shirt, tight Jordache jeans, and a fugly pair of Wallabees. For that manly smell that really turns the girls on, I'm doused in my dad's Aramis cologne. A couple of girls stroll by, so I pull out the omnipresent pocket comb from my jeans and swipe through two perfect feathers on either side of my head. Cheeks dimpled and pimpled, I'm somewhere between a baby face and hormone hell.

"Hey, ladies."

The girls we're checking out have switched from Pez dispensers to birth control pills. They're suddenly sophisticated, refined, and repelled by boys their own age. Especially ones that reek of their old man's cologne. I'm still a kid. I haven't done anything cool yet, like hotwire a car or get busted for weed. Mike and I are hustling hard, but the amusement park queens, crowned with crispy bangs and sporting sly smirks, pass us by.

We finally slide into our roller-coaster seats. As the ride starts off slow and ramps up, I forget about the crowds, Mike, and missed opportunities with the Cinderellas and Snow Whites in our midst. I have never been in love. I don't know what it feels like. Maybe it's like sliding into a Matterhorn bobsled and holding on for dear life. There's an element of danger at every turn. There are dark caverns, steep hills, and claustrophobic tunnels. There is the foreboding specter of the

Abominable Snowman lurking like God or Satan behind sheets of ice. And then you plunge into the unknown. Do you hold on in fear or release your grip and accept the moment?

That shit is Freudian, all day long, and it's all I understand about the future. I lift my hands up and let go. Splash.

As we exit the ride, amusement park queens who blew us off earlier are sashaying our way singing the innocent earworm "It's a Small World" in less than innocent halter tops and cutoff shorts.

"Mike, check 'em out."

God, I wish I was famous. Then it hits me. There was a television show on at the time called *Lucan, the Wolf Boy*. A wild child raised by wolves is captured by hunters and must journey, as the opening says, "from savagery to civilization." I convinced myself that, from a distance, if you squint your eyes, I kind of look like Wolf Boy.

As the girls walk by, I make Mike create a ruckus by running up to me and asking for my autograph. I impersonate the star and revel in the adulation. I'm sure they'll figure out I'm just some idiot, but that's how badly I want fame.

To this day, if someone asks for a picture or autograph, no problem. I'm happy to take the time. Being famous was something I wanted my whole life, and these people watch my shows and are the reason I have a career. Pictures, autographs, anything they want. Might even sign *Love and Kisses, John Stamos*, and leave Wolf Boy out of it.

"It's a Small World" fades away with the girls flipping their hair and by divine musical intervention I hear a muffled melody faint in the distance.

More like I *feel* it. It's not so much a sound as a sensation. A wave of warmth floods my chest and wraps around my heart. I can't resist the call. With each step, the sound grows stronger, pulling me closer, and I feel a palpable connection to it.

The song is "Sloop John B." The band, Papa Doo Run Run. A soundalike surf band. Not the real thing, but an incredible simulation.

As I reach the front of the stage, the music drops out and it's just voices, an immaculate a cappella harmony.

"*Home, let me go home . . . why don't you let me go home? . . . I feel so broke up. I want to go home. . . .*"

The parts start to overlap and intertwine, and I'm covered in goose bumps. The tune ends, and I stand there captivated, awestruck. I want more. I need more.

The stage begins to descend into the ground. The Tomorrowland Terrace stage, or *the up-and-down stage*, is on its way down, and the band is waving good night to the euphoric crowd.

"Good night? What? No! Come back up, guys!"

"They're done," Mike says, and he suggests we come back tomorrow night. And that's what we do. And the night after, and the night after that.

When I realize Papa Doo Run Run is just a cover band, I hightail it to the primary source. I get my hands on an eight-track of *Endless Summer*, The Beach Boys' compilation album. I become obsessed with oldies stations that play them, like K-Earth 101.

Mike Love came up with the title and helped with the song selection. *Endless Summer* goes to number one and is certified triple platinum. A new generation of fans get turned on to The Beach Boys because of that album, and I'm one of them.

I discover that Mike Love's parents live only a few miles from where I go to school in College Park. I ride my bike there and look through the windows, where I see gold and platinum Beach Boys records hanging on the walls. I stare and dream.

In 1979, The Beach Boys are on their *L.A. (Light Album)* tour, performing at the Universal Amphitheater. My Aunt Susie has season tickets and knows how much I love the band, so she invites me. The Beach Boys are my very first concert. I get decked out in my best velour. Sure, it's warm outside, but I have to look cool. They will close the top of this concert space years later, but on this balmy summer evening, it's an open-air venue with millions of stars shining down on us. Everything suddenly feels right in the world.

Brian's intricate melodies incorporate unconventional chord progressions to create a sense of tension and release. Mike is more straightforward, with catchy lyrics and repeating hooks that paint a picture of optimism, hope, and good vibes. Along with Carl and Dennis Wilson and Al Jardine, their music just moves me. It's that simple. The Beach Boys' music is heart music. It bypasses the brain and goes straight to the heart.

I have this fantasy where Mike Love steps up to the mic and says, "Our drummer just broke his finger and can't play the show. Anyone out there know how to play our songs on drums?" Of course, I'll shoot my hand up and declare, "Me! I do!" Little do I know that very scenario almost happens.

Recently, at dinner with Mike Love, I tell him that the first concert I ever went to was The Beach Boys at Universal Amphitheater.

"My Aunt Susie took me. If you would have told me . . ."

"Man, Dennis was drunk that night," Mike shares. "I grabbed the jug of orange juice and vodka he had been swigging and threw it over the fence. Dennis was so pissed, he tried to jump me during 'Little Deuce Coupe.'"

What? I can't believe that innocent night was filled with so much drama.

Mike says a little wistfully, like it's all water under the bridge now, "Security drags Dennis offstage and I'm following right behind, trying to get some punches in. When he tries to snatch the hat off my head, I grab his hand and twist it so hard I nearly break every one of his fingers."

I think to myself, *Man, so close.*

I tell him, "I didn't see any of that."

He slowly turns to me and says, "Your aunt must have had shitty seats."

3

BIG NOSE STUDIOS

Superheroes all have their origin stories: Captain America overcomes polio, Batman lives to avenge his parents' brutal murder, and Spider-Man was bullied before being bitten by the radioactive arachnid that set things in motion.

Here's my origin story.

I got a black eye over a girl in high school and swore that my nemesis, a bastard named Rick Clarke, would live to regret giving me that shiner.

I play Tri-Toms in the marching band at John F. Kennedy High. We're practicing in full uniform for our big trip to Ireland, where we'll compete against other bands from around the world. As we're marching down the street, this kid who's relegated to playing cymbals because he's got no rhythm leans over to me and says, "Hey, Stephanie Small thinks you're cute and wants to go out with you."

"What?!"

I stop in my tracks, and the kid behind me bumps into me, nearly knocking off my tall faux-fur busby hat. I recover and fold back into formation, but marching is the farthest thing from my mind at the moment.

Stephanie goes to an all-girls Catholic high school nearby. She's smart and a natural beauty. I can't believe she's interested in a band geek like me.

"How does she even know who I am?"

The kid starts to answer but misses his one and only cymbal cue and gets chewed out by the band director.

"Gosh darn it, you made me miss my cue!"

"Not my fault you have no rhythm," I say.

"All the girls know who you are, John Stamos!"

What? For as long as I can remember, I've been pretty much invisible to girls. I'd try all sorts of things to get noticed, like showing off my drumming skills or pulling silly stunts like "accidentally" tripping over folks in the courtyard, pratfalling, spilling lunches everywhere. That's just me, I didn't know how to be any different. But they'd usually just roll their eyes, call me corny or a cheeseball, and look right past me at the jock, the preppy trust-fund dude, or even the male teachers. They had no use for an immature goofball like me.

After a while, I stopped trying so hard and just kept marching along. This revelation from a kid who sounds like he admires *me* is the cymbal crash that wakes me up.

Everyone says you have to learn to love yourself from within, but sometimes it takes looking at yourself through someone else's eyes to start understanding your worth. We always pick the best looking, smartest, richest, most successful person in any room and feel like we're lacking, but if you look over your shoulder there might just be someone looking up to you. To a kid banging a couple of Zildjians together, I was the shit.

I start looking around more and notice the kid's right. Shy smiles beaming through braces, furtive looks between a couple of cheerleaders passing notes in math class, giggling girls lingering by my locker, and suddenly I start to come to life. Is that a JS in a heart on a Trapper Keeper?

My spine gets a little straighter from the attention. I put more into my appearance, maybe ease up on my dad's cologne, but I don't change who I am. In fact, I lean into it even more. I get a sense early on that trying to be part of some sport or clique, or flashing a bunch of money around isn't as important as figuring out what is unique about yourself.

"I go to CCD with Stephanie's sister, she's the one who told me and I swore I wouldn't tell you," says my new admirer. "So keep it quiet."

That night, I'm at a block party a few miles from my house, telling anyone who will listen that Stephanie Small is madly in love with me. Like a game of telephone with two cans and a string, the story gets passed from house to house, finally reaching the last party on the block, the cool kids' party. A football player doing a beer bong gets wind of the news and spits out his brewski.

"My girlfriend wants to go out with Big Nose Stamos?" Rick Clarke says.

He laughs in front of the crowd, playing it off like it's a joke. Like I'm a joke, then heads out to hunt me down.

By this time, I'm sitting in a car with a friend, babbling about Stephanie Small's obsession with me. I hear a knock on the glass. A jock. I roll down the window and—

BAM! Dude sucker punches me square in the eye. Everything is happening in slow motion. Bam, bam, bam, he lands more punches to the face, ear, and head. I try to punch back, but my head is down, and I can't really see, so I start punching the hell out of the interior roof and window frame. I've only been in Wild West stunt fights, no real ones. I bang up my knuckles but never land one on Rick's face.

"So, you're telling everyone my girlfriend wants to go out with you, Big Nose?" he yells.

"Listen, man, she was the one . . ." I try to reason with him.

As I plead my case, ten douchebag letter-sweater replicants emerge from the shadows ready to kick my ass.

"Get out of the car!" he demands.

Fuck that. I tell my friend, "Step on it!"

She peels out, sending the jock-straps jumping as we speed off into the night.

There's no talk of bullying back then, no counselor to run to. The embarrassment and humiliation eat me up inside. I walk around with a pit in my stomach every time I hear Rick Clarke wants to beat my ass again. I fear going to school and careen around the corners with caution.

One day, as I'm walking to class, the kid from marching band comes running up to me out of breath. He asks if I've been to the boys' bathroom, and I respond with a hesitant no.

When I walk into the bathroom, my heart sinks. Someone has written a chilling message on the mirror: *You're dead big nose.* Those venomous words cut me to my core. And as I look at my reflection, my black eye fading into shades of yellow and green, I come to the conclusion that I can't take this anymore. I need to do something drastic to put an end to this torment. There is only one thing left for me to do.

I gotta get famous.

So famous that I'll have one of those personal trainers who will teach me the ancient art of Brazilian jujitsu. Then, at our high school reunion, I'll take a break from picture taking and autograph giving, and saunter over to Rick with a sly grin on my face. I'll unleash the dreaded Butterfly Sweep move on him then proceed to give him a stylish black eye to match his pouty expression, right in front of our former classmates who now all happen to be Big Nose fans.

Every time I hit a new milestone in my career, I think of looking him up and taking him down. I'll invite him to a Beach Boys concert to watch me play drums while the girls all scream my name. He'll have a backstage pass waiting for him so he can come shake my hand after the show. But instead, he'll be met by my gigantic bodyguards, and they'll beat him black and blue as the crescendo of my drum solo drowns out his whimpering cries.

Now one hopes time and experience dull memories of yesterday's torment. No resentment, no regrets, no hard feelings. Fame and fortune are secured, the bully is forgiven, and everyone moves on. But, like a phantom limb in war, a black eye from a high school nemesis itches for eternity.

I sometimes still dream of finding Rick and telling him to his face: thank you. I'll thank him for the inspiration to strive, the trajectory of my career, and each small success that was driven by his cheap blows.

I'll tell him, "Rick, I don't think I'd be where I am today if it weren't for you." I'd shake his hand, walk away, then over my shoulder I'd leave him with one more thing.

"Oh, and Rick, I dated Steph for around two years and she said you're hung like a finch, is that true? Have a nice day, pencil dick!"

Of course, we are unreliable narrators of our own experience, and what we consider our first drive is often just a punch in the face that is too obvious. Our real motivation rarely comes from revenge. Let that black eye fade and open your eyes to what comes next.

It's the summer of '77 and my dad has a friend, Doc Manos,

who is the athletic director at Huntington Park High School. They're using the space to shoot a big prom scene for a romantic musical comedy about a greaser guy and his bobby socks babe. It's a Romeo and Juliet–style love story set in the 1950s, filmed with the topical issues of the 1970s, and starring a bunch of "high school kids" played by actors in their late twenties. None of it makes sense, but it doesn't matter. Doc snuck me on to the set of *Grease*, and it's magical.

There are so many lights, cameras, and people. There is a big cowboy figure that says, "Rydell Ranger." I ask a little too loudly, "Why is that cowboy wrapped in toilet paper?" A crew member shushes me and says, "It's crepe paper." Must be a Hollywood thing.

Someone yells out, "Quiet on the set," and everything goes silent. All the bustling, banging, and blustering is hushed, and I can hear my own breath. It gives me chills.

Someone else bellows, "Places, everyone."

My heart starts to pound.

A bunch of ladies in puffy dresses and men with greasy hair walk to the middle of the basketball court and stand on little pieces of tape. What's the tape for?

"Cue playback," someone says officiously. Music blasts. I can't tell where it's coming from. There's a band on a platform at the other end of the gym. Greaser guys with shiny tuxedos are doing the opening drum rhythm for a song called "Hand Jive." The noise blasts through the cavernous gym, echoing like crazy. The floor is vibrating but the band isn't actually playing. They're faking.

Now I'm totally confused and want to ask a million questions. The voice of God yells, "Action!" Everyone gets a little more animated and a spotlight shines on a door.

Out struts John Fucking Travolta.

I don't know the meaning of the word "charisma" at that

point, but I learn the essence encoded in the concept when Travolta moves like a panther parting the crowd in that iconic black suit with a pink shirt, white socks, and pocket square. He's oozing charm and radiating an aura of greatness.

"That! I want to be that!"

He dances, sings, captivates with every word, and gets the girl . . . and the other girl. I start assessing my skills on the spot. I can't sing or dance, so that's out. My brain doesn't understand melody, but being a drummer, I understand rhythm. Tempo. Timing. Still, you'd think some of that would transfer into dance moves. Nope.

I always dreaded school dances. Got so embarrassed. I had all the grace of the Scarecrow in The Wizard of Oz, but when I tried out for the role in our school play, they stopped me after the line "If I only had a brain" and asked if I knew how to do makeup.

John Stamos: Can't sing. Can't dance. Can't act. A triple threat. What I do have is perseverance and a simple but effective formula instilled in me by my parents: If you want to do something, just do it. No obstacles. No roadblocks. Work your ass off and do it.

I start my Travolta transformation by becoming The Wizard of Oz of my own life.

The lesson is clear: what I need to make it in showbiz is already within me. I have enough brains, courage, and heart to make it, and while I'm not wearing ruby slippers, I might have had the power of Elvis's blue suede shoes to click together. "There's no place like Hollywood. There's no place like Hollywood."

I have my first drama teacher, Mr. McGinnis, to thank for another defining moment of inspiration. He takes students on field trips to Hollywood to watch tapings of TV shows. He sees my fascination with all of it and conveniently looks the other way as I sneak backstage to explore.

"Just don't miss the bus," he says.

I'm starting to figure out how everything works. When we're in the audience for a show like *Fernwood 2 Night*, I say, "McGinnis, if you want to be on TV, shown on camera, sit here in this seat. They always show this section of the audience!"

We finally get around to watching a taping of my all-time favorite show, *Happy Days*. Of course, it's The Fonz I connect with most. Not just for his effortless cool, but also his sense of honor and loyalty.

There is a young comedian in the audience. He's wild and exploding with energy. Can't sit still. He isn't known yet, but McGinnis says, "That guy's going to be a star one day." I ask for his autograph. "*Dear money, send Mom,*" he writes above his signature—Robin Williams.

4

THE KEY AND THE KEYHOLE

Trying to achieve sex symbol status growing up around strong, opinionated sisters ain't easy. The sisters snort and roll their eyes at such foolishness, my mom never really acknowledges the man within the little boy she loves, and then there's my dad, who sets such a solid example that being some cheap playboy seems like failing the family. I get the message at a young age that women are valuable and due respect.

While my mom stays at home to care for the family, my dad never hangs money over her head. He perceives her work as equal to, or above, his job. Despite grueling hours, my dad feels like he might have the easier gig. She says many times how grateful she is to my dad that she can stay home to be a mother, to have time to get involved with various charities, and to spend her days taking care of the family she loves. She's proud of that.

One of my mom's notes, attached to the spiral rings of a small pocket diary, reads,

World . . .
Don't tell me
that I didn't work on
I was and still am
CEO of this household!
L.D.S.
1-14-11

I prefer women to men bosses any day of the week. I know that most women in high-profile positions have to put in twice the work to get there, work doubly hard to maintain it, and consistently outperform to overshadow some of the mediocrity of their male counterparts.

Because of my upbringing I learn that "no unequivocally means no." I never want to be presumptuous or cross a line no matter how wildly the hormones rage.

Before I get any of this, my earliest memories of trying to understand women are more about titillation, such as sneak peeks at my mom's *Cosmopolitan* mag in the section "Cosmo Tells All." Hot stories and women in underwear. I can't wait for the monthly subscription to arrive.

Then my friend Mike and I find an extremely graphic magazine in a phone booth that takes it up about seventeen notches. I can't take my eyes off these stirring images, trying to make sense of what I'm seeing.

"So that's how you put the lime in the coconut," I say.

I come home from school one day and find a book about sex sitting on my bed. I guess this was in lieu of my parents having the birds-n-bees talk with me. It's some archaic thing full of supposition, sly similes, and goofy metaphors. I open the first page and there is a giant key. On the next page, a giant keyhole. I don't get past the first two pages.

Girls love guys in bands. Since I can remember, I've always dreamed of being in one. The thought of jamming with other musicians sounds cool. My desire is fueled by my love of music, and it excites me to think about the creative energy that could come from working with others who share that passion. Also, girls love guys in bands.

My first band is called Destiny, a trio with my good friends Philip and Habib Bardowell. Super-talented brothers. Most of our gigs are family parties and school events. My dad carts us around with our equipment loaded in the back of his El Camino.

One night after a gig, as he and Philip are packing up our gear, instead of helping, I'm jive-assing a group of girls who have flocked around me. Phil says to my dad, "Man, look at Johnny. He could get any girl he wants." My dad turns to Phil and flatly says, "Well, not *any* girl." And he's right. My first fumblings aren't the stuff of lothario legend.

In high school, I'm in another a band, called Crosswinds. We practice at the house of our bass player, Loretta, because she has a liberal, hippie mom who's Eastern European and doesn't care if kids have a beer.

I'm seventeen and a half, and sex is on everyone's brain, with the number one topic being when and how we are going to "lose it" and to whom.

Philip and Habib happen to be hanging out one night after band practice. Someone mentions weed, and Habib whips out a sandwich bag full of sticks and stems. They know I don't smoke but want me to try.

"What's the big deal?" Habib asks.

"No biggie," I say, trying to be cool. "Spark that bad boy up."

I know how to do this, I've been watching my parents smoke my whole life. In fact, my mom tells a story about taking me to the pediatrician and, smack-dab in the middle of the checkup, my mom and the good doc decided it was time to take a smoke break, right there in the sterile confines of the doctor's office. There I was, splayed out on the examination table, as bare as a newborn babe (literally), when I decided to display my newly acquired skill—peeing like a champion racehorse. A golden arc of liquid rebellion jetted out with such precision that it made a splash landing in the doc's shirt pocket, giving his precious pack of cigs an unexpected bath. That'll teach him to smoke on the job!

I proceed to take a long hard drag, just like my parents do.

"Hold it in, man," Phil says. I hold it in as long as I can. The room goes silent waiting for my reaction. I cough so hard that it feels like I'm choking up a lung.

Everyone laughs and I just give a carefree shrug, not letting on that my throat is on fire.

After a few minutes, I start to feel slightly light-headed but good. We laugh and listen to music. I say, "This feels good, guys."

In this exploratory state of being, in an environment of openness just down the street from my parents' house but a world away, surrounded by hormonal peers, an apparition floats into the room, parting the haze of smoke: a blonde, Nordic goddess. The mythical Ani is Loretta's sister: great laugh, beautiful, large braless breasts.

"The party's over. Go home!" she says. No nonsense. The guys file out of the place with hangdog expressions.

"Johnny, sit down, I'll get your keys."

Like a setup from a *Penthouse Forum* "You'll never guess what happens next" letter, I cannot guess what happens next. She playfully tosses me the keys to the El Co, but they end up landing right in my lap. "Oops," she says, "I'll get them." Initially, her search remains on the outer territory of my pants, but soon enough, she ventures inside. Oh, now I get it. This is how the whole key in the keyhole thing starts: with real keys.

Okay, so this is going to happen, huh? Most of it is a blur, but she's gentle, sweet, and helpful because I have no clue how any of it works. That ridiculous key and keyhole book didn't describe a tall Viking chick who looks like she just stepped out of a Frank Frazetta painting. She jumps on top of me and does most of the work, putting my hands and mouth where they should be and then lets nature take care of the rest.

I'm thinking, *This is what the whole world revolves around? It hurts!* Eventually, when the pain subsides, I understand. Damn.

I walked in a boy and I'd love to say I walk out a man, but I walk out a boy who is no longer a virgin. The next day my friends come over to hear the story of what it was like to have sex. They fashion a crown out of branches and twigs to place on my head. "You are no longer the Virgin King!" Weirdos.

"Before you tell us all the horny details," Habib says, "we gave you oregano to smoke last night. It wasn't pot."

They all laugh, and I want to strangle them. Maybe the oregano was an excuse for me to feel like I was crossing boundaries, being adult, being bad. The good feeling must have been organic, a readiness to try new things, who knows.

I bullshit through the sex story, casting myself as the stud and leaving out Ani's coaching, experience, the pain, and the confusion.

I am now a member of the I've-Finally-Had-Sex Club, but Club Fame still remains elusive.

5

FLASH IN THE PANTS

It's the era of disposable teen idols, throwaway child stars, and hunk-of-the-month-club magazine cover boys.

"I don't want to be some flash in the pants," I say in front of a bunch of strangers in my first acting class.

We sit on a stage and talk about our dreams, career ambitions, and where we see ourselves in the future. Everyone laughs, and I don't get that I've misunderstood the common cliché "flash in the pan."

My friend Jim Warren gives me a primer on "flash in the pants" versus "flash in the pan" after class. "So, flash in the pan is a guy who has a few seconds of fame. Flash in the pants is . . . well . . . I don't really know what you mean there."

"Okay, fine. I get it, I messed up the term," I say. "My point is I don't want to be a one-hit wonder, a here-today-gone-tomorrow kind of guy, a wham-bam-thank-you—"

"I get it," Jim says.

"No, actually you don't."

My mom gets me a small-time agent for some small-time

gigs. I do a commercial for the Long Beach department store Buffums. I get a Coke commercial with America's favorite clean comedian, Bill Cosby. I guess our chemistry is nil and the ad never runs. It's hard to imagine everyone's trusted TV dad, the pudding pop guy, becoming a roofie rapist. If you would have told me.

I become friends with a singer and actor from The Young and the Restless named Michael "Rock On" Damian. He is a good guy and connects me with movers, shakers, and kooks in the industry.

He introduces me to an editor at Tiger Beat. Doreen Lioy is a pasty, virginal, lonely soul who gloms onto my family fast. She puts me in the magazine before I have any real credits to my name. She loves my mom's nurturing ways. She even calls her "Mom," and our family sort of adopts her. She spends holidays at our house.

Since biblical times, there have been "forgers of idols," and L.A. in the 1980s is the Sodom and Gomorrah of selling unattainable beauty and sex for a coin. The Tiger Beat headquarters, or Dream Factory, as they call it, is not as dreamy as one would think. No glitz, no glamour. Fluorescent overhead lighting illuminates a normal-looking office space with blown-up magazine covers lining the walls. The enterprise is owned by the Laufer brothers and run by a skeletal staff of an art director, photographer, and a few all-powerful editors like Doreen.

On the periphery, there are creepy dudes posing as "press agents, photographers, managers." Slick Svengalis who are nothing but bottom-feeding scavengers. The Devil makes deals with pretty prey: sign here to swap your soul for a few seconds of fame. Grifting predators lurk the streets of Los Angeles waiting for the next farm-fed, wide-eyed innocents to step off the bus, willing to do just about anything for a shot at the big time. No one touches me. I develop a gut instinct at a young age that will stay with me for life: I know who to trust in an instant (I SEE YOU), who to avoid after a quick conversation (I HEAR YOU), and when to haul ass (FUCK YOU).

My naivete is my greatest appeal and oddly an ally in staying safe. In the moment, it all seems exciting and fun. It takes years to reflect on the darker side and learn about some of my fellow young hopefuls not lucky enough to escape the gropers and groomers. Talented kids like Todd Bridges from *Diff'rent Strokes*, Mackenzie Phillips from *One Day at a Time*, and the Coreys (Haim and Feldman) who were in every hit movie of the 1980s. Their stories and struggles are their own to tell, but it's hard to look at reruns on television and know how many adults just stood by while they were being hurt.

My mom keeps a close eye on me and for the most part stays on the sidelines, but the formidable presence of Loretta Stamos ensures that any sharks looking for young chum in the talent pool stay far away. Still, even under watchful eyes, there are sketchy motives in this photographer, that low-budget director with a leering gaze, or popular acting gurus running recruitment centers for dubious spiritual enlightenment.

I'm ready to move from magazines and commercials to a real role I can sink my teeth into. I get accepted to Milton Katselas's acting school at the Beverly Hills Playhouse. The real deal.

Katselas trained under Elia Kazan and Lee Strasberg. His method produced gut-driven actors with edge, like Gene Hackman, and stunning stars who shone in every role, like Michelle Pfeiffer. If you got it right, you were part of a canon of greatness. He also had a knack for bringing out the best in comedic actors like Alec Baldwin, Tony Danza, and Ted Danson. I want to do that kind of acting, where I nail a dramatic scene, then pivot on a dime to make people laugh.

I'm a terrible driver and have a hopeless sense of direction. I'm a human compass of confusion. To get anywhere, I use something called The Thomas Guide. It's a big, complicated map with microscopic veins and arteries representing the stop-and-go side streets pulsing through the city. I'm always late. The first night at the Beverly Hills Playhouse, I try to slip in quietly so no one notices, but I get chewed out by the wannabe Milton who runs his intermediate classes.

I see two attractive women onstage in the middle of a scene. They are playing the roles of friends meeting in a diner. Mia, the teacher's assistant, sits me down and piles workbooks on my lap. I'm excited to dig into Milton's renowned approach to the craft and career of acting. I leaf through the texts and the curriculum is heavily focused on the attitude of the actor. He describes an artist like a camera lens aperture, the brighter the spirit—the more light you are willing to let in—the brighter the performance. Piece of cake.

I look up from my books, and the two girls onstage, supposedly still sipping shakes at the diner, are now topless and slowly stripping off the rest of their clothes. This ain't the Yellow Basket. Tonight's exercise is one designed to help conquer stage fright. I guess if you can stand in front of an audience naked, you can bare your soul in a scene?

Then, a non sequitur after *Boobs in a Greasy Spoon*. A guy gets up and begins a long, emotional monologue. He's having trouble remembering lines. Finally, he looks down and flatly says, "I have pancreatic cancer. I'm dying." He takes us through his journey, shares the pain of his prognosis, and begins to cry. "Today is my last day with all of you." Everyone in class is crying, including me, and I don't even know the guy. It's heartbreaking to see a young, talented kid so full of promise be cut down in the prime of his life. Then, like emerging from a trance, he stands up straight and announces, "Um, sorry. I don't really have cancer. I've always had a problem crying in scenes and . . ."

It's a bit? The students start screaming, "Fuck you! That's fucked-up! How dare you!" They throw crumpled-up papers at him. I toss a pencil at his foot.

It's hard to figure out where I fit in. I'm not here to roll around onstage naked or lie about dying for attention. I want to learn, but I can't lose myself in showboating exercises that don't feel genuine.

After class, I'm walking to my car and Mia runs out and hands me my workbooks. "Hey, you forgot these."

She adds an extra book, the size of a brick, to my stack. "Start with this one," she says, smiling. "I think it will open your eyes to some amazing things. A couple of us are getting together to talk about it tomorrow around five P.M. Come meet us. The address is 5930 Franklin Avenue, Hollywood."

"Dad, you have to let me off early today, I need to go meet some students from my acting class."

"Why?" he gripes.

"Because I want to be an actor."

I crack open the book while on my shift at Yellow Basket. There's a lot about control: controlling your reactionary mind, controlling energy, controlling space, and controlling time. Where's the part about acting? And who's this L. Ron guy who wrote a bunch of his opinions in here? I thought Milton was the teacher. I can't control my navigational skills and now someone's trying to give me a roadmap for my mind. I'd rather stay lost.

I zip up to Hollywood and pull into the parking lot of a building that is grand, ornate, and creepy as fuck—a cross between Chateau Marmont, Disney's Haunted Mansion, and a mental hospital. The Church of Scientology Celebrity Centre International.

I walk in and I'm overwhelmed by the opulence and excess. Every window is heavily draped, there are antique objects, modern displays, and the joint is trimmed in oligarch-gold. The interior is as nuts as the outside: a mobster's manor reimagined as a *Star Trek* set.

In the theater, with her artsy black turtleneck, the Beverly Hills Playhouse teaching assistant is all business, but in the soft glow of these antique chandeliers, Mia emerges from the shadows like a vampire and greets me with a sweet smile. She's short, buxom, flirty, and slightly dangerous, like some bubbly 1950s actress you find out is into satanism.

"Did you start reading the book?"

I bullshit my way around the question. "Yeah, gotta get those audits and control time and whatnot . . ."

"Excellent," she patronizes. "Let's get a read on your Thetans."

I don't know what she's talking about and I must seem reluctant because she becomes seductive. "Come on, cutie, I won't bite. Not hard anyway."

She takes me into a weird little office where a weird little man shows me a weird little machine that has a bunch of knobs, levers, and gauges to measure my weird little soul. All I can think about is the Wayback Machine from *The Rocky and Bullwinkle Show* deployed by the genius beagle, Mr. Peabody, and his adopted human boy, Sherman, to time travel through different dimensions.

"This is an important religious artifact," Mia shares. "It monitors the psyche, mind, and spirit."

I'm handed two round things that look like cans. I put one to my ear and the other to my mouth and mimic talking into an old-timey telephone: "Hello, there."

Mia suppresses her irritation with me, and the weird little man gives her a withering look. He pinches me on the hand. Ouch. I pinch him back. He begins to question me about committing crimes, asks if I have negative thoughts about Scientology or L. Ron Hubbard, and probes into some strange sex inquiries. The Wayback Machine needle jumps up and down erratically.

There are hushed whispers in the corner, and Mia looks disappointed. I am whisked out of the room and sent on my merry way. Apparently, I'm not Scientology material. Darn it.

When you grow up in a family like mine, there's no chance eye-rolling sisters will see you as someone who could ever learn the great secrets of socioemotional control, nor do I think my no-bullshit dad will support me bearing witness to the esoteric teachings of Xenu. My mom has many crosses in all sizes around our house and makes us sing "Happy Birthday" to Baby Jesus each Christmas. In words, deeds, and cards effusive with guiding sentiments, she always reminds me where I come from:

Dear Johnny~

God looked all over heaven to find the most special baby boy. It was you, then, God gave you to Dad and me to cherish forever.

It was such a happy day and you have continued to make our lives happy.

Thank you Johnny, I love you more than you'll ever know.~

Forever,
Mom

XO XO XO XO

There's no concept, cult, or congregation that competes with a mother's love.

6

THE YELLOW BASKET BANDANNA

I start daydreaming. Crazy stuff like playing music with The Beach Boys or being given the keys to Disneyland so I can take over the whole park and skip all the lines. Or even having my own sitcom.

Not so fast. My dad slows my roll. It is imperative that I go to college and get a business degree so I can take over the burger empire he's building for me.

I can probably grow the franchise, become a hometown hero, drive a red Porsche off a used-car lot each year, and retire with a pad in Cypress and a summer timeshare in Lake Havasu. I'd consider that a success standing in the footsteps of a great man.

But I miss the first semester of community college. Not for lack of trying. I drive a few miles to register but can't find the little sign-up room, so I drive home. (I may have stopped at Knott's Berry Farm on the way.)

"That's it," my dad says in a threatening tone. "If you don't register and get your ass a business degree, I'm done with you. You're out and on your own!"

This is a do-or-die moment, my last chance. I have to get on a TV show.

Everyone is watching a soap opera called *General Hospital*. College kids rearrange their class schedules to make sure they don't miss an episode, and bingo halls postpone draws so Grandma can catch "her stories." It's a series about a hot-blooded hospital in the mythical town of Port Charles. I get a call to audition for the role of a character described as a street punk named Blackie Parrish.

General Hospital has more viewers than any other daytime soap. Thirty million people tune in to watch the wedding of the century. The lead character Luke drunkenly rapes the lead character Laura. The daytime supercouple are betrothed in a romantic wedding that makes virtually every magazine cover in America. A night of brutal violence ending in white lace and roses is indicative of the lusty lawlessness of the era.

The pre-#MeToo world is messy as hell. Somewhere between the idealism of the 1960s and the hangover of the 1970s emerges a generation trying to figure itself out. There are so many options to screw yourself and others over, a wild time to be innocent and unaware.

Blackie Parrish is described as a street urchin from New York. I go to the library to look up what being an "urchin" means: "A kid, usually an orphan, who has lived on the streets for most of his short life. Survival is a matter of stealing whatever is needed, doing odd jobs." Perfect typecasting (except for the orphan part, living on the streets, and thievery. The only thing I ever stole was some Halloween makeup from Gemco, a department store near my house).

I don't have that East Coast swagger and dangerous edge necessary for the role. They are looking at a kid named Brian Robbins, who later stars in *Head of the Class* (and goes on to be the head of Paramount Pictures). The kid has the street cred I'm lacking. I need to go to the source, the power, the oracle: Travolta.

In *Saturday Night Fever*, John Travolta has a specific walk. With his tight, waist-cut leather jacket, he struts in perfect cadence with the Bee Gees' "Stayin' Alive." I want that walk. My slow California stroll needs some East Coast energy.

I also need a look. A leather jacket. My dad's Members Only is too flimsy. A baby-blue, collarless windbreaker won't cut it. My mom has a beautiful leather coat stashed in the back of her closet. It is voluminous and lengthy.

Now, to find the New York vibe along the mean streets of Cypress. Knott's Berry Farm and Disney are my hard-core hunting grounds, but there's not much "edge" among fruit pickers and talking mice.

I cruise in the El Camino up to Hollywood a few hours before my audition in search of the seedy streets that will inspire the strut I need to win the part. I end up on Santa Monica Boulevard. It feels New York-y to me. There's a lot of people drinking at outdoor bars. Lots of men. Mostly men.

After three failed attempts to parallel park, I find a spot in front of a club called RAGE. That feels right. Need to tap into the fury, the fire, the rage. I step out of the El Co in my mom's badass leather ready to work.

At first, I start with an aggressive, throbbing, forward-moving energy leading with the lower torso but also engaging the hips. Nope, not cool. I need to take it down. A slow swagger loosens me up, and I settle into casual confidence. By adding just enough bounce to the ball of the foot, I go Travolta-lite while speeding my tempo back up. It helps to mentally hum "Stayin' Alive."

Once the rhythm and musicality are fully realized in foot, leg, and ass, I advance to facial expressions. Eyes are looking straight ahead but hungry. Features are flat but hard. Add an Elvis lip curl.

I'm fully in character: New York street urchin ready to steal shit and break hearts.

"Get it, girl," someone purrs from an alleyway.

Girl? I guess I do have long hair, and my mom helped me feather it with her curling iron this morning. I have some Sun In still streaked through my mane left over from the summer. A guy whistles at me from an outside bar. It's strange attention, but I'm making an impression. I'll take it.

I feel like my look needs one more accessory. Suddenly, the image of Chachi, played by Scott Baio, from *Happy Days* comes to mind. He seems like a street kind of guy. I remember that he always has a bandanna tied around his thigh. There's a lot of stores with bandannas in all colors along the boulevard. I walk into a nice bodega and pick out a snazzy yellow one to tie around my leg.

The gentleman behind the counter says, "You know, today is your lucky day because this particular bandanna comes with a free back massage!"

"I appreciate that, sir," I say, "but I'm on my way to an audition."

I show up at the *General Hospital* casting office ready to rule the world: hot strut, Mom's leather, feathered hair, and a yellow bandanna around my thigh.

I thought that for sure I'd be auditioning on a dramatically lit stage or one of the hospital sets I saw on TV, but I'm escorted into the first of many functional offices without a scrap of atmosphere that makes you drearily aware of the gap between the Hollywood fantasy and stark reality.

The boss man I need to impress is Marvin Paige. He's an old-school operator decked out in polyester, giant aviator glasses, and a turquoise western bolo tie. He has a quiet, watchful kind of power that doesn't assert itself right away.

He nods and looks me up and down as I shift my weight from foot to foot, anxious to get things going.

There's another guy with a slightly smug expression sulking in the corner. He's blond with a mustache and slick style. Does he have a prosthetic hand with a cigarette lodged between the rubber fingers?

He raises his eyebrows dubiously and sighs a withering sigh, like he's put out to amble over and offer a limp handshake with his other hand. "I'm Skitch Hendricks, assistant casting director. Let's see what you've got, kid."

I take a deep breath, walk out of the office, then burst back in with my meticulously rehearsed walk and then start pacing the room wildly. I launch into my first line, "*I'm talking about a couple guys jumping me, baseball bats in one hand, brass knuckles—*"

Skitch Hendricks interrupts me.

"Stop moving around so much. Stand still and say the lines. You don't need to walk around."

Well, shit, all that strut-and-swagger work down the tubes. I try to relax, shake off my energy, and take another deep breath. *Get back into character and say the lines, Stamos.*

"*I'm talking about a couple guys jumping me, baseball bats in one hand, brass knuckles—*"

"Hold on," Skitch breaks in again. "You into golden showers?"

"What?" I ask. I don't know what he's talking about.

Skitch shakes his head. "Wearing a yellow bandanna around your thigh means you want someone to pee on you. I hope you haven't been walking around all day like that."

Pee on me? There's a whole wild world out there I know nothing about. I was going for the Chachi look, and now I'm wondering about the private kinks of the *Happy Days* star.

Marvin looks mildly amused. "All right, knock it off, Skitch. Start the scene over, dear."

Dear? Between losing the swagger and learning about erotic watersports, I'm thrown off my game and struggle through the scene.

As I walk out, Brian Robbins passes me on his way in. He has shaggy dark hair, slightly disheveled clothes, and a big, toothy grin. He looks the part.

"Yo," he says.

Yo sounds so New York.

I step out into the overly bright light of late afternoon Los Angeles feeling dejected. I blew it. No strut, just a shuffle back to the car. I'm still wearing a yellow bandanna signaling the universe to piss on me.

My story is one of constant struggle, endless waiting, and overcoming great obstacles. Or not. That was my first audition on January eleventh, I get a callback on the twelfth, and a final callback on the thirteenth. They tell me the news that I got the part of Blackie Parrish right then and there.

"Report to Stage Twelve tomorrow morning, six A.M.," Marvin says. "In two weeks, your first episode will air, and you will be coming into millions of living rooms all across America! Brian Robbins will play your sidekick."

I'm overwhelmed, excited, and nervous. Damn. I hope they don't shoot on Sundays, or my dad won't let me. That's Yellow Basket's biggest breakfast shift, and I'm his Sunday guy.

My first call is always to my family. My mom picks up right away. Her voice is filled with such hope. "Hi, Johnny, how did it go?"

She is holding the phone out so all the family members in the room can hear.

I sigh, sounding depressed, and say, "Bad news . . ." I let the pause linger. "I got the part!"

Screams on the other side of the phone. My dad chimes in, "Just make sure you get Sundays off!"

It's a quick, take-it-or-leave-it offer: four hundred dollars an episode, and if I happen to stay on longer, four fifty. That's a fifty-dollar bump in the second year. It would take me twenty weeks to earn that at Yellow Basket. I'll take it!

Thursday, 5:15 A.M., I arrive early to my new home, Sunset Gower Studios. Even with my history of bad directions, I remember my dad always saying, "If you're five minutes early, you're ten minutes late."

I roll the window down at the guard gate. "Hi, my name is John Stamos, I play Blackie," I say to the Black security guard. He looks at me for a long beat, shakes his head, and waves me through. Whose idea was it to name the character "Blackie"?

There is a receptionist sitting behind a large desk in the lobby answering phones and checking people in.

"Hello, Mr. Stamos." Mr. Stamos? I look around to see if my dad is behind me.

"I'm Sandy and I'll show you around today. Your dressing room is down the hall and to the left. Two doors down from Mr. Springfield's," she says.

"Mr. Springfield, as in Rick? Rick Springfield? NO WAY!"

I idolize Rick Springfield. His debut album *Working Class Dog* spawned the classic "Jessie's Girl." It starts with a distorted, grungy guitar riff followed by his breathy voice bemoaning his best-friend's girl. He's the coolest—tall, handsome, a pure rock-n-roller, and talented. If John Travolta is the unreachable pinnacle, Rick Springfield–level acclaim is a lofty goal to strive toward.

I imagine all kinds of scenarios where he's my best bud, big brother, mentor. This is going to be great. Just me and Rick hangin' out. I think about us running lines, jamming on guitars in his dressing room or mine. Maybe we'll even write a few songs together, who knows.

Sandy shows me the ropes. The dressing rooms are downstairs

in a maze of hallways. Large pictures of cast members hang on the walls: lawyer-turned-cuckold Scotty Baldwin, club-owner-turned-rapist-turned-loving-husband Luke Spencer, and the wealthy Quartermaine family, who oversee a dynasty of delicious deception.

It won't be long until my picture is hanging on the wall of fame right next to them.

My character is slated for only a few episodes, then he'll be killed off.

Blackie Parrish will die over my dead body. I'm going to make him so compelling, so honest and real that they'll have to keep me around at least a month or two.

"You see these different colored carpets?" Sandy says. "They delineate where cast members like you can walk and what areas are off-limits. Bright green carpets are a go, red carpets are a no. That's where the producers, casting, and writing staff offices are located."

She makes it sound like a secret lair guarded as closely as a vault holding the nuclear codes or the Price Waterhouse safe containing the sealed envelopes of Academy Award winners.

We weave carefully along sanctioned paths of correct coloring. After my bandanna experience, I'm freaked-out about the secret symbolism of different hues. I don't want to walk down any yellow carpets.

The next stop is hair and makeup. Without warning or fanfare, I'm introduced to an idol.

"Mr. Springfield, this is John Stamos. He'll be playing the role of Blackie Parrish."

My hands are sweaty. He looks even more like a star than he does on his album cover. He's got a feminine quality up close: perfect skin, big eyes with long lashes, full lips.

"Hey, man," I say with a half-wave, extending my clammy hand.

Rick is in the makeup chair with a stylist trying to fix his hair. He barely looks up as he rudely pushes the stylist's hand away from his head and waves her off. I've never seen that before. Why would anyone do that?

He's holding a hand mirror up to his chiseled face, futzing with his hair, moving it from looking perfect on the left to raking his hands through until it looks equally perfect on the right. He gives me a nod without breaking eye contact with himself.

I guess he's done making my acquaintance.

I start to head out. "See ya, Rick!" I shout over my shoulder a little too eagerly. "By the way, 'Jessie's Girl' is the greatest song ever . . ." Sandy grabs my arm and pulls me away.

Rick is at the tail end of his contract and wants out. He had moderate success in Australia but was a complete unknown in America until he landed the role of Dr. Noah Drake on *General Hospital*. His record hits number one, and now he's a giant sex symbol. Rather than credit the hyperventilating housewives and horny teens who discovered him because of his soap gig, he tries to distance himself from his star-making role to be a full-time touring rock star.

I'll see this over and over again: actor strives to be seen by anyone, gets a break, solidifies stardom, and becomes reticent to talk about those early days or the first fans who parted with apron change and babysitting money to support their journeys toward success.

Still, when I see a disaffected, ungrateful, mildly irritated Rick Springfield preening on his throne, I'm enamored.

"Come on, come on," Sandy says. "We have four minutes to get you to your wardrobe fitting. You cannot be late."

I'm hustling down the hall behind her and in the distance, I hear a gruff voice, scratchy as sandpaper, getting louder and louder. Sandy and everyone around us freeze in their tracks, heads bowed, eyes to the floor. They roll into themselves protectively like pill bugs.

Around the corner comes a woman about four foot six in heels. Her hair is in curlers, and a harried stylist is trying to take them out on the run. An entourage of seven people with yellow legal pads, most of them even shorter than she is, are writing down everything that comes out of her mouth.

". . . And make sure that cue for Scotty comes much sooner. Pace, pace, PACE!" she shouts.

She's chewing gum like a panther chewing on a human heart. There's spittle coming out of her mouth as she speaks. She's decked out in a designer suit with designer bags under her eyes. I've never seen a woman so wild but in control, powerful, and scary-cool. Her words are intelligent, her moves aggressive. She runs the place: Gloria Monty.

From Allenhurst, New Jersey, to Rancho Mirage, California, Gloria's journey has taken her from being a theater student to becoming a moneymaking powerhouse in the industry. She parlayed her master's in drama from Columbia into a successful summer stock role, leading workshops for icons like Marlon Brando and Tony Curtis.

As executive producer for *General Hospital*, she saved the show from cancellation when it was struggling for viewers. She created space to introduce younger characters, adding the sex appeal and romance that attracted a youthful audience, the coveted female nineteen-to-thirty-four-year-old demographic: teen impulse buyers and shoppers for the household. It's a demo daytime TV hadn't captured yet. Cut from heartthrob to lip gloss to detergent. Make the sale.

General Hospital is her last big horse in the Hollywood race. She knows how to pace a show, starting each scene with a strong entrance, keeping the action moving, and ending with a powerful exit. She's cultivated the show and trained it into a thorough-bred. I'm the latest pony in her stable.

Almost passing me by, she doubles back and gives me a strong hug, her big curlers scratching my baby face. "There he is! My new Blackie Parrish! Look at you . . . just darling!" She pinches my cheek a little too hard.

Everyone is terrified of her, but I'm not.

"So, they tell me you're from Orange County—" she begins.

I interrupt. "Sorry, Ms. Monty, can we talk later? I have one minute to make it to wardrobe. I'm getting a real leather jacket today, and I can't be late."

Everyone freezes. No one walks away from Gloria Monty.

She smiles and reclaims the moment. "What are you all staring at? The kid doesn't want to be late." I know from that moment that she likes me, and I like her.

I'm rushed through wardrobe, where I am transformed into Blackie Parrish: leather jacket, boots, a dirty sweater. I feel cool. Off to hair and makeup, where I let them do whatever they want to me. No pushing hands away like Rick.

P.K. Cole, the makeup artist, is a true-blue California 1970s bronzed beach girl with sun-bleached hair. She does her thing and swings me around in the mirror to see her creation. Blackie is wearing so much makeup he looks like a wax figure from Madame Tussaud's with very heavy guy-liner.

P.K. laughs. "When the lights and cameras hit you, it will look great!"

I don't care. I feel pampered and special. I've never had any-one examine my face in such detail, adding foundation to make it glow, then powder to minimize shine. Every hair on my head is contemplated and considered before being lightly sprayed into an immovable coif.

Over little speakers that hang in the hallways, I hear, "Moving to item fourteen. Sport Center. I'll need Rick, Lesley, Rose, Luke, Bryan, Spike, Scotty, and please welcome our newest cast member, John Stamos, who plays Blackie! Places, please!"

I hear a smattering of applause down the corridors.

"How exciting!" Sandy says as she guides me down the green-carpeted pathway to a large soundproof door.

"That door is too heavy for me," she says. "This is where I let you off. Break a leg!"

Like Glinda the Good Witch, she flies away before I can ask her why I should break my leg.

I use all my strength to open the heavy door that leads to a flight of stairs. I climb up, a tad out of breath, and encounter another portal to pass through. When I open the next door, the scene magically transforms from the dull dun of industrial offices to a Technicolor wonderland.

I feel like Dorothy in Oz, but instead of the yellow brick road leading to Emerald City, there's a place called Port Charles, comprised of a few familiar sets: the hospital rotunda, Ruby's Diner, and the Waterfront.

The Waterfront is where poor Blackie Parrish lives on the streets. There's a loose homage to Elia Kazan's On the Waterfront where a young Marlon Brando emotes, "I could've been a contender. I could've been someone." Because it's the 1980s, the potentially downbeat tale of a homeless kid gets a Rocky-like, inspirational storyline.

I step onto the set. I meet Chris Robinson, who plays Rick Webber, and Denise Alexander, who plays his wife, Lesley. They will eventually adopt my character. I learn quickly they don't say "Action!" on this set. The stage manager counts down from five to one, but never says the number "one." In five, four, three, two . . . silence. I'm waiting for one.

There are around thirty people, cast and crew, with all eyes on me because I have the first line. Seems like an eternity before Chris Robinson whispers, "They don't say 'one,' just do your line."

I'm already a ball of nerves, now add embarrassment, a pounding heart, and top it off with a little anger at myself. Fuck it! I've prepared for this moment my whole life. I make an entrance with my walk, and explode into the scene like a runaway stallion. I have the wildness, recklessness, and fearlessness that comes with no experience. I'm energized, full of ideas colliding at once and living out the scenes in the moment without overthinking. Although we grew up in very different circumstances and lived opposite lives, I know how this guy feels. I get him.

Some of it is brilliantly grounded and emotional, flickers of that elusive Travolta charisma. Some of it is shit, but it's a glorious, unabashed shit with no fear of failure, no judgment, and a complete lack of self-consciousness. The inner critic is dormant, and a guileless kid is finding his voice in real time.

The stage manager calls out, "Aaaaand we're out!"

All eyes are on me but this time they seem impressed. The sound of heels echoing in the cavernous stage gets louder and more reverberating as they move closer. Everyone tightens up. It must be Gloria. Her minions almost bump into her as she makes an abrupt stop in front of me. She stares at me, chomping on her gum, and nods her head yes up and down, up and down. She gives me a big smile and she's off. Click, click, click go the heels; chomp, chomp, chomp goes the gum.

My plotline evolves from sleeping out in the cold to helping clean up the corruption and crime on the docks. I get Teen Time up and running, a sports complex where the wild urges of inner-city youth simmer during games of basketball. The work feels natural and easy.

Cast members call me "the sponge" because after I finish my

scenes I stay to watch and learn. Tony Geary, the guy who plays
Luke Spencer, is mesmerizing. He's got this regular guy's face,
thin frame, and a frizzy perm, but when the camera hits him, he
holds everyone's attention with his ferocity and fixed gaze. He
is intense but energetic. His pauses draw me in. I initially think
I need to fill every moment, but he teaches me there's a power
in silence. There's something cool in restraint. I'm studying him
closely and figuring out how to use it in my next scene. One of
the producers tells me it's time to go home.

"Johnny, your mother just called!"

"Okay, in a bit." I try to spend as much time as I can on the
set. I like hanging out with my TV family, but I'm still living at
home with my folks and working at the Yellow Basket.

My dad is encouraging with the Hollywood stuff but still
forces me to pull shifts on Sundays at the restaurant.

Even after the show starts airing, I'm flipping eggs on the bus-
iest day of the week. People come in and say, "I'll have the ninety-
nine-cent special, wheat toast, and . . . wait . . . aren't you the guy
on . . . ? Nah, make my hash browns a little crispy and egg whites
only please!" Damn, the egg white guy.

Eventually, girls start coming around. More and more each
week, draping themselves along the counters, asking for autographs, nursing sodas until I finish my shift. I'm getting too
well-known for Sundays at the Yellow Basket and need to have a
heart-to-heart with my father.

"Dad, I'm kinda famous now, can I quit?"

"Nope. You're my Sunday guy. I need you."

I'm not sure if he kept me working on Sundays because he
thought this acting thing was not going to last. Or he wanted to
keep me humble. Or maybe he just liked the fact that my newfound fame was attracting customers and business was booming.

"C'mon, Dad! You told me I could go for it. You encouraged me to focus on one thing and not be a jack-of-all-trades. I'm making progress, but I need rest. I need time to study my lines. Plus, I'm tired of smelling like French fries on Mondays."

He snaps, "Oh, you think you're too good for this place?" and I quickly respond, "No, not at all." I don't want to disrespect him as I'm grateful for all the years of hard work he put into taking care of us. "Please, Dad."

I can tell he knows how important this is to me. Then he says, "I'll think about it."

The discipline my father instilled in me, along with his respectful way of treating others, I carry all the way to Port Charles. Once he sees that, he gives me his blessing to leave the apron behind and says, "Knock 'em dead, my boy."

And just like that, I go from serving up discount breakfasts on Sundays to spending every day of the week on daytime TV serving up my heart on a platter.

7

TINKERING W/THE TIP

That nose. It bothers me. When I see it on TV for the first time, it's all I can look at.

I'm increasingly self-conscious and discreetly block scenes to ensure my good side is in view of the camera. Fixating on my nose is beginning to detract from my performance. Plus, the early years of bullying by the Rick Clarkes of the world have me ready to make a change.

Everyone who gets a nose job tries to find some excuse other than vanity, but let's call it what it was—vanity.

I have a few weeks off, so I tell everyone I got a job offer and it doesn't conflict with the show. I didn't say what kid of job. My mom helps me through the whole thing. We get a referral for a doc from my parents' best friends, Cookie and Gus. Their daughters, Pam and Andrea, got nose jobs, so my mom figures they have an in. They fixed my folks up on a blind date, so it seems fitting they help me fix my nose up.

When I return to the set after some healing, I think I'm

pulling a fast one. Chris Robinson points to his nose. "So, exactly what kind of job did you get on your break?"

I'm not all that happy with it. My nose looks kind of pushed up like Peter Pan or something. So on my next hiatus, I have it redone by Michael Jackson's plastic surgeon. Who better to handle the delicate task of resculpting my nose than the man who created a whole new face for M.J.?

I haven't even been on the show for a year and I've already graduated from the youthful newbie to the double-nose-job guy.

Doesn't matter though because something about the life-and-death drama of the hospital and the libidinous lives of those who orbit this place of hope and healing captures young and old alike. From sweet sixteen to septuagenarian, I'm building a wide fan base.

My parents don't have a clue how to help me navigate this brave new world, but they do have some commonsense know-how that helps me avoid some of the pitfalls of fast fame.

Before there is a term for it, Loretta Stamos is a classic "mom-a-ger." This is not to be confused with the controlling stage parents that swarm so many young actors. The stage parents push their kids into the business, raid their piggy banks, and live vicariously through their precocious children. They twist with jealousy and grovel with greed, handing over their freckle-faced progeny to the first poseur with a PO box for an office and a matchbook cover for a business card.

My mom figures if I want to continue doing this work, she'll make sure I'm safe, supported, and having a good time. It matters to her that I don't get so swept up in the moment that I lose my connection to family, friends, faith, and fun. She enjoys being on the periphery of the industry and only asserts herself if someone tries to fuck with a Stamos, any Stamos.

Despite all the breathlessness and betrayal on camera, the cast and crew of General Hospital are protective and kind. I'm nice to everyone, work hard, and if I follow some of the stars around like a puppy, it's because I want to learn from them. People respond to wide-eyed admiration and genuine appreciation. I want to be part of their family, and something about my unspoiled openness makes even the most world-weary actors shield me from the sex, drugs, and sleaze that are the outer rings of this strange little planet.

Still, not everyone is a fan.

In between shooting scenes, I stalk Springfield and try to become friends. Music echoes in the hall and draws me in. He's strumming his acoustic guitar in his dressing room. I hang out and listen in. I sheepishly move my head along with his playing. Without acknowledging me or missing a beat, he slams the door shut in my face. Oh, well.

My mom and relatives pen as many letters as they can to ABC: "Keep Stamos!" Not enough to make a dent, but their dogged devotion keeps my confidence up, and I give my all in every episode. Instead of Blackie getting killed, poor Brian Robbins's character takes the hit. I feel full of life.

As the weeks go by in a blur, Gloria Monty keeps putting me into more and more episodes. My part is expanding. Sometimes I have twenty to thirty pages of dialogue a day. I love every minute of it. Kin Shriner, the actor who plays Scotty Baldwin, is older than me and takes me under his wing. Where Rick Springfield is dark and brooding, Kin is blond and bright. He's a focused actor on set but with an easygoing way when he's not on camera. I'm starting to collect signed eight-by-tens from the cast for my dressing room walls. Kin's says, "John, keep looking up to me, I won't let you down." And he hasn't.

Blackie is his flunky, and I like doing scenes with him, but our energies are totally different. He gets mad when we're supposed to enter a scene in a "two-shot." I'm moving at the speed of light, and Kin is more laid-back. The cameraman can't hold both of us and is confused about which character to follow. Over the loudspeaker, the voice of Gloria booms, "Boys! I need you to stay closer to each other. I can't keep you both in the shot. Someone needs to speed up or slow down, I don't care who." Then we argue about who should acquiesce. It's usually Kin.

After hours, all is forgiven.

General Hospital is cultivating a cast of young performers. Demi Moore is one of them. She's a firecracker with a gravelly voice and a big laugh. She's only a half year older than me, but infinitely more sophisticated and worldly. She's seen a few more things than I have.

Recently, I run into Demi at a party celebrating Jamie Lee Curtis's Oscar nom, and as we're catching up, a writer friend of ours, Ali Adler, completely fangirls out on us.

"Oh my god, *Blackie and Jackie!*" she says. "Did you two ever fuck?"

We both look at each other, wondering what the other will say.

Demi pauses to think about it. "I don't know if we slept together. I think we fooled around though."

I just smile. Then ask if she remembers back in the day when we all went to see Rick Springfield at the Universal Amphitheater.

I don't care if Rick allows me to get close to him or not, I'm his biggest fan, and seeing him in concert is something I've looked forward to for a long time.

The audience is filled with thousands of screaming teens and a handful of parents monitoring the frenzy. We get there after the lights go down and slide into our seats. Amazing show! I know every song. Damn, look at him, I can't believe I work with this guy. He is masterfully managing the mood of the moment and moves into a heartfelt song called "April 24, 1981." The touching lyrics memorialize the passing of his dad, and he sings directly to his father, asking questions about his spirit's journey and "the great unknown." I haven't lost a pet goldfish at this point so the moment is lost on me.

Turns out they're filming the concert for a Rick Springfield Special. When he hits the emotional peak, the house lights come on so the audience can be filmed expressing muted appreciation of this sentimental song. And that's when the first few teen girls see me slumped in my seat. There is a high-pitched scream, another, and another. "It's BLACKIE!"

Kin grabs me. "Let's get out of here!" We burst out of our seats and start running toward the exit.

Rick's eyes fill with emotion as he eulogizes his dad. As cameras capture the heartfelt moment, frenzied girls chase me and Kin up the stairs, all the way to the top of the theater, and with a burst of energy, we blast through the doors and sprint to the lobby.

"Blackie! Blackie's here!"

The buzzing gets louder as girls begin to multiply, drawing new bees into their swarm. We dart past concession stands stocked with "Singing Doctor" T-shirts and around corners, trying not to get stung.

We lose the mob for a second, duck into the men's restroom, and barricade the doors. We're doubling over laughing and push against the door as hard as we can to hold back the mayhem. Some poor dad at a urinal is interrupted midstream and pees all over his shoes in the melee.

I think about Rick Springfield onstage finishing his song in chaos. I realize I have as much of a chance to play drums with Rick's band as I do to sit in with the Beatles, Stones, or Beach Boys.

The next day at work, Kin is pissed at me.

"It wasn't my fault those girls started screaming," I say.

Kin accuses me of trying to get recognized on purpose.

"No way! The last thing I want to do is upset Rick Spring-field."

"Well, you did," Kin says. "Guys like him don't like being upstaged by punks like you!"

Upstaged? By me? No way.

We are walking by the front reception area where all the fan mail is kept. Overflowing bags stuffed with thousands and thousands of fan letters. Sure, there are probably some for Tony and Kin, but I'm betting most of them are girls telling Rick they've broken up with Jessie and are ready to be his girl.

"Look at this," I say. "That guy probably gets more mail than Santa Claus. He's hardly worried about some peon like me."

"You don't know that, John," Kin says, huffing his way to his dressing room.

I look around. No one in sight. The secretary must be in the bathroom, so I decide to take a peek into the overflowing bags.

Now, if I were living in a soap, dramatic music would swell, my eyes widening with surprise, the camera zooming in for a close-up of the letter in my hand addressed to John Stamos, then panning out for a wide shot of more and more letters for Blackie Parrish, John Stamos, Blackie Parrish, John Stamos . . .

Turns out I'm getting over ten thousand letters a week. Staffers pile them into the back of my dad's car. What am I supposed to do with all of them? My mom, sisters, and I open them and read all the lovey-dovey, gushy stuff teenage girls are writing me. Letters in curlicue penmanship on specially selected stationery sprayed with 1980s perfumes like Love's Baby Soft and Charlie.

My mom takes on the responsibility of answering mail until it gets to be too much. She hires a service but still oversees the content of the correspondence. It is very important to her that they single out all the letters from handicapped or sick kids so that I can write something special to them.

Reading about the struggles of young people throughout the country, I see how light and easy my life is right now. Kids in wheel-chairs, young kids with cancer, and children recovering from the worst kinds of abuse reach out. Maybe they relate to the issues my character is going through, or the hospital settings they've become familiar with. Maybe they just dream of some thrill-a-minute life in a town like Port Charles where everyone is beautiful and brave.

8

NEET GIRLS

As my popularity rises, I'm given more screen time, which is definitely driving up my fan mail, and with that comes a flurry of personal appearances, press events, and talk shows. For my first big morning show, *A.M. Los Angeles*, with some guy named Regis Philbin, my dad reminds me to keep it light and funny.

"Stay on your toes with that Regis guy, he's tricky!"

I get my first big commercial endorsement gig. I'm the new spokesperson for NEET, a depilatory for women's legs. It makes no sense, but I'm surrounded by hotties with hairless legs wearing next to nothing, so it's not the toughest check to cash. My tagline is, "I looooove girls with great lookin' legs. I loooooove NEET girls." Nicolas Cage will credit this commercial for his vocal style in the film *Peggy Sue Got Married*. (He gets panned for that choice. Sure, pal, blame it on me.)

I'm especially loving the car show circuit. Detroit Auto-Rama, Knoxville Car Extravaganza, Phoenix Championship Auto Shows, Boston Budweiser World of Wheels.

I take a red-eye on a Friday after work, land at around 6:00 A.M., go to the hotel to get myself dolled up (usually some Blackie leather look or a T-shirt pandering to whatever town I'm in: JOHN STAMOS LOVES CLEVELAND!), and show up Saturday for my first appearance.

I'm finally famous enough to have a bodyguard. Pauley B is a greaser on steroids. He has a shoe-polish black pompadour with gray sides and hulking muscles flexing under cut-off shirts. I bring him along when I'm carrying cash. He can also bust a little brawn when I need crowd control.

Tens of thousands of teenage girls and their mothers line up around the building and promoters pack them in shoulder to shoulder until the auditorium looks like a sea of bobbing perms. I walk in, and the place goes crazy. It's a real rock star moment, minus concert lights, smoke, and talented musicians. There are industrial lights, maybe a few mothers smoking Virginia Slims on the sidelines, and the only talent I display is the penmanship speed I perfected signing my John "Stamos" Hancock at amusement parks when I was fakin' it till I made it.

I get asked to sign everything from breasts to diapers, but there are strict rules. I can only sign autographs on the eight-by-ten glossies fans have to purchase at the venue.

I do the afternoon show from 1:00 to 3:00 P.M., then another from 7:00 to 10:00. Party in my room until midnight, get up, do another appearance on Sunday from noon to three, and rush to the airport to fly home so I can be on set bright and early Monday morning.

Sometimes they'll send along twelve Playboy Playmates with me, and other times it might be the hot ingenue du jour.

And on that jour, in Allentown, PA, at Agricultural Hall for the twenty-fifth Custom Car Show, November 5 and 6, 1983, it happens to be Heather Locklear. I have such a crush on her, "America's Sweetheart," with natural beauty and talent. I think

I'm in love. She stars as Sammy Jo on *Dynasty*, and I'm just a peon on daytime. She probably has no clue who I am. So, for now, I content myself with stealing glances at her from across the auditorium amid the muscle cars, admiring her Farrah Fawcett hairstyle framing a flawless face.

At one point our eyes meet as she looks up from signing autographs, and she flashes me a radiant smile that embodies the innocence and optimism of the eighties—I melt. A few minutes later, I receive a note from her that reads, "Hi cutie, meet me at the bar in our hotel after the show, xo Heather." If you would have told me . . .

I arrive at the bar early and slam a bunch of drinks to calm my nerves. She shows up in a short white sundress and says, "Let's play quarters." Before I can say I need a break from drinking, she blurts out, "With tequila shots!"

She turns out to be an ace at the game, making me drink even more. When it's my turn, I not only miss the glass with the quarter, I miss the entire table. I'm hammered. She's done with games and whispers in my ear, "Meet me up in my room in twenty minutes. And don't be late."

My heart is racing and my mind goes into overdrive as I sprint to my room to freshen up.

When I get there, the room starts spinning, round and round and round. The next thing I hear is POUND, POUND, POUND. It's Pauley, banging on my door, telling me I'm going to be late for the show.

Show? But . . . Quarters? Heather? Quarters. I struggle to form a coherent sentence. It turns out that it's the next day and I've apparently passed out on the floor, but not before barfing all over the bed first. Never made it to Heather's room.

I don't see her again until many years later when we cohost *Dick Clark's New Year's Rockin' Eve* special. She starts out understandably cold because she thinks I stiffed her, that I stood her up. We laugh and end up playing quarters again after the show. I've brushed up on my game over the years.

I'll do about three or four car shows a month. Always returning to Orange County with a bag full of cash (sometimes up to ten grand) and walking through the front door, bragging about my big weekend as my dad shoves a pooper-scooper in my hand and tells me to go clean the dog crap in the backyard.

It's a strange dichotomy: I'm starting to feel like a superstar on the road while still shoveling shit at home.

I'm not much of an athlete, but I can't pass up the opportunity to play a charity baseball game against my all-time favorite show, *Happy Days*, and its incredible cast.

If seeing Travolta sets a bar, and working with Springfield sets an expectation, then meeting Henry Winkler sets a tone that will last a lifetime. He is one of my heroes. Fonzie, Arthur Herbert Fonzarelli, the Fonz. For all his tough-but-tender, leather-clad affectations on-screen, Winkler is a rare gentleman and a serene figure in person. The guy who made the phrase "Ayy, sit on it!" famous has a master's from the Yale School of Drama.

I shake his hand. "Nice to meet you."

He looks me in the eyes and smiles. "No, it's nice to meet *you*."

There is a kind of person who doesn't just want to be seen and acknowledged but seeks to learn more about you; a guy who doesn't look over your shoulder to see if someone more important has entered the room. That's the spirit of the Fonz and the reality of Henry Winkler.

I think to myself, *I'm going to treat people the way he treats me.*

I go from a few shots in the teen rags to being plastered on the covers of *Tiger Beat*, *Teen Beat*, *Super Teen*, *Sixteen*, *Seventeen*, *TeenSet*, *BOP*, and any other publication selling daydreams and zit creams.

I'm sandwiched between features about Ralph Macchio, Rob Lowe, and Menudo. I'm photographed at a petting zoo with my hand on a zebra. The headline reads: "Blackie's Animalistic Side." I'm peppered with pressing journalistic questions like "What is John Stamos's favorite color?" They throw me in a pool atop an inflatable raft with pink-and-purple-colored lighting that matches my socks. My shirt is wide open to my belly button and I'm holding a volleyball for some reason.

Doreen Lioy, who gave me my first layout in *Tiger Beat* when I was a struggling nobody, wants me to be exclusive with her publication. I'm naturally a loyal guy, so I want to do right by anyone who does right by me. She has remained such a close friend of the family. I do my best to sit for new photoshoots and fulfill "breaking news" interviews like the hot cover story "John Stamos: His Family or YOU—Must He Choose?" I'm trying to spread my wings beyond the teenybopper audience, but Doreen seems to want to keep me forever young.

"He has this boyish charm about him. He's become like a little brother to me," she says. "The first time I saw Johnny flipping burgers, I was . . . captivated."

Everyone in the Stamos household and surrounding neighborhoods is on high alert in the summer of 1985. At my birthday party, we huddle around the TV watching the news. A San Gabriel couple has been brutally murdered. The husband was shot in the back of the head. The wife was raped and then killed. L.A. County Sheriff Sherman Block speaks directly to the cameras: "Richard Ramirez, you cannot escape. Every law officer and every citizen now knows exactly what you look like and who you are." They flash a mug shot of Ramirez.

Doreen is mesmerized by Richard's face. She leans over to my mom and whispers, "He has that little boy quality that Johnny has. Don't you think there's something . . . captivating about him?"

"Doreen!"

"Oh, I'm just joking."

My mom does not find it funny. Richard Ramirez looks nothing like her precious Johnny.

An American serial killer, rapist, necrophiliac, pedophile, robber, and Satan worshiper. A man who inflicts physical and emotional pain on his victims in unimaginable ways, yet Doreen Lioy is "captivated" by him, too.

Many of the murders are taking place just a few miles from my house in O.C. I come home late one night from a Beach Boys tour to discover my dad sitting on the porch in his underwear, bat in hand, ready to protect his family. Ramirez targeted yellow houses, and Bill Stamos was not going to repaint.

Doreen and Richard communicate by telephone through a thick plexiglass partition, but even at that distance, Doreen feels she's finally "the apple of someone's eye."

"He's Rudolph Valentino, Mick Jagger, and the Boogeyman all rolled into one. I love him."

Doreen leans into her identity as an idol maker. For her, Richard is just like the pretty boys that came before him. She grooms him for the first day of his trial like she's styling a cover shoot for *Tiger Beat*. She buys him large, black, Porsche-type sunglasses so he can close his eyes behind them. She dresses him in a shirt and tie, with a black leather jacket.

My mom is in shock. She knows my dad will flip the fuck out if he finds out about this. But it's hard for my mom to turn her back on Doreen like everyone else in her life. My mom always looks for the good in people, but this is a tough one.

"Listen," Doreen says, "I'm well aware that you may think I'm crazy or naive. But I believe in him."

"Doreen, honey, I watch the news," my mother says. "There are dozens of women who are in love with him."

"I'm a virgin, and Richard knows it. That's why I'm different."

"But what about children, Doreen? You've always talked about having a family someday."

"He's worth any sacrifice, and I know that dream will never come true. I've just replaced that with a different dream."

"Which is?" my mom asks, not knowing if she really wants to hear the answer.

"Which is becoming Mrs. Ramirez. I'm going to marry him, and we'll be together for the rest of our lives."

My mom can't keep this a secret from my dad. Doreen and my mom now have to correspond by mail.

"Loretta," Doreen says in a hopeful tone as my mother answers her call, "I want you to be my matron of honor."

It's this phone call that makes my dad realize Doreen is still calling his house. He grabs the phone from my mom and screams, "Listen, you desperate psychopath, you leave my wife and my family alone! And tell your boyfriend to save you a spot in hell!"

He slams down the phone, nearly shattering it. His hands are shaky. He can barely pour vodka into his glass.

Being a teen idol suits me just fine for now. Look beyond the corniness of the images and writing and you'll see a kid on fire. It's a hell of a ride, and I'm up for all of it. This is what I wanted my whole life. Some busy days it's like an out-of-body experience where I'm floating overhead watching someone else live out my dreams. At other moments, I'm so present and almost exploding with the realization that I'm famous, girls are interested in me, and somewhere out there, that bully bastard Rick Clarke sees the eyes of his girlfriend glide over my mug sneering at him from a magazine cover.

Some nights I stay at Kin Shriner's bachelor pad up on Beverly Glen so I don't have to drive all the way back to Orange

County after working late or if we go out on the town, hit up a few clubs. Being under twenty-one, my options are limited.

"I know a place we'll get in," Kin says with a mischievous grin. "Chippendales!"

Wait. Isn't that the male strip club where beefy, overly tanned dudes gyrate on bored real estate agents and repressed secretaries?

"Forget it, man." I hold my hands up to let him know I'm out.

"Trust me," Kin says knowingly. "The dancing boys go on from eight to eleven. At eleven thirty, they open the place up, and it's a nightclub."

"Huh?" I don't get it. We show up and Kin's friend sneaks us in the back door a half hour before it's open to the public. We're the only two men in the club. All heads turn.

I look at Kin and smile. Now I get it. We are meat in the lion's den. Freshly stamped, grade-A steak and the big cats are three hundred hopped-up housewives slipping off their seats, looking to sink their teeth into something sweet and juicy. But we are more like peacocks than carrion; we show up, fluff our feathers for a while, and fly home. On our way back to Kin's Bev Glen bach pad, I fall asleep curled in a ball in the back of his '77 dark blue Cutlass convertible.

Early the next day, as Kin shuffles out last night's date, he always finds me downstairs, eating cereal and watching Saturday-morning cartoons.

Across the street from the studio, at the corner of Sunset and Gower, there's a strip mall that looks like an old *Bonanza* film set, called the Gower Gulch. In the 1940s, the place was a hangout for wannabe cowboys trying to get hired as extras in the westerns filmed at our studio. The *General Hospital* crew loves a sushi restaurant in the complex, called Amagi. I stroll over sometimes, but I'm not a fan of uncooked fish. I'm also underage and strait-

laced when it comes to work, so I'm not about to drink sake on
the job.

"Amagi. You comin'?" Kin asks.

I hold up my script. "Nah, gotta study."

I have a ton of lines, but I'm pretty quick if I sit and focus.
My mind is uncluttered by other responsibilities, so it's easy
to learn them, especially if they're well written. With the halls
empty and everyone pitching sake across the street, I leave my
door open and dig in.

An attractive woman walks by and smiles. She's tall and
poised, with dark hair and an easy, elegant walk; the kind of girl
who glides.

"Hi," she says. "Can you tell me which way is casting?"

I babble something and notice a large modeling portfolio
under her arm.

"Are those your headshots?" I ask.

She smiles again. "Yes, do you want to see them?"

I nod.

She walks me to my couch, sits me down, unzips the big
black portfolio, and begins her show-and-tell.

"Oh, um, that's beautiful . . ." I'm stammering. Each page
she turns reveals more and more of her body. From sweater, to
swimsuit, to lingerie, to . . . tastefully nude, totally nude, and
now we're getting into gynecology textbook territory.

My face is hot and red. She isn't a *Cosmo*-tells-all model from
my mom's monthly subscription, and she isn't the girl-next-
door Playboy Playmate. She's a Penthouse Pet, posing in ways I
have never imagined possible.

Act cool. Pretend this happens every day of the week.

"So, uh, where are your commercial shots, like throwing
a Frisbee, skateboarding, or riding a horse?" I ask, trying to
joke around.

She stands up, closes the door, and starts removing her clothing. She's not in the mood for laughs. We have sex on my little couch in my little dressing room. It's hot, breathless, and all brand-new for me, but as soon as it's over I'm thinking, *She knows I can't get her a job on the show, right?*

She looks at the Snoopy clock on my desk, jumps to her feet, and washes herself up in my little sink. She dresses as casually as she undressed and heads off down the hall.

There is this awkward thing about fantasies being fulfilled. It's a wet dream that teens rub one out to, but the reality doesn't factor in the lack of connection, courting, and closure. You don't imagine the corporate furniture, fluorescent overhead lighting, eight-by-tens signed by cast members covering the walls, and how weird you'll feel in the moment.

You don't account for the swift gathering of garments and splashing sounds of the sink. Wham, bam, thank you, ma'am. The Penthouse Pet seeks to star in legit shows with old casting couch methods, likely learned from pervy execs. The new kid in town she seduces is still too young to toss a shot of sake across the street.

"Dear Penthouse Forum, you'll never guess what just happened. . . ."

I arrive early for work the next day and head to Kin's dressing room. Before I can kiss and tell, he trumps me with breaking news.

"Hey, congrats on your Emmy nomination!" he says casually. What?

"What did you say?"

"Emmy nominations came out just now, and you got nominated. After only one year!" he says, busting my chops but looking happy for me.

The other actors on the show seem surprised or envious. This is a big deal, a dream that never even crossed my mind. A dream that gets better with each sleep.

The Emmys are held in New York. Sitting next to my mom, I nervously await my category: Best Supporting Actor in a Daytime Soap. A cute, baby-faced actress from another soap reads off the nominees. My name gets a big round of applause.

"And the daytime Emmy goes to . . . ," she says, taking her sweet-ass time opening the envelope, "Darnell Williams, Jesse Hubbard on *All My Children*."

The first Black man to win in the category. Good for him. I don't get the statue, but my mom and I have a wonderful time. "Don't worry, Johnny, you'll win next year."

Years later, the pretty young soap star who fumbled with the Best Supporting Actor envelope will be cast as my girlfriend in a show about three bachelors trying to raise a house full of rascally little girls.

Nice to meet you, Lori Loughlin.

9

Slappin' Skins w/the Candy Man

General Hospital is so popular that everyone wants to be on it. A musician is booked for a guest spot and as I leave for work, I ask my dad, "Hey, you know a guy called Sammy Junior something?"

My dad looks at me like I'm a dumbass.

"Sammy Davis, Jr., is the greatest entrainer that ever lived. He can sing, dance, act, and play instruments. You don't know 'The Candy Man'?"

"You mean the song that creepy candy store owner sings in *Willy Wonka*?" I ask.

"Why do you have to make a joke about everything? You want to be a well-rounded entertainer, you need to know who these legends are, Johnny. Frank Sinatra, Sammy Davis, Dean Martin, they're the kings."

"What about Elvis? He's the King."

"Elvis couldn't shine their shoes. Look, Sammy is a hell of a drummer, ask him about drumming. He'll like that," my dad instructs.

So it begins. Our ongoing debate about who's cooler, Elvis or Frank. I promise my dad I'll do a deep dive into Frank Sinatra's music if he does the same for Elvis.

I put a quote in my yearbook about the link between music and life. It was a line from German philosopher Friedrich Nietzsche that read, "Without music, life would be a mistake." My dad thought it was stupid. I don't think he knew how important music was to me. Of course, he didn't think it was so stupid when I went on to play drums with The Beach Boys, John Fogerty and Bruce Springsteen, BB King, Willie Nelson, Little Richard, America, Tom Jones, and many more greats over the years.

Sammy is playing the father of a character named Bryan Phillips, portrayed by actor Todd Davis. His character is Eddie Phillips, an old nightclub singer and recovering alcoholic who's dying of spinal cancer. He's in Port Charles to make things right with his estranged son. Just as the community center my character helped establish is about to close, Eddie shows up for a charity show to save the day.

I'm realizing it's rare for there to be a solid storyline for the Black actors on the show, on any show. There's a subtle Jim Crow segregation in soaps that I don't understand in the moment: limited screen time, separate makeup and hair rooms, fewer lines. I don't get it, but I notice it.

Around this time, I form a new band with two estranged members of Papa Doo Run Run, Marky Star and Jimmy D. Armstrong, a big get for me. We call ourselves The Bad Boys, although we aren't.

I keep asking to play drums on *General Hospital*, but Gloria doesn't exactly take requests.

The director takes me to meet Sammy on the Waterfront set. When he walks on the set, he's already dressed in his costume: dark suit, white shirt, dark tie, 1950s Vegas suave. I'm starstruck.

He's smaller than I expected, yet he radiates an energy so massive that it fills the entire room. He sees me and strolls across the set, his rhythm so fluid it is as if he is performing a silent dance number. He reaches out to shake my hand, and I'm struck by the depth of his dark eyes, one genuine and the other a gleaming glass replica. (My dad failed to mention the glass eye part.) Now I'm really dumbstruck and can't muster a single word. Sammy senses this and his smile spreads across his face from ear to ear. He says, "Hey man, I'm a big fan."

Still at a loss for words, I remember my dad telling me to talk about drumming. So instead of something civilized, like "I'm a big fan of yours as well, Mr. Davis," I whine to him, "They won't let me play drums on the show." I ramble on about my drumming, and how I love playing, just like him.

"I wish they would give me a shot. I know they'd be impressed, but they keep saying no."

In that iconic, warm timbre, he says, "That ain't cool. Hold on, man." I like that he calls me "man."

He smiles and scuttles off somewhere. When he comes back, he's stern with me. "Listen, in the middle of the scene, just do what I say."

"Huh?" I ask.

"Just do what I say!"

Okay, Mr. Davis, Jr., sir.

My character, Blackie, is the host of the benefit. I'm wearing a tux as I introduce Eddie Phillips. *"We're talking about saving the Waterfront Sport Center,"* I begin. *"This is not just a place to hang out, it's a place to be proud of. And now, without further ado, please welcome Mr. Eddie Phillips."*

He's set up to perform several songs, so there are instruments on the stage. He gets on the mic and goes off script. *"Blackie, you play drums, don't you?"*

A completely flustered Blackie Parrish walks onstage and mounts the kit. Sammy sidles up to the piano to count off, "One, two, three, four." He begins to plunk out a jazz number, and I'm right there with him, smiling on the outside and dying on the inside.

Sammy challenges me with the cameras rolling. He's getting a kick out of it. He throws it to me for a drum break. I blast out some fast paradiddle thing on the hi-hat and throw it back to him. He picks it up, and with his fingers floating along the keys, he gives me that big grin of his.

It's a defining moment in my life. There are forty years that divide us, but we're speaking the same language in this moment: music. There is a look from the sage to the student that says, "Welcome to the club, kid."

We just keep jamming; no one dares stop us. The brass from the New York ABC offices, writers, and producers on the Gower lot and ABC execs in L.A. all have the live feed, and crowds begin to drift toward the monitors. Big shots, assistants, and secretaries gather around to see the kid and the Rat Packer go, man, go!

They finally stop us because we need to shoot the next scene to make our day. The whole stage erupts in applause. Sammy comes over and gives me the greatest hug ever.

"In five, four, three, two . . ."

Without missing a beat, Sammy Davis, Jr., falls back into character. "Blackie, don't worry about it, man, that sports center is gonna be all right." His face is twisted as he acts out the faltering health of his dying character.

Then in a heartfelt moment to his son, "If there's one thing I've learned in my life," Sammy/Eddie says with conviction, "it's that in the final analysis all you've got left is family; not money, possessions, not even adventure means a thing."

The last time I see Sammy Davis, Jr., is at the Greek Theater a few years later. He's been diagnosed with cancer, like his character Eddie, and he's in bad shape. He wants to say hi to me after the show. I'm sitting at the bar backstage, and Sammy floats into the room decked out in a white suit, cape, and cane. He comes over and gives me a frail hug. This hug feels different from the one he gave me on the set.

"Thank you for what you did for me. They never would have let me play music on *General Hospital* if it wasn't for you. Now I have my own band on the show called Blackie and the Riff Raff, and there's a whole storyline to go along with it," I tell him.

"Blackie and the Riff Raff?" he says, shaking his head and laughing. We laugh together.

He asks the bartender for an Orange Crush, and orders one for me. As the drinks hit the bar, Sammy says, "The cigs and the dope, I don't miss. The booze I miss." We hold up our soda pops for a toast. Sammy dies a few months later.

10

GOLDEN HANDCUFFS

As my popularity rises and I keep delivering in my scenes, I'm given the heaviest storyline to date. Blackie's mom dies. It's the first time playing one of those deeply dramatic scenes about loss.

I walk down the hallway, staying on the green carpet, of course, and open the door to the stairs that lead to the stage. I stop.

I flash back to myself at ten years old. I remember being at the foot of the stairs in my parents' house in Cypress. "Noooooooo!" my mother is screaming. "Nooooooo." She just learned that her own mother died of a pulmonary aspiration at dinner that evening. It's the exact moment I understand the concept of death, and from that day forward I obsess over my mom or dad dying. The thought of it can make me burst into tears on the spot, so these scenes should be easy.

I'm at the set a little early to pace around. I'm going to kill this dying-mother scene and win the Emmy this time. My mom will be there in the audience, and I'll give a speech crediting her for the inspiration for the performance of a lifetime.

Jerry Blumenthal, the stage manager, asks if I'm ready. I nod.

Chris Robinson, in Rick Webber character, is trying to calm Blackie down. "It's okay to be sad, let it out."

I start to say my line. Nothing. I'm empty. I spit out, "The world isn't fair!" I'm watching myself act, throwing out everything I've learned about performing and giving up on my instincts. I stop and ask if I can start over. I never do that.

Chris tells me it's fine. "You're allowed."

What the hell did I learn from Milton's class? Uh, get naked? No. Wait, I'll make a big announcement that I'm dying of pancreatic cancer. I'll make everyone cry, wallow in their grief, and play the scene filled with heartbreak and devastation. Then, I'll tell them it was just an exercise I learned in acting school, they'll fire me, and I can finally weep for real.

Gloria Monty's voice comes over the loudspeaker. "Come on, dear, we're waiting." That doesn't help.

I try a different tactic, telling myself, *My Mom's dead. My. Mom. Is. Dead.* Then my subconscious says, *No she's not, dummy, she's alive and well, teaching CCD at St. Irenaeus today!*

Time for Stanislavsky's "what if" method. It allows an actor to imagine the given circumstances as if they are really experiencing them in real time while simultaneously acknowledging that these circumstances are make-believe. "What if my mother is dead?"

Jerry counts it down and I'm off to the races. It's flowing. Real. Blackie tells Rick Webber how unfair life is and I feel it in my bones. I'm in the zone.

Peripherally, I catch someone putzing around in the distance. I try to ignore it and go on, but the person is making a racket trying to set up what looks like a director's chair. I hear a popping sound. What the hell?

I draw on flare-ups I've seen when fellow actors are disturbed during powerful scenes. Someone like Chris Robinson will just start yelling out of nowhere for somebody to get out of his "eyeline."

Initially, I don't relate to the concept because there are always twenty people standing around all the time: boom operators, folks pulling cables, wardrobe, directors, and other actors. Now I get it.

For the first time, I really lose it on set and yell out, "Will someone get that old woman out of my eyeline!"

That old woman is Elizabeth Taylor. There she is, in all her lavender-eyed glory, poised in a director's chair, sipping champagne. She is a fan of the show, and a few months before I started, she showed up for a brief, scene-stealing role as Helena Cassadine, wearing a diamond-festooned turban.

She's there visiting Tony Geary and wants to watch me do a scene. Chris quickly tells me who she is, and I'm so embarrassed. I can't believe I lost my shit in front of Elizabeth Taylor. My dad is going to kill me. I mute my tantrum, apologize profusely, make some excuse about calling her old, then slither back to the set and continue the scene. This time, I cry my eyes out.

Because the show is such a hit and I've got some buzz around me, I'm booking more gigs than ever for my band The Bad Boys. I have to squeeze music in between personal appearances for everything from the thirty-fifth annual Catholic Breakfast for Actors to judging wet T-shirt contests for MTV's "Spring Break in Fort Lauderdale." Trust me, the irony of this dichotomy is not lost on me.

I want to get more serious with my music. People are trying to talk me into doing an album, like Michael Damian or Leif Garrett. I start to get caught up in all of that, then realize I'm fooling myself into thinking I'm a real singer, a real musician. I'm not.

I feel a creeping restlessness. My dad would sometimes call me a jack-of-all-trades, master of none. I need to master a few more things. Go to the next level of drumming. Study guitar and piano. Work with a vocal coach. And follow my dream to be on a sitcom. Find a character like the Fonz on a Garry Marshall–type show that will turn me into a household name.

My contract is up soon and big-time agents start to sniff around. "Are you happy with your reps? Are you doing what you truly want to do?" Truthfully, I don't know.

Gloria and the higher-ups at ABC get wind of my desire to move on. They start throwing dough at me to add years to my contract. A lot of dough. Enough to buy my dad a new car and finally get rid of the El Co. I can take my sisters and my mom on a shopping spree. It's all so confusing to me.

My dad knows nothing about showbiz but everything about life, a hardworking man of character. He used to talk about "golden handcuffs," those wonderful but confining aspects of life that ensure comfort at the cost of growth.

His golden handcuffs were working for his dad on his tomato and eggplant farm in Mexico. He fell in love with a young beauty and part-time bathing suit model named Loretta, who lived in Los Angeles. His choice was to live comfortably, supervising conveyor belts sorting bad tomatoes, or tell his dad that he was in love and wanted to have a family and a restaurant of his own to provide for them. That was his happily-ever-after life. He made the right choice.

I corner my dad and start rattling to him, "I'm scared and don't know what to do, Dad. On one hand, I love being on the show and I know I'm doing good work, but it sort of doesn't matter. It's still a soap opera, with soap opera lighting, overdone hair and makeup, cheesy storylines. On the other hand, they're offering me a lot of money. Big money, but I'd have to be there a lot longer."

He calmly says, "Did you just say you'd 'have to' be there?"

"Yeah, I said I'd 'have to' be there . . ." His silence conveys a profound message. In that moment, I get it—I should *want* to be there, not *have* to be there.

"Follow your heart, Johnny. Be kind, be appreciative, be grateful, and leave with class," my dad says.

It's all I need to hear.

Gloria Monty takes me to lunch for my twentieth birthday. I've grown fond of her during my time on *General Hospital*.

We walk into an old-school Rat Pack hangout in Beverly Hills called La Dolce Vita. Our lunch is more of a shakedown than a celebration, so the mafia-style joint seems fitting. Dean Martin is dining nearby. He's alone, but the crisp, white-clothed table is set for two. Apparently this is his signature move so nobody tries to join him.

Gloria waves and Dean squints through glasses with frames so large they're like a pair of sliding glass doors over his eyes. She tells me that Dean Martin is sitting nearby.

"That's Dean Martin?" I ask.

My dad told me about him. He says I need to study guys like him, not sure why. "Mario, dear, meet Mr. John Stamos," Gloria says, introducing me to the waiter. Eager to meet Dean Martin, I throw a little wave across the room. Mario is guarding Dean's peace.

"Mr. Martin prefers not to be disturbed," he responds politely. Yet, catching my eye, Dean beckons me over.

Accompanied by Gloria, I approach the legend. She introduces me as her show's star, but adds that I'm getting a bit antsy and considering leaving.

Looking at Dean, she urges, "Share your wisdom about the value of commitment, Dean."

After a long pause, the aging crooner turns back into the King of Cool. A mischievous grin spreads across his face and, leaning in, he whispers to me, "Get out while you can!"

In that moment, I understand why my father encourages

me to learn from greats like him. Gloria immediately ushers me back to our table.

Once there, the mood takes a sharp turn. The lightheartedness is replaced by gravity. Gloria is pleasant but distracted throughout the meal.

She's sharpening her shiv and loading her pistol under the table. Her perfect bouffant is sprayed into Aqua Net submission, an immovable helmet as stiff as her resolve. Eye makeup shadows her gaze; red lipstick softens a weary, impatient smile.

Having already chosen to end my *General Hospital* contract, I'm putting my mental energy into selecting dessert.

Gloria leans in close. "Answer me something, won't you, dear?"

I knew this was coming. The offer I can't refuse. The big hit.

"Are you one hundred percent sure about your decision to leave my show, dear?"

I try to be honest and respectful. "Gloria, I am so grateful for everything you've done for me. Please know how much you mean to me. Your mentorship, friendship, and faith in me are gifts that will stay with me for the rest of my life. Without you, I'd still be flipping burgers at the Yellow Basket. But I want to be on a sitcom. I want to be funny."

She doesn't say anything. I don't say anything. Then, "You want to be funny?" I slowly nod yes.

She laughs at me. It's a laugh that starts at the mouth and never quite makes it to the eyes. I imagine a pearl-handled .22 pointed at my brazen balls.

As the waiters grind giant peppermills over tableside Caesar salads and ol' Dino gets served a whiskey aperitif, Gloria fires her shot.

"You know, if you leave, dear, you'll never work in this town again."

11

THE CHASE

I go from chasing fame, chasing women, and chasing that elusive party monster "happiness" to tripping and falling into a joyfully boisterous teen idol fantasy. It's a miracle and a mindfuck. I'm on top of the world, flying high and living my best life. In other words, I'm a full-blown, natural-born sucker ready for my first big heartbreak.

It's my last week of *General Hospital*. My exit storyline is a dark narrative twist involving unintentional manslaughter, where I inadvertently cause the death of my girlfriend, Lou. In a tragic sequence of events, a push leads to Lou tripping and falling, then hitting her head on the table, resulting in her untimely death. Blackie goes to jail. Any fleeting thoughts of me changing my mind and staying on the show are decisively extinguished. I'm in the makeup chair with P.K., hoping she'll take it easy on the contouring.

"P.K., why don't we try no mascara today?" I suggest.

"Teri Copley thinks you're sexy!" she interrupts with excitement.

"Who?" I ask her reflection in the mirror.

"Teri Copley! She's on a sitcom called *We Got It Made*. She's newly single and wants to go out with you."

We Got It Made is the kind of quintessential short-lived 1980s show you'd miss by blinking: kooky premise with sexual overtones (two bachelors hire a hot housekeeper or "maid"), stars the requisite blond bombshell, and features a series of slapstick gags designed to highlight the lead character's jiggle jugs. It's a less-clever *Three's Company* copycat.

"I've never seen it," I say, "but, you know, I'm really flattered." I shrug it off.

P.K. holds up the week's *TV Guide*, with Teri Copley on the cover. My heart stops. She's a modern Marilyn Monroe in skintight jeans, suspenders, and a pink shirt unbuttoned right down to the precipice of cleavage.

"Doesn't she remind you of Marilyn—" P.K. begins.

"Uh-huh," I say, snatching the magazine right out of her hand.

I have an infatuation with the iconic film star and can't take my eyes off the photograph of Teri. They have the same halo of blond hair framing heart-shaped faces. They both have bright blue eyes and cherry-red lips. There is something in the sweetness and roundness of their features that is familiar and timeless. Marilyn could look a little sad and haunted, but Teri was all Norma Jean: perky, personable, and ready to take on the world. She has an all-American wholesome sexiness that's quite hard to find in Los Angeles.

P.K. can tell I'm curious. "She's kind, just like you, and I know you guys would really like each other. She's tired of dating around. What do you say?"

I've never been in love. I fall into whatever-this-is just by looking at her picture.

"Yeah, so it wouldn't hurt to get to know her," I say casually. It will take a couple of months before we can finally meet.

Even before my contract is up at *General Hospital*, I'm already receiving offers and development deals from various networks and studios. CBS makes the best play, and within just a week of my last episode of GH, I start work on a new project, a single-camera, half-hour comedy series titled *Dreams*, revolving around the story of an unsigned rock band.

Bill Bixby of *Incredible Hulk* fame directs it, and I play opposite up-and-coming brat-packer Jami Gertz. This is not the straight-up, multi-cam sitcom I was looking for, but my new fancy agents at the William Morris Agency think it'll be a high-profile show, with potential to be a hit.

Andy Borowitz, creator of *The Fresh Prince of Bel-Air*, who goes on to become a premier political satirist, creates this show as well.

MTV is getting hot, and the idea is to do a show like *The Monkees*, where the fictional band does an album, makes videos that play on MTV, and we find success in all mediums.

One problem: I'm the only real musician in the group, and even that's a stretch.

Jon Peters, Barbra Streisand's hairdresser-turned-boyfriend-turned-de facto manager, is executive producing. There's a lot of that kind of thing happening around me—folks who subvert the ol' nose-to-the-grindstone ladder of leadership and slip into success with sex.

Peters is burly, arrogant, hairy, and scary. There's something off about him; a loose cannon.

He wants me to sing "Jailhouse Rock" on an episode, and I'm not feeling it.

Instead of discussing alternatives with me (I mean, after all, there are a lot of songs out there), the dude erupts in anger, yelling, forcefully pinning me against a wall, practically knocking the wind out of me.

I can't believe it. No one in a position of power has ever done something like this. Not even my father. I feel violated.

Loretta Stamos is not pleased and immediately contacts CBS executives to let them know that any further physical aggression toward her son will not be tolerated. CBS assures her that they understand and that it would not happen again. It does not.

But it's my initiation into the ugly side of Hollywood, the first time I understand how the big boys silence with violence.

Dreams gets canceled after thirteen episodes.

But that's okay, because just as I'm losing one dream, another walks into my life.

When Teri Copley and I meet for the first time for a casual date, she opens her mouth and speaks with a soft, breathless tone that makes me melt. I've never felt like this before. It's indescribable, but I'll try. There's an ugly-sounding Danish word for this beautiful feeling: *forelsket*. It's the first spark of infatuation, euphoric bliss, intoxication, and that smitten moment just before you fall off the cliff into love.

Teri and I date for close to a year and things keep getting better and better. We hit up my old haunts like Knott's Berry Farm and Disneyland, but also end up at Hollywood after-parties and premieres. We go bowling and eat at Bennigan's like high school kids.

My sexual experiences are limited to just a few girls. Where Ani's teaching moments end, Teri steps in seamlessly and introduces me to new and unexplored territories. We role-play, with her taking on the persona of Marilyn Monroe while I assume the role of Bobby Kennedy (or JFK, or Frank Sinatra, or Joe DiMaggio, or Arthur Miller with the glasses, when I'm feeling particularly daring). Despite Teri being a woman, like Ani, I still feel like a boy trying to keep up with her pace. It will take me some time to outgrow my Orange County upbringing, but I see no reason to rush the process.

I'm still living at my parents' house in my decked-out converted garage: brown shag carpeting, built-in Formica shelves, wood paneling, lobby cards from *Grease* covering the walls, ceramic faces of the Marx Brothers and James Dean, a giant poster of me that my mom had framed, my *Soap Opera Digest* award, and Loretta Stamos's most infamous keepsake: my tonsils in formaldehyde. Check it out, Teri: Shangri-la.

My new blue nine-piece Ludwig Vistalite drum kit, which looks like plexiglass cylinders, takes up practically the entire room. This is where I rehearse with my group The Bad Boys. The place is soundproofed with a faux wall, which also hides the washer and dryer and mostly quells the sound of the whishing and whirring.

"Don't mind me," my mom would say, waving her hand, "just grabbing Johnny's clothes out of the dryer so they'll be clean for work in the morning. Sorry for the interruption!"

Teri has been through a marriage, divorce, pregnancy, and the stresses of motherhood. She's been ogled and objectified in a business that exploits youth and beauty. We're not far apart in age, but we're worlds apart in experience. This is becoming a theme in my dating life. In the moment, I can't see it as a problem.

She's everything I'm looking for in a woman. She has an adorable daughter, Ashley, from a former relationship, and I love the idea of stepfatherhood. I'm starting to imagine our little family coming together. I'm dumbstruck and goofy in love. I could spend the rest of my life with her. Who knows if I'll ever find love again? Why not take a chance?

I'm on the road a lot, doing car shows and gigs with my Disneyland heroes, Papa Doo Run Run. I want Teri to come see me in action, but she doesn't. She always seems to have an excuse not to join me.

I call her from the road, but the girl who breathlessly picked up the phone after one ring is now giving me busy signals and dial tones.

When I get home, I call her throughout the day and into the evening. No response. Strange. We've gone from talking on the phone every few hours to silence. She's probably just occupied with a modeling gig or auditioning for something. I leave a message on her machine. She usually calls back in less than five minutes when I do that. Hours go by. I leave a message, then another message, okay, now my messages are getting a little weird, but I'm worried.

By the time I fill up her answering machine, I start feeling funny about the whole thing. Should I drive up to her house? Nah, don't want to look desperate. After all, she's the one who chased me.

I'm pretty confident in the relationship and have finally found someone I can be vulnerable around. I'm not going to mess this up by acting insecure. Just need to hit the hay and relax. I toss, turn, and get about thirty-six minutes of shut-eye before the sun blasts through my blinds. I think about how Elvis put tin foil on his windows when he stayed at hotels.

It dawns on me that I forgot about Teri having to deal with her daughter's father, Chip Mayer, this weekend. That's it! Chip is a dark-haired, burly-chested, handsome hunk whose claim to fame was being replacement beefcake for one of the Dukes of Hazzard. I'm not threatened by him. I trust Teri. I mean, sure, they had a baby together and probably planned this whole future, but you know, she's with me now. I take a good look in the bathroom mirror and pump myself up. "Hey, John Stamos, you handsome bastard." Standing in the same ratty pajamas I've had since junior high with bedhead, I look more like a mixed-up kid than a serious suitor. "There's nothing to worry about," I tell my reflection.

I peel out of the driveway so fast, the tires of my pop's car squealing down Carob Street on my way to the 605 out of Cypress. I'm probably overreacting. But I am stressing. I'm sure I'll get there and she'll be in her front yard waiting for me with open arms and a big smile.

I'm such an idiot.

I jam an eight-track into the player, Elton John's *Madman Across the Water*. The first song is my favorite. It's about a blue-jean baby ballerina with pretty eyes and a pirate's smile. It makes me think about Teri. I roll down the window and sing at the top of my lungs, "*Hold me closer, Tiny Dancer!*" And as I count the proverbial headlights on the highway, I'm pulling up to her cute little house in the Valley.

No lights on, no movement behind the windows. There's a car parked in her driveway. A black 1957 Porsche 356 Speedster, vintage convertible. Strange. I shuffle to the car with my stomach sinking and take a quick look inside. There's a hairbrush, keys, boxing gloves, and a half-unrolled poster of my girlfriend, naked, barely covered by a white sheet. Half of her butt is showing. I've never seen this poster before. Must be new. My mom loves Teri, but she's not going to like that one. It feels like that J. Geils Band song where the guy finds out his angel is the centerfold.

I try the front door, but it's locked. Why don't I have a key? I check the side door. Locked. Teri and I sometimes sleep in the guesthouse, so I go around back. The blinds are closed, but the door is slightly open. I take a peek inside and see four feet protruding from the shabby chic, floral print duvet that once kept me warm.

My Tiny Dancer is in bed with Mr. Porsche Speedster. They are sleeping. I can't tell who he is, but I recognize Teri's ass barely covered by the sheets. It looks like her new poster. My heart is beating out of my chest. My mind is racing, and the room is spinning. I feel like throwing up all over her white shag carpet. It's my worst nightmare.

I try to hold back tears. Time slows until I'm frozen. I can't breathe. A few tears roll down my face, and it pisses me off. They snap me out of my daze, and I feel angry and confused. I could explode.

Do I pull him out of the bed by his hair, kick him in the nuts, and beat his ass? She's my girlfriend. Who is this piece of shit? He looks familiar. Content bastard. He rolls over, exposing his ripped abs and muscular body.

Fuck it, I'm gonna run like hell. Not the time or place to save an ego that's shot to shit. I veer backward into the yard and sprint down the driveway.

But Teri used to chase *me*. Why am I the one running out here alone?

I fly past the Porsche, but something stops me, and I look inside again. I grab the poster and unroll it. I stare at the two-dimensional, half-dressed woman that I thought I knew. She's signed the poster, with little hearts, "My Dear Tony, I'll love you forever. XO, Teri."

Tony? Who the hell is Tony?

I jump in the El Co, start the car, and Elton John is still singing, and that's when it hits me. I mouth the words to his most famous lyrics and realize the name of my rival: "Hold me closer, Tony Danza. . . ."

12

DOWN THE RABBIT HOLE

I can't get out of bed. I'm depressed. My thoughts are racing. *What's Teri doing, who's she doing it with?* I've always had allergies, but I start chugging extra Dimetapp prescription syrup to make me drowsy enough to temper the heartbreak. The saccharine grape elixir clears up my congestion and helps me slip into the sweet relief of sleep.

I'm hopeful work will help; it doesn't. I'm cast in a silly Irwin Allen two-part made-for-TV fantasy musical of *Alice in Wonderland* opposite Harvey Korman, another legend I don't get until it's too late. *Blazing Saddles, Young Frankenstein,* and the *Carol Burnett Show?* I mean, come on, he's one of the comedy greats!

First day of shooting, I'm two hours late. They throw a costume and wig on me and hustle me to the set. I'm on Tragic Young Romantic time, half-past despair and a quarter-to-cryin'. Harvey is understandably cranky, but it's hard for him to stay mad at a mixed-up kid who looks like a Renaissance pleasure fairy with a Dorothy Hamill pageboy.

I babble about my fresh heartbreak, and he's sympathetic.

He says, "Assist, don't resist." He demonstrates with his hands. When he says assist, he's knuckle to knuckle. When he says resist, he pulls them apart. Weird. But I think he's telling me to go with the pain instead of fighting it. Accept this moment but don't waste energy trying to go against it. It's hard to take love advice from a guy dressed as a giant king from a game of lawn chess.

As we start our musical number "The Lion and the Unicorn," I get a quick glimpse of myself on a monitor, and I'm mortified. This isn't where I pictured myself at this point in my career, and the look in Harvey's eyes suggests that he feels the same, making the whole thing even more depressing.

The experience is a far cry from what I had hoped for. I thought it could be a moment of levity, a brief reprieve from the heartache I'm feeling. It is not. However, an interesting opportunity is on the horizon, which just might be exactly what I need to break out of this funk.

I get an offer to play Lance Stargrove, a young James Bond type in a movie called *Never Too Young to Die*. "Enough with TV," I think. "This'll be my breakthrough. I'm going to be a movie star!" George Lazenby is playing my father. He was an OG James Bond once, and once only, in *On Her Majesty's Secret Service*. That's all I need. Just one shot at 007.

KISS legend Gene Simmons plays the evil hermaphrodite, Velvet Von Ragnar. Robert Englund, of Freddy Krueger fame, plays an evil dude, and rounding out some of the finest thespians ever assembled for an artistic masterpiece like this is Prince protégée Vanity, who plays my love interest, Danja.

If working alongside Harvey Korman in a Little Lord Fauntleroy costume depresses me, being serenaded by Gene Simmons in full drag with prosthetic boobs singing "It Takes a Man Like Me, to Be a Woman Like Me" makes me want to quit acting and pursue my childhood dream of a life in puppetry.

My character, Lance, is a gymnast, so I put all my heartache energy into training. After a few weeks, I bust my ankle trying to do a double-flip-twist thing on the trampoline and I'm in a cast for a month. That should have been my first sign that none of us are ever too young to die—on the trampoline, or worse yet, on the silver screen.

When starting a new project, there's usually a meet-and-greet cast dinner and tonight it's at a restaurant on Sunset Boulevard called Le Dome. Mere moments after meeting Vanity for the first time, she's giving me a hand job under the table. Not even sure how it starts. I'm making small talk as she rearranges a napkin in my lap and the next thing I know she's all in. It's exciting but nerve-racking. She maintains a slight smile and looks attentively at the director, who's discussing the nuanced attraction between our characters, Stargrove and Danja. Nothing nuanced happening under the table. At the same time, the producer is making introductions. I hope she doesn't shake hands with anyone.

It's not the first sexual experience I wanted after a big breakup, but it's the one I got. Probably pretty common stuff for rock stars, but I feel self-conscious with everyone sitting there. Beyond awkward. I mean, Freddy Krueger is watching.

"Can I get you something to drink?" the waiter asks him.

Now would be a great time for Robert Englund to say, "I'll have what he's having."

Like a James Bond martini, I'm still getting shaken but not stirred under the table.

In addition to suspect dinner etiquette, on our first day of shooting on the set, Vanity goes full Al Pacino in *Scarface*. She grabs any prop weapon she can get her hands on and unloads clips all over the place, even when we're not rolling. This gal is working out sex and violence issues and I'm trying not to be the next

Jon-Erik Hexum, who just recently accidentally killed himself with a prop gun on the set of his television show *Cover Up*.

Her real name is Denise, but she insists I use her stage name.

"Vanity! Call me Vanity!" she says.

When she gets out of control, I get under her skin. "Lighten up, *Denise*."

Looking back, I feel for her. Her dad abused her until he died. Then she was modeling at seventeen and molded into the sexpot image by influential men who wanted to make her their "Nasty Girl." She ping-ponged from freebasing cocaine to tripping on the stronger drug of evangelical religion.

I imagine a lot was done to her and somehow doing a little something to a younger, inexperienced guy and waving machine guns around gave her a feeling of reclaiming power.

The movie comes out and it's a steaming pile of embarrassing shit. I thought I'd impress Teri by being a movie star, but the whole production gets panned by critics and bombs spectacularly. What kind of delusional thinking made me assume I'd be the fresh face of the next Bond franchise?

Years later, I'll find the humor in it all. It's the best, worst thing you will ever see. I hope one day it takes off like *The Rocky Horror Picture Show*, with all its campiness, but in this moment, it's the lowest point of my career, and doesn't do much for my broken heart. I go to a drive-in to see it and drive out of my own movie. A new low.

But that's all about to turn around with a frantic phone call from Jimi Jo, the bass player for Papa Doo Run Run, who is like an older brother to me and is one of my best friends. "J, get your ass to Disneyland, we need you!"

"What's up?"

He just yells, "Now!" and hangs up the phone.

I get my ass to Disneyland and find Jimi Jo at the Carnation Plaza Stage. It turns out they need me to fill in for drummer Krazy Jim Shippey, who's unable to perform with Papa Doo Run Run due to an unfortunate case of the runs.

Jeffrey Foskett, a member of The Beach Boys' band, is also hanging out and joins Papa onstage for a few songs. He sings "Lucille" and "Roll Over Beethoven." I can't believe the range this guy has. He hits high notes with an easy, effortless falsetto that soars above the music, as only a young Brian Wilson could. His control, range, power, and versatility make him a true master and leave a lasting impression on anyone who hears him, especially me. I play drums that night with an intensity and passion that I have never tapped into.

I guess I impress Jeff, and our little jam session will turn out to be a pivotal moment. He will later serve as a bridge between me and The Beach Boys, changing the course of my life forever.

Jeffrey and I are becoming good friends. He knows how down in the dumps I am about my first major breakup and offers to help get me out of my funk. The Beach Boys are playing at Jack Murphy Stadium in San Diego after a Padres game. He doesn't promise anything but says he might be able to introduce me to my heroes.

Jeff says, "Come backstage the second they end the last chorus of 'Fun, Fun, Fun.' They'll head back to do an encore, and after that they'll jump in their cars and split immediately to beat the crowds leaving the stadium."

On May 8, 1983, a voice booms throughout the stadium: "Ladies and gentlemen, please welcome, from Southern California, The Beach Boys!"

The crowd goes wild, stomping their feet, shaking the stadium like an earthquake.

They perform their biggest hits.

Toward the end, I hear the familiar guitar riff that kicks off "Fun, Fun, Fun." I'm nervous as hell by the time Daddy takes the T-Bird away for the final time.

A security guard leads me onto the field and points me to the backstage area. All of a sudden, I hear screaming. It sounds like a horror movie. I look over to see what the commotion is all about, and I see about twenty or thirty teenage girls freaking out. Turns out the commotion is me.

The entire group of cheerleaders are coming my way. I smile and wave sheepishly. They take off, running toward me, I take off running away from them, and the chase is on. I bolt like hell. Since we're on a baseball field, I round the bases like an idiot, then take off to the outfield where the girls are gaining on me. I'm a terrible runner.

Oh look, there I am, larger than life on the jumbotron: a dorky, skinny-legged kid in Jordache jeans with a mullet that looks like a crow died on my head, being outrun by a bunch of screaming teenagers.

I'm breathing so hard I feel like I'm going to pass out. I see a sign for the backstage area. I pivot toward it as I whip out my pass and slip through just in time for security to close the door behind me to muffled screams.

I'm completely out of breath. I'm sweaty. My hair is . . . well, my hair is still perfect. I'm bending over and gasping for air. The room is suddenly silent. Mike, Carl, Al, and Bruce, The Beach Boys, are all staring at me in horror (and these guys spent time with Charlie Manson).

I've never wanted to slither out of a room and under a rock faster.

Mike Love, the P. T. Barnum of the band, asks, "Who's that?"

Jeffrey turns to Mike and says, "That's my friend John Stamos. He's on a soap called *General Hospital*. He's a great drummer."

Mike says, "Do girls chase him and scream like that wherever he goes?"

Jeff says, "Yep."

Without missing a beat, Mike says, "Get him onstage!"

In the same spontaneous way Sammy Davis, Jr., got me to play on General Hospital, Mike Love points me toward the drums. Holy shit, this is it. He steps up to his microphone, and I hear one of the most iconic and distinctive voices in all of rock-n-roll. "Ba, Ba, Ba, Ba . . ." Just like that, I find myself playing "Barbara Ann" with my idols.

A stadium packed with fifty thousand fans are all singing, dancing, and clapping in unison to a rhythm that I'm creating with my hands and feet. It's an unbelievable feeling. I've imagined this scenario a million times, but the reality of it all is beyond my wildest dreams. The minute it ends, I want to do it all over again. It's like great sex; that lusty, primal moment where you suddenly find your groove and figure everything out.

Little do I know this one-night stand will be a lifelong love affair. Right now, it's just a great feeling that I am ready to re-create at work, in life, and in love. I've fallen down the rabbit hole, and I don't want to return to the ordinary world ever again.

13

SATANS AND SAINTS

In July of 1985, The Beach Boys are asked back to perform at the annual "Sea to Shining Sea" July Fourth concerts, in D.C. and Philly. A few years before, they had been ousted from playing at the concert by Secretary of the Interior James Watt. He declared that the "hard rock" group drew the "wrong element" and replaced them with Wayne Newton. This didn't fly with First Lady Nancy Reagan, who was more of a "Surfer Girl" than a "Danke Schoen" dame. James Watt not only had to grovel to get the Boys back, but President Reagan also awarded him a trophy of a plaster foot that had a hole in it, symbolic of Watt having shot himself in the foot.

The concerts always feature guest star friends of The Beach Boys, and my name comes up to sit in on drums. Carl Wilson, the band's musical director, asks Jeffrey if I could make it through a few songs.

Jeffrey says, "Are you kidding? Stamos is a badass drummer and a good human as well. Of course, he can handle a few songs. Hell, he could play the whole set!"

When I arrive at the Watergate Hotel, in D.C., Jeffrey is in the lobby waiting. He gives me a big hug and says, "Let's go, we need to meet up with Jimmy and go over the songs he's playing with us."

"Jimmy?" I say. "Who's Jimmy?"

Next thing I know, we are standing in the Watergate Presidential Suite with Jimmy's roadie/assistant/handler, Phil Carlo. "Come on in, boys."

It's the biggest suite I've ever seen. It's the size of a house. I'm in awe. Floor-to-ceiling windows with waterfront views, massive couches upholstered with a giant flower print, an imposing fireplace, a bar, a library.

Just then, Jimmy Page comes around the corner. Wiry, skinny, moving up and down as he walks in like a Slinky.

Oh, that's Jimmy. Phil does the intros. "This is Jeffrey Foskett, the guitar player for The Beach Boys." Then looks to me with a blank stare.

Jeff jumps in. "This is John Stamos from *General Hospital*."

"You're a doctor?" Jimmy asks, taking a big swig from the largest bottle of Jack Daniel's I've ever seen. He holds it out for us to share a drink.

"No, thank you." Then I politely ask him, "Do you have a light beer, Mr. Page?" He looks confused, then disappears.

Jeffrey zips off to another room to check out Jimmy's guitars. Phil follows, leaving me alone with my hands in my pockets.

There's a strange chill in the room for such a hot day. Not an air conditioner chill, something different, a little creepy.

On the other side of the room, near a large overstuffed floral couch, are two large Anvil cases covered with a hippie tie-dyed sheet.

Everything has gotten quiet.

I plop down on the couch, and the giant cushions practically swallow me up.

Then a tiny, skinny, curly-haired girl pokes her head out from between the two Anvil cases.

"FUCK!" I scream.

Then she screams, "Fuck!"

She looks young but roughed up by life; rode hard and put away wet, as they say. She's in all-black, wearing some sleeveless, witchy dress. She looks hungry.

Jimmy waltzes in, and she quickly ducks back between the cases like a little bird in some gothic cuckoo clock. Jimmy sits next to me, completely oblivious, and calmly pulls an acoustic guitar to his chest and hands me a light beer. I suck it down. Fast. My heart is pounding out of my chest. Jimmy Page is unquestionably one of the most influential, important guitarists and songwriters in rock history.

"What songs am I playing on?" he asks me in a soft voice.

He's composed. He soothes my nerves with his calmness.

"Well, I'm sure you'll be playing on 'Barbara Ann.' That's a big sing-along song they do during the encore."

"Oh, right," he says. "How does it go?"

I'm floored. This guy who is asking me how to play "Barbara Ann" is the same guy who wrote "Stairway to Heaven." Stairway. To. Heaven.

Okay, maybe he's never heard "Barbara Ann."

I tell him. "It's just a one, four, five progression in the key of F sharp."

He explodes. "I CAN'T FUCKING SOLO IN F SHARP! Goddamnit! What about 'Help Me, Rhonda'? What key is that in?"

I screw up my face like I'm about to take a punch and eke out, "C sharp?"

"I CAN'T FUCKING SOLO IN C SHARP, MAN!"

The skinny girl pops her head back out from behind the Anvil fort. "Jimmy? Can I come out now?"

"No!" he screams.

What the fuck is going on? I've had nightmares about being chased by chainsaw-wielding clowns that were more fun than this.

Thankfully, Jeffrey comes back.

"Yell at him!" I say, pointing at poor Jeffrey. Let him take the blame.

Jimmy and the girl take off to another room.

Phil tells us Jimmy is tense.

"I know the feeling," I say, wishing them a good night. I need to get out of here before I get cursed or something.

"All right, Stimity Stame," Jeff says, using one of his many nicknames for me, "get some sleep." He and Phil were off to find Jimmy. As I slink out, and against my better judgment, I peek into another Anvil case that happens to be open. Maybe Goth Girl has a twin getting ready to "Jack in the Box" me?

Nope. Just a wooden baton with a grotesque mask that looks like it's carved out of bone, a mother-of-pearl inlaid cross wrapped in something that looks like bloody twine, a crow's head with a beak, and a baby bat.

In less than twenty-four hours I'm about to play the first real concert of my life with my childhood heroes, but I go to bed thinking about that little bat. Is it real? And if so, should I report this to PETA?

Morning comes quickly. I jump up and put on my show clothes: white and gray plaid linen pants and a baby-blue shirt. I slap on my backstage pass with a big number 1 (all-access, baby) then fluff up my hair a little higher than usual in preparation for the humidity.

The day begins at Washington Union Station, where the band will travel by train to Philadelphia. Besides Jimmy Page, other guests joining the band will include Christopher Cross, Joan Jett,

The Oak Ridge Boys, and for some reason, Mike invites Mr. T. He figures Mr. T was in *Rocky III*, the film took place in Philly, so . . .

"Do you have any musical talent?" Mike asks him.

Mr. T says, "No, but I did play Clubber Lang, and that sounds like a drummer, so I'll play drums."

"Who is going to tell Mr. T he can't play the drums?" Mike declares, so a third drum kit is added to the already overcrowded stage.

It is hot in the passenger car. Mr. T gets so rambunctious that he knocks out a window.

As we get closer to the gig, in the distance we see the Philadelphia Museum of Art, with the seventy-two stone steps that Rocky famously ran up and down getting in shape for his big fight with Clubber Lang.

"I'll get you, Balboa!" Mr. T. then comes running through the train, and right on cue, someone feeds him the setup to his most iconic line in the film, "Do you hate Rocky?"

Mr. T says, "No, I don't hate Balboa. I pity the fool, and I will destroy any man who tries to take what I got!"

Then he moves from car to car, doing his bit for passengers all the way through the train.

Jimmy Page, looking elfish and elegant in a cool black, white, and pale-pink vintage floral Hawaiian shirt, sits next to Goth Girl, who is wearing the baby bat as a necklace. (Ahhh, baby bat mystery solved.)

Mike Love is a man with a beautiful vision to save the world. He founded the Mike Love Foundation with the idealistic goal of ending world hunger (small goals, according to Mike). When he speaks about these aspirations, he has a way of inspiring others to believe that they, too, can accomplish anything. I am in awe of his philanthropic spirit. Being on a train with Jimmy Page and Mike

Love is like rolling with Satan and a Saint. One wants to control the mysteries of the universe with magic, and the other wants to unite the earth with good vibrations. I'm just here to play drums, man.

Onstage, Mike Love describes this massive gathering of a million fans who line the Ben Franklin Parkway as, "A blur of jubilant humanity."

I stop and take it all in. One million people. A sea of faces and outstretched arms extended toward the stage, resembling undulating waves that crash against it. The fans in the back disappear into the surroundings like mist on the ocean, while their collective screams meld into a single roar like the sound you hear when you hold a seashell to your ear.

Jimmy Page doesn't drown out The Beach Boys, as some feared, but complements them extremely well. He gives the songs some rock edge but never muddies their quintessential California sound. It's clear Jimmy is having a good time. If he's nervous, it doesn't show.

I play drums as Jeffrey belts out a powerful vocal on Little Richard's classic "Lucille," just like we did when we first met on the Carnation Plaza Stage at Disneyland with Papa Doo Run Run. Only difference is today we're on the steps of the Philly Art Museum, playing for a million people, and Jimmy Page is shredding the guitar solo.

I am truly humbled. Who would be bold enough to even think about dreaming this big? Oh yeah, me.

Winding up the show in Philly, Mike Love invites all the guests up for "Barbara Ann," then calls out, "Everybody, don't forget John Stamos up here! He just joined us on drums. Do you remember him from *General Hospital*? Stand up, John!"

I stand on my drums, a move I cribbed from Krazy Jim from Papa Doo Run Run. The women scream.

"The girls love him!" he shouts.

We launch into "Barbara Ann," and it turns out Jimmy Page *can* solo in F sharp.

After the show, teeming with adrenaline, I'm springing down the stairs of the mammoth stage. I spot Jimmy.

"See, Jimmy, the audience really loved you! I told you there was nothing to worry about. Did you see all the rock-n-roll salutes the crowd gave you?" I say, demonstrating the standard hand-horns gesture of head-banging concert aficionados: index finger up, middle fingers down, pinky up, and thumb in.

He looks at me, perplexed, his head cocked like a puppy hearing a high-pitched sound. Then it appears something dawns on him.

"Oh," he says with a tinge of relief, "I fought they waz hexing me now, didn't I?"

We're all loaded up in the private DC-9 that American Airlines provided per their deal with the Mike Love Foundation.

This is the first private plane I've ever been in, and I'm loving everything about it. Except for Mr. T, who is fired up and won't stop talking. Finally Carl, who never raises his voice, turns to him and says, "Shut the fuck up!"

We're running late as we touch down at Washington National Airport. We pile into three large buses and take off with a phalanx of police cars leading the way. Sirens are blasting through the streets. Feels like a stressful situation, but not for me. At this moment, I'm living my very best life.

When we finally arrive, we're late and everyone is in full panic mode. One of the tour managers, Joel Gast, and a rep from the U.S. Park Service approach me. "Stamos, we need you to go out there and get the crowd to calm down."

"Excuse me? What do you want me to tell seven hundred and fifty thousand hot, drunk, constipated people?" I ask, ready to shit my own pants.

Now we know why my mom covered me with a blanket when she brought me home. *"You were a homely little baby."*

My dad teaching me the importance of balance early on (btw, I still have those undies).

The less homely I got, the bigger my ears grew. Even trade.

I'm incredibly lucky to have the most supportive sisters in the world, Janeen and Alaina. They helped make me the man I am without judging the little boy I was.

Me trying to impress a
girl with puppets—her
reaction is the reason I
became a musician.

My first drum set: Tony the Tiger.

My dad bought me a real blue sparkle
kit after I practiced all summer long.

Band geek and proud of it.

Me and my best friend,
Mike Owen, sporting
our velour on our way
to Diz. "Hey ladies."

"*I'm talking about a couple guys jumping me, baseball bats in one hand, brass knuckles in the other!*" My first day as Blackie Parrish on *General Hospital*.

Gloria Monty and me with our Soap Opera Digest Awards. She was my earliest mentor and the reason I have a career.

Me, Demi Moore, and Tony Geary. Tony was the best actor I'd seen up to that point. I would stay after my scenes just to study him.

"Blackie, you play drums, don't you?"
Hanging on the set of *GH* with
the man responsible for my
musical career on television,
Mr. Sammy Davis, Jr.

The man who took me under
his wing at *General Hospital*,
Kin Shriner.

Teri Copley, my first but not my last heartbreak.

"No, it's nice to meet you."
Me and the Fonz,
Henry Winkler, at a
charity baseball game,
Happy Days vs. *General
Hospital*.

Me with the Signals: Sharon Coker,
Loretta Grikavicius (younger sister to
Goddess Ani), and Matt Caver.

My first band, Destiny, with Phil
and Habib Bardowell

The night I smoked oregano leaves after my friends told me it was pot. Oh, and also the night I lost my virginity.

Doreen Lioy, editor of *Tiger Beat* magazine, called me her little brother. She called my mother Mom. And called Richard Ramirez, the "Night Stalker," her husband.

The making of a teen idol.

Lori, couldn't you have said my name at the Daytime Emmys instead of the name of the guy who actually won?

My mother with Frank Sinatra right before Jilly Rizzo almost tackled her.

Me, Frank, and Paula Abdul. "Smoke one for me, Johnny!"

My first time onstage with The Beach Boys and about
one million fans. That's the crowd they asked me to tell,
"Back up or they'll shut down the show." I've never felt
one million people turn on me so fast.

Jimmy Page.

July 4, 1985, Washington, D.C.

Brian Wilson: God Only
Knows where we'd all be
without him.

Bruce Johnston, Brian Wilson, Jeffrey Foskett, and
me at the piano at the Four Seasons in Montreal,
July 3, 1995: "Rock, Roll, Rockin' and a Rollin'."

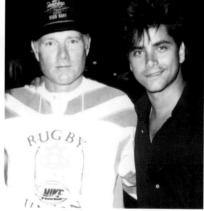

Me and Mike Love before a show at
Mud Island in Memphis.

"Tell the audience to stop pushing and crowding one another or The Beach Boys will not perform, and everyone will have to leave the premises immediately."

"So, you want me to give an ultimatum to that massive crowd?"

A local DJ, Smokey Rivers from WAVA, gets on the mic and announces, "Ladies and gentlemen, give it up for Blackie!"

Race riot, anyone? Even back then, not the most PC name. Luckily, as soon as they see me, they mostly get it. They begin to clap and scream. It gets louder and louder until it's deafening. I don't know what to do.

I yell out something amazingly uncool. "Are you ready to rock out, D.C.?!?"

They roar. Jimmy Page hexing signs pulsate in the air.

"So, guys," I say, holding my hands up, "the U.S. Park Service asked me to come out and tell you all to back up and stop pushing or they're going to cancel the show."

Suddenly, the seven hundred and fifty thousand people go from screaming for me to booing at me. I quickly switch to kiss-ass mode. "Let me finish! I told the Park Service guy that you beautiful people can do any damn thing you want! God bless America and thank you!"

The crowd cheers uproariously and I walk offstage to angry faces, sheepishly giving them an "I tried" look.

It's SHOWTIME!

The Beach Boys finally hit the stage around nine thirty.

Mike Love starts the show. "Sorry we're late, but we're here to express harmony and good vibrations!"

They open with their classic "California Girls."

"*Well East Coast girls are hip I really dig those styles they wear. . . .*" That's as far as they get. . . .

BA-BOOM! Fireworks wait for no one.

The beautiful explosions drown out the next couple of songs.

Bruce Johnston says, "This next one is from our album *Pet Sounds*," followed by the optimistic opening melody of "Wouldn't It Be Nice." While he couldn't make the Philly show, a trim, beardless Brian Wilson joins in on a keyboard called a keytar that hangs around his neck. He takes the lead vocal and sounds almost like he did on the record.

Not one ounce of my past heartbreak matters at this moment. I am delighted, grateful, and just wish my family was here to see me. In the future, anytime I join the band at an important show or on tour, I'll insist my parents come along.

Mike brings up Jimmy Page and says, "Like we promised, Stairway to Rhonda!" and they break into "Help Me Rhonda." Page, once again, kills the solo.

Now it's my turn. I play on a John Fogerty cover called "Rockin' All Over the World."

Carl Wilson sings lead and picks me to play this song. It's a slamming groove, four-on-the-floor, with a Rolling Stones feel. It's like "Tumbling Dice" but faster.

I've played drums for years, but nothing prepared me for a show like this. There's so much sound swirling around with at least seventeen elite musicians onstage. I have no choice but to play as hard as I can. I hold my left stick the wrong way, using the fat end to bash the snare drum. My arm whips up and down for power like I'm snapping someone's ass with a wet towel.

I tap into a kind of control I never knew I had until this very moment.

Don't listen to the crowd. Don't listen to my heart beating out of my chest. Fuck these nerves.

Before the show, Carl Wilson tells me to watch his elbow for time. I watch it from behind, going up and down, up and down, as if he's sawing a piece of wood. He's the one I have to impress. I cut out every bit of outside noise and only focus on what's needed to survive. I do that for at least three more minutes until the song ends. I feel like I've just boxed ten rounds and won.

"John Stamos on the drums!"

Carl turns to me like he's in slow motion, smiles, and nods. He approves. Then, everything goes back to normal speed; in fact, it feels faster.

I start to leave the drums, but Carl motions for me to stay. A vote of confidence. It means everything to me.

The band gives the crowd a raucous version of "Fun, Fun, Fun," and a few more fireworks blow in the background as Jeffrey, Bruce, and Brian Wilson sing the falsetto part at the end, "Oooh, oooh, oooh," and the entire audience is right there with them. It's a sensation that's difficult to put into words, something so pure, stunning, and quintessentially American.

When the song ends, Mike says, "Try to leave the place a little bit clean and for heaven's sake, be nice to each other. Do unto others and all those simple things. We'll be back to catch you again sometime. God Bless. We love you!"

July Fourth 1985 was to be the last time The Beach Boys play on the Mall. They get banned from the annual celebration by the National Park Service, who feel a "family-oriented" program is better suited. They're looking into the possibility of having a military band perform. They want a more patriotic-type ceremony in keeping with the holiday. More patriotic than America's Band? The only way The Beach Boys could be more patriotic is if they sang The Star-Spangled Banner dressed as the Founding Fathers while shooting apple pie from a T-shirt cannon.

In 2019, doing a hosting gig for PBS's A Capitol Fourth, I invite them to make a triumphant return. They're the perfect band for the perfect time. America is divided like never before, but The

Beach Boys bring folks together with songs that everyone can agree on.

The then-president of the United States, Donald Trump, holds a dark, foreboding rally by the Reflecting Pool as I share my speech on the Mall.

In an article for the *Washington Post*, reporter Dan Zak wrote "Evening in America; What It Felt Like on Trump's Fourth of July."

A nearby stack of speakers thundered with Sousa marches until TV star John Stamos kicked off the Capitol Fourth concert.

"I see a mosaic of different histories," Stamos said, his voice piped all over the Mall, echoing into a garble.

MAGA acolytes were blowing whistles in support of the president's speech.

A band of young white supremacists began to confront protesters.

"All part of the fabric that makes us an American family," went the disembodied voice of Stamos.

A scowling man in a MAGA hat put his fist near a protester's face and turned his thumb down. Dusk was falling. The whistles reached a shrieking volume.

"Let's love each other as citizens," Stamos said, and the whistles kept going and going and going.

In many ways, my speech about family and love was just stuff I learned from The Beach Boys. The things that separate us seem small compared to what should draw us together. Politics are divisive. Music unites. Narrow ideologies limit us. Curiosity and creativity invite us to imagine endless possibilities.

The Beach Boys represent all the best of who we can be: generous, talented, brilliant, benevolent, and divine. God only knows where I'd be without them.

14

THE ODD COUPLE OF MENTORS

Garry Marshall calls himself my "godfather" of showbiz. He is much more to me than that. Garry is one of those people who always comes through with his promises or commitments. He presents me with an Icon Award. He makes a beautiful speech at the unveiling of my star on the Hollywood Walk of Fame. He puts me in one of his movies (although I get cut, but he proudly tells everyone they can see me in the "deleted scenes" if they buy the DVD). One day, he says to me in his thickest Bronx accent, "I'm going to recommend you for a part in a new TV show my friends are producing. Can you play guitar?"

His friends are Tom Miller and Bob Boyett. The TV show, *Full House.*

I met Garry while doing a show called *You Again?* with Jack Klugman, my first mentor.

Jack plays my father, a boring supermarket manager whose life gets turned upside down when his teenage son, whom he barely knows, shows up to live with him.

Every young actor in town was clamoring to play opposite

Jack Klugman in his return to sitcom television. If Ben Stiller was the front-runner, I was the back-lagger. NBC didn't think I had comedy chops. Ben grew up in the comedy royalty household of Jerry Stiller and Anne Meara. They only knew me from *General Hospital*. They refused to cast me. I know Jack came up against similar obstacles transitioning from his dramatic work to *The Odd Couple*. Maybe he could relate because I later learn that Jack says, "If John Stamos doesn't do the show, then I don't."

Jack becomes like a second father to me after my father dies; he becomes the next important male figure in my life that I want to make proud.

On punch-up night, Jack takes me to the writers' room and says, "Sit in the corner, watch and learn, and don't say a word."

He calls in his comedy legend cronies to watch the run-through, then go over the script line by line, make it funnier, work on story and structure, and brighten and tighten where needed. I am in awe watching these kings of comedy work. Garry Marshall, Harvey Miller, who wrote *Private Benjamin* and *The Bob Newhart Show*. Jerry Belson, a joke genius who wrote on *The Dick Van Dyke Show*, *The Lucy Show*, *The Tracey Ullman Show*, and co-created *The Odd Couple* with Garry. Saul Turteltaub and Bernie Orenstein, who ran the second season. Jerry Stahl, who would go on to write his memoir, *Permanent Midnight*. If I open my mouth to make a peep of a suggestion, I'm pelted with crumpled-up paper balls.

The opportunity to be in that room is a defining moment in my life, and I am grateful to Jack for giving it to me. The valuable lessons I learn contribute significantly to my work on *Full House* and the rest of my career.

The last time I see Jack is when he surprises me at the Walk of Fame star ceremony. I look into the crowd, and there he is, in his wheelchair, looking sharp as ever with his cool hat. He isn't supposed to speak, but he asks for the mic at the last minute and announces he wants to adopt me, but my mom won't let him.

I owe Jack a debt of gratitude for introducing me to Garry, whose friendship I've cherished for years. Garry has a knack for discovering new talent and launched many careers, but none more famous than the casting of Julia Roberts in Pretty Woman. For some reason, Garry always wants me to meet Julia.

"You're both nice people, have good mothers, you should get to know Julia. She's a good person, like you."

Sure, Garry, would love to. Who the hell wouldn't? Unfortunately, over the years, it never happens.

On a sad day in July 2016, I get a call from Garry's longtime right-hand woman, Heather. She asks if I'd like to come to the hospital and say goodbye to Garry. It should be quiet this evening. Garry is dying from complications of pneumonia following a stroke.

I am extremely busted up. My hero will soon be gone. A kid who dreamed of being on a sitcom like the ones Garry did is now alone in a dark hospital room saying goodbye.

Well, almost alone.

As I bend down and tell Garry how much I love him and what he means to me, I hear sniffles from a dark corner across the room. Out from the shadows steps Julia Roberts.

"Hi, John, I'm Julia. Garry always wanted us to meet. And here we are."

She gives me a friendly hug, and although he is in a coma, I swear I see a smile on Garry's face.

15

YOUR BABY'S A PIG

JESSE COCHRAN mid-twenties, exterminator by day, rock-n-roller by night, a rebel, a ladies' man, cynical streak, not a big fan of children. Walks across the messy living room.

JESSE: "Your baby's a pig."

It's a harsh thing to say about future billionaire twins who will one day rule the fashion world, win multiple CFDA awards, and make enough money to buy the soundstage we're on.

If you would have told me.

Jeff Franklin, the man who created *Full House*, has always been my kind of guy. When we meet, Jeff is young and ambitious. He looks like every other cool guy writer in the 1980s: mulletesque hairstyle, leather jacket, white sneakers. He's charming and kind and has infectious energy when pitching his ideas, but the thing that attracts me to him the most is that he comes from the Garry Marshall camp. He actually ran the number one hit show *Laverne & Shirley* at the ripe age of twenty-three. Wow.

Jeff sets up a lunch meeting and we hit it off immediately. We talk Elvis, girls, movies, girls, music, and girls. We spend too much time trying to figure out if we've dated the same women or not. I like him and feel like I've known the guy forever. We spend an hour and a half together and not one word about this new show we're supposed to be discussing.

As I'm hopping in my car at the valet, Jeff shouts out, "What about *Full House*? Will you do it?"

I trust him and feel we're cut from the same cloth. Plus, it turns out there's no crossovers in our dating history either.

I smile. "Yeah, I'm in."

Executive producers Tom Miller and Bob Boyett are legends in my eyes. They've also worked with Garry, producing some of his biggest hits: *Happy Days*, *Laverne & Shirley*, *Mork & Mindy*, you name it. These are the exact people I want to be working with.

I'm being told, primarily by my agents and managers, that *Full House* will sort of be like their hit *Bosom Buddies*. Three buddies versus two, and no cross-dressing. Perfect. The kid angle will be fine, as long as it's way in the background. I don't want to play second fiddle to some rug rats. The only thing worse would be adding cutesy animals.

Franklin sets up a chemistry lunch with me and Dave Coulier, an up-and-coming comedian who is up for the role of Joey Gladstone.

I'm late, rushing, and get into a fender bender at the valet in my baby-blue Mustang convertible.

Apparently this is funny to Dave and Jeff, who are sitting at an outside table, busting up.

I join the boys and Dave waxes on a bit too seriously about comedy, and specifically his comedy and how it sets him apart from other comedians. Call me nuts, but don't you have to be funny to call yourself a comedian? I don't feel the connection, or the funny. It's like some kind of Amway sales pitch.

As soon as I get home I call Jeff. "You're kidding, right? That guy is what we call NF, not funny!"

Jeff pleads with me to give him another shot. "Just come out and watch him do his act," he says.

The next night, Jeff drags me out to Igby's Comedy Cabaret. Dave walks onstage and blows my mind for the next hour and a half. It's a brilliant performance. He has this Robin Williams sense of rapid-fire impressions. He does a full-blown reimagining of *The Wizard of Oz* called *The Wizard of Odd*. He does every voice, every sound effect. Spot-on.

I go backstage. "And why couldn't you have done that at lunch and saved me a forty-five-minute car ride?" He laughs, I hug him and tell him how talented he is. I can't wait to work with him.

A few years back, when Jeff was a writer on *Bosom Buddies*, he met a stand-up comedian who was doing the audience warmup: Bob Saget. Jeff befriended him and told him he'd like to write a sitcom for him sometime. Bob just brushed it off. "I do stand-up, I'm not really an actor." Jeff didn't seem to care. When the time comes to cast Danny Tanner, Bob's on a show in New York, CBS's *The Morning Program*, and isn't available.

Dave and I do readings with a bunch of Danny Tanner wannabes. I start to feel like I'm the one being auditioned, but Jeff assures me that's not the case. "Just trying to get the right mix." They go with an actor named John Posey.

Jeff sees Jodie Sweetin on an episode of Valerie Harper's show *Valerie*. She's a lively little one with blond ringlets and has a knack for wide-ranging expressions. She's perfect for the role of Stephanie Tanner.

For the older sister, D.J., he wants a more serious, subtle performer and chooses Candace Cameron. She can handle the weight of the central storyline, which brings a ragtag group of guys together under one roof to deal with the loss of her mother.

The last casting call is for Danny's littlest daughter. Two adorable munchkins, Mary-Kate and Ashley Olsen, are cast in the role of Michelle. They have big blue eyes wide with wonder. As identical twins, they can take turns sharing short takes without spending long hours on the set.

I'm thinking they've put a lot of work into casting these kids who are just going to be in the background, but I admire Jeff for his attention to detail. Good for him.

Mid-March of 1987, a few days before we start shooting the pilot at the Sony Studios lot, Stage 28 (the same stage where they shot portions of The Wizard of Oz), we all gather for a table read at the Century Plaza Hotel. The script is aptly named "Our Very First Show."

The place is buzzing. I'm introducing myself to everyone, and the moms of the little kids are swoony General Hospital fans. As folks crystallize around me, I realize I'm "the name" on the show and there's a lot riding on my shoulders. No worries. I'll knock this out of the park.

Jeff says, "Welcome, everyone." He introduces the cast one by one. I get the biggest response. Jeff continues: "This is the beginning of a wonderful journey called Full House." Once again, the place erupts in applause.

Legendary sitcom director Joel Zwick shouts, "SHUT UP!" He's a screamer, but a lovable screamer. He reads the opening stage directions.

SCENE ONE

FADE IN:

I'm getting really excited. Not nervous at all, just ready to knock this reading out of the park.

INT. LIVING ROOM—MORNING
THE TANNERS LIVE IN A WARM, HOMEY
TWO-STORY HOUSE IN SAN FRANCISCO,
WHICH IS PRESENTLY NEAT, CLEAN,
AND APRIL FRESH.

Everyone erupts. If a stage direction is getting this kind of laugh, I'm going to kill.

ON THE MANTEL IS A PHOTO OF DANNY,
HIS LATE WIFE, PAMELA, AND THEIR
THREE GIRLS.

Ahhhh, everyone melts.

ACTION!

Jodie Sweetin, the little scene-stealer, has impeccable timing and is cuter than a bag of sleeping kittens. She gets the first big laugh. She blows the roof off the place. The audience roars as she impetuously demands I play ballerina with her. It drowns out my next three lines. I laugh along and blend into the background like pink bunny wallpaper. My initial excitement of landing a multi-cam sitcom is fading fast. I can already envision a future where the adorable child characters with their annoying catchphrases become sensations, while the rest of us exist to support their punchlines. Once the kids hit puberty and

transform into awkward teenagers, I'll be buried in the grave-
yard of forgotten surrogate fathers from shows like *Webster* or
Diff'rent Strokes.

With every big laugh she gets, I slip lower in my seat until
I'm practically under the table. The rest is a blur to me.

The final scene calls for the whole cast to gather around a
baby's crib and sing the theme song to *The Flintstones*. By the time
we get to "Have a Yabba-Dabba-Doo Time," I'm having a Yabba-
Dabba-Don't Time. The reading ends, thank God, and I head to
the lobby as fast as I can, avoiding everyone babbling how great
it went. I dig through my pockets for change. I jam a quarter into
a pay phone, get my agent on the line, and gently suggest, "Get me
the fuck off this show!"

I'm dying to pull the rip cord on this family-friendly hell,
but I'll fulfill my contractual obligation to shoot the pilot. Keep
it professional. The thing will crash and burn faster than my reputation, and I hope I can salvage some dignity with my next
project. For now, stay cool. Control what you can control.

My character's original name is Adam. Not funny. A terribly
unfunny name.

"What name do you want?" Jeff asks.

Off the top of my head, I say Jesse. Jesse was the name of
Elvis's twin brother who died at birth, and if I'm going to die in
this pilot, I might as well go out in style. Jeff loves the idea (not
the dying pilot part, the Jesse name change part).

If being upstaged by a pixie phenom isn't bad enough, I get
shouted down by screaming babies in stereo on day one. I'm trying to get through a scene, and the cutesy twins are crying their
heads off. They'd rather be anywhere in the world other than that
set, and I'm right there with them.

Joey and Jesse are saddled with the task of changing Michelle
when Danny is called into work. First, we run her down the

stairs, I have her under the armpits, and Joey is holding on to her cute little chubby legs. "Step one, step two."

We get her in the kitchen, and Joey wants to put her in a pot. I admonish him by saying, "Whoa, whoa, man. That's a living thing. You don't just stick it in a pot. Use the meat rack." Funny line if you could hear it over the wailing screams.

Of course, when it's time for Stephanie's line "Are you going to cook Michelle?" not a peep from Mary-Kate and/or Ashley. The audience laughs hysterically.

Then, like the little rug rat is punking us, she starts screaming right when Joey's line comes out of his mouth: "We're changing her diaper." She clams up when Stephanie says, "Then how do you roast a turkey?" Four-minute laugh, easily.

The scene continues. I'm trying to get my funny lines out between the baby's wailing as we remove her soiled diaper with tongs. Then we squirt water from the sink sprayer at her little tushy and dry it with a fan, "Fan her fanny, Fan her fanny," before diapering her with floral kitchen towels and plopping her in a plastic bag.

As much as I want to give the munchkin the benefit of the doubt, I don't. Let's be professional here. Buck up. My career is on the line, Mary-Kate and/or Ashley. Now it's my turn to scream. "That's it!" I bark at Jeff and the Miller-Boyett bros. "It's either me or them. They're not going to work out. They'll ruin this show *and* my career."

Be careful what you wish for. When you get your way in Hollywood, there's usually a catch. I send the Olsens and their diaper bags packing, and a new set of perfectly behaved twins are paraded onto the set. They are quiet, calm, and homely as hell. I know, I'm one to talk. For the longest time, the neighbors thought my parents got a pet monkey. But here's the difference: I wasn't trying to be in show business yet. "Jeff, could we please bring back the Olsen twins?" I say sheepishly. I may have misjudged the situation. It turns out that Jeff didn't allow them to go too far, they were actually waiting backstage. I can't help but wonder if Jeff deliberately chose the homely twins fully aware that I wouldn't like them and would beg to get Mary-Kate and Ashley back.

By the time daddy Danny comes home, the living room is a disaster with Michelle's clothes strewn everywhere.

"Whoa! What happened? What's with all the dirty baby clothes?" he asks.

Dave's character, Joey, says, "I'm sorry, Danny, but every time we tried changing her, she'd dribble, or drool, or spit up."

My character is less apologetic. "Your baby's a pig."

The audience explodes, and with that line, everything changes. The pilot ends up testing through the roof, and "your baby's a pig" is the highest testing moment in the whole show.

The show is the perfectly wholesome family programming ABC is looking for, and they give us a pickup not long after we shoot the pilot.

But Jeff seems unsettled for some reason. "What do you guys think of John Posey?"

Uh-oh.

As fate would have it, Bob Saget gets fired from his show in New York around this time and moves back to Los Angeles. He's looking for work. We shoot a secret test with Bob on the *Perfect Strangers* set, another Miller and Boyett hit. Bob's still green, but he's funny, and the three of us automatically have the kind of chemistry you can't buy.

"Bob Saget is not an actor. He hasn't done shit!" the studio execs bark at Jeff. "We've spent millions on this pilot and it tested through the roof. The show is picked up as is. Why take this chance?"

Jeff submits a reshoot budget. "Trust me on this one." And they do.

"Ballsy move for a thirty-two-year-old first-time creator/ showrunner," I tell him.

Jeff shrugs his shoulders. "I had a gut feeling, and I believe Bob is the guy."

I'm grateful for Jeff's gut because it turns out to be a casting move that will change my life forever and ignites a career for Bob Saget that will keep the world laughing for years to come.

September 22, 1987, *Full House* premieres, and the general feeling is tepid.

The *New York Times* says, "And so it goes, one predictable situation following another, with the actors frantically trying to keep the patient from becoming a full-fledged corpse." Wow.

Another reviewer writes, "This show won't last till Thanksgiving." But he doesn't say which Thanksgiving.

Our regular Friday slot has us leading the night followed by a show called *I Married Dora*. It's an architect-falls-in-love-with-his-housekeeper show. It's tanking, and we were going down with it. Jeff, Bob Boyett, and Tom Miller have that "we're on the bubble" feeling. And they are right. The president of ABC, longtime showbiz muckety-muck Brandon Stoddard, calls them in for a meeting to ask why ABC should pick up the back nine episodes and not cancel them midseason, like Dora-the-housekeeper.

Jeff starts pitching future episode storylines, but Brandon seems to be a bit glazed over, and it looks like the meeting is coming to an end. As they start to shuffle out, Tom and Bob, ever the politicians, thank Brandon and assure him that if *Full House* doesn't make it, they have a slew of new shows coming his way. But Jeff isn't giving up so easily. "Hold on a second, I want you to see something."

Tom and Bob just want to get the hell out and cut their losses. They're not big on surprises. Through fake smiles they say, "Let's go, Jeff."

"Hold on." He rolls some footage that hasn't aired yet.

Jesse and Joey are huddled around Michelle in her high chair. I'm pouring cough medicine for Michelle, and she won't take it. Our characters are clarified: Dave in his wild shirt trying to mollycoddle the kid, and me in black pants, a leather vest, and wallet chain, watching him fail miserably. Joey makes a spaceship sound, spins the spoon toward Michelle's mouth, purposely misses, and feeds me the cough medicine instead. I get fed up and pour another spoonful for Michelle, who then drinks it no problem. Our chemistry has grown into something powerfully irresistible by this time. Brandon Stoddard is mesmerized.

"That!" Jeff says. "That's the show. At its root it's about parenting. Guys that don't know how to parent, learning to be parents. And all the single-guy stuff, and the kids with each other, can be B and C stories. But what drives the show is parenting stories. We've got these amazing kids. We've got lovable guys. That's the formula!"

Everyone's listening.

"And by the way," Jeff continues, "we're doing something no sitcom in history has ever tried to do. We're raising a baby on TV."

Son of a bitch, he's right.

There's something tender and true here if we have enough time to develop it. It's a story critics can get contemptuous about but also one that moms and dads can enjoy with their kids. It's corny as hell but sentimental in a way that feels brave; a vulnerability that is almost retro. There are some groaners that bomb, but enough moments that are endearingly funny.

At this point I start to settle in. Dave and I make each other laugh so hard, we don't want to leave each other's side. Our off-camera shenanigans are not lost on the writers, and they begin writing to our strengths. We have a natural timing together. We work tirelessly before and after hours to make sure our bits are well rehearsed for the run-throughs. If you half-ass these routines, they cut them. My approach has always been, the more rehearsed I am, the more relaxed I look.

Dave and I becoming best friends is throwing Bob off a bit. He was Dave's best friend before I came around. Dave and I are single, living a more carefree life at this point. Bob is married with a daughter and another one on the way. He will eventually have three wonderful daughters, Aubrey, Lara, and Jenny. In his act he jokes their names are D.J., Stephanie, and Michelle.

I tell him that he's the only father out of the three of us; bring some of that to the show. It's an authenticity that I feel Danny Tanner is missing. But he doesn't want advice from me.

I'm spending more off-camera time with Mary-Kate and Ashley. I adore them, and they adore me. Writers start developing more Jesse and Michelle stories, which become a highlight of the show. We have it down to a science; Mary-Kate is stronger in the emotional scenes, Ashley scores in the comedic ones.

"I'm the father of these babies; why is Stamos getting all the good scenes with them?" Bob gripes.

During photoshoots or promos for the show, Bob and I often jockey to be the one holding Michelle. We argue over who should be in the center or do single photos with Mary-Kate or Ashley.

Bob and I are carrying on with our pettiness at a shoot with renowned photographer Annie Leibovitz. She's had enough and kicks everyone off the set but me and Mary-Kate.

She captures a sweet shot of Jesse and Michelle wrapped in a blanket, both somehow looking equally innocent.

It tells the story of the show in a single frame.

I jokingly suggested to Bob that he take off his shirt, grab a binky, and come cuddle with me in the blankie. He doesn't find that funny.

Adding insult to injury, Dave and I are getting big laughs during the tapings, and Bob feels he's becoming the straight man on the show.

He complains to Jeff that he's not being written funny enough. Jeff says, "Let's find a way to make you funny then. Let's amp up the neat freak Danny Tanner stuff." This upsets Bob even more. He hates all the dust-busting crap.

It is crystal clear to us and everyone on the set that our styles clash. Bob is a comic. I'm an actor. If he can't get laughs on the show, then he'll get them from the crew. He's like a junkie and his drug is laughter. He doesn't give a damn about how or who provides those laughs; he just needs his fix. He can't help himself. He has comedy Tourette's.

During our big notes sessions, I'll be in there, trying to figure out how to fix a moment that's not working in a scene.

"Hey, I have a question, do you think my line about the dead fish hurts Joey's joke coming up?" I ask.

"Yup," Jeff says. "Good call, let's cut it. You're good at this, John."

Then Bob will chime in with something like, "Hey, I have a question, John, does your dick have a mullet, too?"

"Come on, Bob, we're trying to work here," I snap at him, which only inflames him more.

He starts humming the theme song to *Indiana Jones* while pantomiming a Japanese disembowelment suicide via hara-kiri. A power play on his part that I can win, but it will take me away from the task at hand. I just want to make the show better.

It becomes a game for him. The more serious I get, the more he tries to sabotage the moment. One of his favorites is when he grabs a fork during a dinner scene in the *Full House* kitchen and pretends to stab his private parts, yelling, "I hate my cock!"

I imagine I cut into his good times by questioning each word in every script. I can be obsessive to the point of making everyone crazy.

"Why does Michelle say 'You got it, dude' here? There's no 'dude' in the scene. It's just her and a turtle," I'd fret, running my hands through my hair, like we were staging *Waiting for Godot*.

Poor Dave, he's the man in the middle, Dr. Phil in "Couples Therapy from Hell."

"Bob's being a whiny, complaining asshole," I'll bitch.

"John's being mean to me. He called me a whiny, complaining asshole," Bob whines like a complaining asshole.

Dave just shakes his head and laughs. He'll say I was a little insensitive to Bob, and he's right. He'll also joke, "Shhhhhh, listen. If we're real quiet, we can hear Bob complaining somewhere."

Bob is the humblest egomaniac I've ever met, but he undercuts his narcissism by being so damn lovable. A walking contradiction, he makes up for his self-inflicted insecurity by being a self-inflicted aggrandizer. One day he thinks he is the least desirable person on earth, the next day he insists every woman guest starring on *Full House* is in love with him. I swear sometimes he thinks of himself as a cross between Tom Hanks and George Clooney. I wonder if I need more of that bravado. Should I be more confident like Bob? I think he's setting himself up for failure. Unrealistic perceptions.

I tell him, "You're projecting too high, Bob. Places you and me will never go. Set your expectations a little lower, then if you get close, that's an accomplishment. That's a win."

Dreaming too big without even getting close can damage the spirit. In Hollywood, there are always a bunch of sycophants promising you you're the greatest and just as many detractors telling you you're nothing. It's a balancing act. Everyone needs a level of self-awareness; you want to be in on the joke.

I know Bob is wickedly talented. I just don't tell it to his face at this point. But If I want to learn anything about comedy, I need to study Bob.

It isn't easy, because of the lightning-speed, nonlinear way his mind works. He'll say something that is not only crossing the line but stomping on it. He'll stop, take a nanosecond, wondering if he's gone too far, and then shrug off any hesitation with a "fuck it" smirk before doubling and tripling down. In legendary appearances on *Letterman*, he's able to crack Dave's impenetrable composure.

"My daughter is home asleep right now . . .'cause we chloroform her!" Bob riffs.

Letterman shakes his head as the audience devolves into chaos. "Now, Bob, you've got to be careful what you say."

Bob takes a beat. "We don't really chloroform her. . . ." Whew. Everyone recalibrates. "We get her *drunk, then* she goes to bed!"

The audience and David Letterman fall apart, and Bob Saget is in his perfect place, sitting there with a virtuous expression after detonating a comedy bomb.

The type of original comedic brilliance that Bob possesses is what earns him respect from peers like Dave Chappelle to Jim Carrey. However, his fast-paced, crude, and irreverent style of humor is not particularly useful on a conventional sitcom format. Certainly not the one we're doing.

Bob and I tolerate each other and attempt to avoid interfering with each other's creative processes, though it can be challenging.

We are still on Fridays, but now they've put *Perfect Strangers* as our lead-in at 8:00 P.M. Good strategy, and we're doing fine. Nowhere near a hit show, but we're finding our way and making quality television.

One day I get a call, and on the line are my agent, my manager, and my lawyer. Now, usually when you get more than one of them, and especially three, it's good news.

"Hey, good news!" they open with. "*Full House* could be on its last leg. You got your wish. Luckily, no one saw the show, so you came out relatively unscathed."

"Well, some saw it."

I tell them about a guy who came up to me, a single dad raising two kids on his own. *Full House* makes his kids feel like they are still a family, even though it's not considered "traditional." I let my team know that the show and cast are starting to mean something to me, and I'm hoping to get another season or two out of it. Silence.

"What? You begged us to get you off this show!" my agent says.

"Well, it turns out, unlike you guys, I have a heart," I say, half-joking.

On the other end of the line, a collective sigh. Then my agent says, "Okay, so there was an idea discussed, but we're not sure you're going to like it."

"Why?" I ask.

"They're talking about putting one of ABC's biggest hits as your lead-in over the summer reruns, but . . ."

"But what?"

With that simple strategy, *Full House* lands in the top ten throughout the summer. We find an audience, and they follow us to season two.

If you would have told me the day I walked into that room and caught my true love in bed with another guy that his show, *Who's the Boss?*, would launch *Full House* into a bona fide hit, making me a household name . . .

Well, what can I say? Thanks, Tony Danza.

16

BEACH BOY BINGO, I WIN!

Nothing makes me happier than someone telling me they got turned on to The Beach Boys because of me. I feature the band on *You Again?* and *Full House* and encourage the guys to join me for countless appearances throughout my career. It's such a gift to be able to introduce people, especially young ones, to the music that has touched my heart. It's one of the small ways I show my appreciation for the profound impact The Beach Boys have had on my life.

The first time The Beach Boys appear on *Full House* in the episode "Beach Boys Bingo," the Tanner family and band gather in the living room on the couch as we all sing along to their first number one hit in twenty-two years, "Kokomo."

Mike will say their guest spot on *Full House* and my being in the video helped the song go to number one. I think it would have done just fine without me, but I'm honored to be part of it.

We are shooting a special for ABC at Disney World's Grand Floridian Hotel. The Beach Boys are featured on The Fat Boys' new single, a cover of "Wipe Out." I bring my girlfriend, Chelsea

Noble, whom I met on the set of *Full House*. After finishing "Wipe Out," their manager decides it might be useful to have some footage of us doing "Kokomo" for potential future use. And since we're all camera-ready from the special (me rocking a lovely fuchsia tank top), we get a few quick takes in before a rainstorm interrupts the shoot and they call it a day. Later, we're invited to an after-party and I ask the hotel's beverage manager, who I'd buddied up with, to send over some champagne. Chelsea decides not to join, so I go solo. The party turns out to be a wild Jacuzzi party with about twelve bikini models from the shoot and just me. Champagne keeps flowing, and the night is full of harmless fun and games.

Suddenly, Chelsea arrives and pulls me out of the Jacuzzi by my ear. She bids goodnight on my behalf, as I'm too intoxicated to speak.

In the future, I try to book a room at the Grand Floridian again. I love the place, but they always seem to be booked no matter how far in advance I try to make a reservation. "Sorry, Mr. Stamos, no rooms are available."

I call a few months later. "Sorry, we're all booked up, Mr. Stamos."

"*You gotta be kidding me!*"

When we shoot *Full House* episodes at Disney World, I discover that I've been banned from staying at the Grand Floridian. Apparently, after the "Kokomo" shoot, while I was on The Beach Boys' private jet on the way to the next gig, the bikini babes continued partying and not only left their bikinis at the bottom of the Jacuzzi, but also a bunch of broken champagne bottles as well. I feel mortified, but I apologize and explain that we had already left before any damage occurred. Thankfully, they understand and welcome me back anytime.

Several of The Beach Boys are practicing T.M., Transcendental

Meditation. They were taught the peace-promoting technique from none other than the Maharishi himself in India, along with The Beatles in the 1960s. Now that I'm spending more time on the road, they feel it's time for me to learn, so I can join the group meditations. Mike Love sends a teacher to my house to train Chelsea and me. I think it's cool and get into it. Chelsea thinks there's something cultlike about it that challenges her Christian faith. Eventually, we break up. I get the T.M., and she gets my TV niece's brother, Kirk Cameron. They meet at a cast pool party at my house. We all live happily ever after in our own enlightened ways.

I play hundreds of shows in the 1980s and into the 1990s with Mike, Carl, Al, Bruce, and on occasion, Brian Wilson.

It's Carl who asks our tour manager, Joel, "When is John coming back out? We miss him. Please tell him to come out again."

It makes me feel good to know Carl likes the way I play drums. It validates me as a musician and not just a pretty face. On the other hand, Mike has no problem with my pretty face and always sees the commercial side of having me out. I sell a few tickets, give them extra publicity, and continue to bring my younger fans around in hopes of turning them into Beach Boys fans.

I'm keenly aware of the delicate balance between bringing my occasionally over-the-top youthful energy to the show while at the same time making sure it does not detract from the authenticity of the music or the band. I am humbled, grateful, and respect them so much. I never forget what an incredible privilege it is to be on that stage with those men. People always say it looks like I'm having the time of my life up there, and I am.

To this day, I remind myself that I'm there to enhance the experience, not take away from it. I hope the fans, even the hardcore Brian Wilson acolytes, know I am one of them—a fan who got lucky.

In season three, Mike Love makes a solo *Full House* appearance on an episode titled "Our Very First Telethon." The whole band returns in season five for the episode "Captain Video."

For the longest time, I find myself obsessed with a little-known Dennis Wilson song from the *Sunflower* album. I believe I'm drawn to it because of the way it beautifully captures eternal love and loyalty. Two things eluding me in real life.

But the song is fitting for the Jesse and Becky story as they become new parents. I even feature our twin boys, Nicky and Alex, in the video. You can catch them somewhere between me waking up nude in a brass bed in the Alamo, and when I'm carefully maneuvering through a fake church, making sure not to whip my hair into one of the eight hundred lit candles.

I am honored Carl, Mike, and Bruce are kind enough to sing their original parts on my version of "Forever."

Watching Carl Wilson, up close, sing with such ease is something I'll never forget.

His voice is otherworldly, angelic, ethereal. The man who sang "God Only Knows" and "Good Vibrations" is singing "Forever" right next to me. Terry Melcher, who is producing their upcoming album, likes my version so much that, with the band's blessing, he includes it on *Summer in Paradise*.

Mike and Jacquelyne Love ask me to sing "Forever" at their wedding. What an honor. My mother and father are there. Jacquelyne is a radiant light in my mother's life, and my mother adores her. They spend countless hours in late-night talks until the day my mom dies. Jacquelyne continues to be like a sister to me, and through life's ups and downs, we've held each other close, offering unwavering support and unwritten promises of forever.

She's simply a beacon of love and I cherish her beyond measure. While singing "Forever," I look down and see Audrey Wilson sitting next to her son, Brian, closing her eyes and smiling as she listens to me sing her boys' song. She comes out on the road sometimes and sits side-stage, singing and clapping with the music. When the show ends, I rush to her, full of adrenaline, and give her a big kiss on the cheek. She calls me hambone and says I reminded her of Dennis onstage.

Dennis Wilson is the James Dean of rock-n-roll. A guy I idolize from the first moment I was aware of him. I know how much his song "Forever" meant to him, and it brings me such joy to share my rendition with a wider audience who may not have had the chance to hear it otherwise. I try to emulate him, play drums the way he did, and even try to sing like him. But as time goes by, the more I learn about Dennis, the less I want to be like him.

Brian is a genius, Carl, an angel, and Dennis, the rebel. He is troubled and suffered years of abuse as a kid. He's known as one of those guys who's generous to a fault. So much so that he gives his house, gold records, and Rolls-Royce to Charles Manson and his family.

In 1968, Dennis meets Manson, a thirty-three-year-old former convict and singer-songwriter who believes he is just one recording contract away from stardom. He preys on Dennis's weaknesses for sex and drugs while trying to get close to The Beach Boys. He feels they can fulfill his musical ambitions. History has recorded the horrifying story. Luckily, Dennis and the rest of the band come out unscathed physically, but there are scars they live with forever.

I regret including the Manson story in the miniseries I produced for ABC called *The Beach Boys, An American Family*. The network was insistent on including more of it. I knew this was a dark stain on their legacy, and if I had the experience I have now, I would have stood up to the network.

Business-wise, it turns out well. It earns high ratings, and we are nominated for many awards. One is an Emmy nod for

Outstanding Miniseries. My second nomination and loss. I feel I let the band, their families, and even some fans down. From that moment on, I decide I will never make another movie about friends ever again. Five people, five different truths.

On December 28, three weeks after Dennis turns thirty-nine, the only surfer in The Beach Boys drowns at Marina Del Rey. He had been drinking all day and dived into the slip where his beloved boat, the *Harmony*, used to be docked before the bank repossessed it. He was trying to retrieve his ex-wife's belongings. Maybe Dennis was searching for his past, trying to find a reason to keep going, attempting to rescue himself. Sadly, he died before telling his story and seeking help. Luckily, I get to tell my story, and when I'm offered help, thank God, I take it.

At his funeral, The Beach Boys perform Dennis's solo song "Farewell My Friend." Dennis would have wanted the band to continue. After all, it's the music that has gotten them through all these years.

The Beach Boys are aware of the unifying power they possess to bring people together spiritually and bridge cultural, societal, and religious divides. Their music has the ability to uplift, inspire, and empower people, even in the most challenging of times. However, this sentiment is about to be tested like never before.

Lung cancer has metastasized to Carl Wilson's brain. Carl was always very private, but the news is about to get out. One day, before a show, I get a message that Carl wants to talk to me.

Am I in trouble? Carl is famous for his "stink eye," usually onstage if you screw something up. Pretty rare that I get it, but I've been a recipient of it a few times over the years. Today, there are no stink eyes, just sad ones. In his dressing room, he tells me he's been diagnosed with lung cancer. Before I get a chance to respond, he assures me he will beat it.

"You promise?" I say to him.

"Yep. I just wanted you to hear it from me before you hear it from anyone else. See you onstage."

I visit Carl and his wife, Gina, who happens to be Dean Martin's daughter, at their house. Gina plays a bootleg cassette tape of her dad and the Rat Packers Frank and Sammy to cheer Carl up. Doesn't really work. Carl seems tired but optimistic and determined not to let this fucked-up disease take him down. Gina gives me the tape of her dad to take home.

Carl returns to the road and does his best to get through the shows. It seems therapeutic for him. I'm so happy to see him out there, even if he has to sit most of the show and is wearing a wig and fake beard because of the hair loss from the chemo.

I join them on August 3, 1997, at the Blockbuster Pavilion in San Bernardino. I am still hopeful, and the last time I check in, Carl is on the upswing and on his way to kicking this thing. His doctors are on hand when he performs. Before the encore, I am standing on the side of the stage with them and say, "It's amazing that he's doing so well. He's going to beat this, isn't he?"

Both look at each other, then at me. "Umm, no. It's all through his lymph nodes. He's a goner. Sorry." They seem so cold.

The opening of "Barbara Ann" starts up, and Carl calls the doctors out to play guitar and sing along. They wave to the crowd like they are going to save his life. Fuck. You. It pisses me off that they are onstage having a rockin' good time right after they drop that news on me. I don't join them.

Carl Wilson dies on February 6, 1998, at the age of fifty-one. This is devastating to his family, fans, and friends, but it is especially hard on the remaining members. Mike Love seems to be taking it the hardest. Two Wilson brothers gone way too soon.

During the live shows, I have the honor of introducing "God

Only Knows." I cut together a beautiful video montage of Carl over the years. As the video plays on the giant screens behind us, the band accompanies him with music and background vocals as he sings his lead. Not a night goes by that I don't cry during Carl's performance of "God Only Knows."

17

SMOKE ONE FOR ME, JOHNNY

Don Rickles is introducing celebs in the audience at a Sinatra concert.

"Let's see, where's John Stamos?" Rickles asks. "He's probably sitting in the cheap seats in the grass. In fact, he's probably smoking grass."

Frank Sinatra grabs the mic from Don and says, "Smoke one for me, Johnny!"

If you would have told me, back when I was having those animated discussions with my dad about whether Frank or Elvis was the cooler icon, that one day Sinatra would address me personally before an audience of twenty thousand and, most significantly, in front of my father, I would have told you that you must be smoking grass.

I lean over to my father and say, "Elvis who?" My dad is right, Frank is the real king.

From that day forward, following my dad's advice, I immerse myself in the Rat Pack. And soon I actually complete the final piece of meeting this trifecta of talent and get to introduce my dad to the man himself.

On an episode of Full House, D.J. is trying to think of a fake name on the fly during a phone call. She looks at posters on her bedroom wall. One is Paula Abdul, and the other is Janet Jackson. She comes up with the name "Janet Abdul."

That year, I get a call on the set of Full House from my publicist, Greg Alliapoulos. "So, Paula Abdul finds you attractive for some reason and needs a date to go to the Grammys. Personally, I think she needs glasses."

Greg likes to take the piss out of me, like most people I surround myself with.

Our first date is the awards ceremony, and Paula looks as golden as a Grammy in a lamé gown fringed with tinsel and a cute little diamond cutout baring her midriff. We barely have time to chat before we are thrust onto the red carpet. She's kind and considerate, a powerhouse onstage, but adorable and approachable up close. She's the biggest singing star on the planet, and people are knocking me over to get to her, but she's unaffected and humble. She wrinkles up her nose and shrugs like, "Here we go!"

The next morning, there are tabloid shots plastered everywhere: "Paula Abdul and John Stamos Dating!" We are? If the Enquirer predicts romance, why not make them right for once?

We travel. We have dinners with her famous friends, like Elton John. We spend time in London, where we stay in Michael Jackson's suite at the Lanesborough Hotel. On our first night there, I pass out during an intimate moment. Jet lag doesn't discriminate, even in the middle of a romantic interlude. I'm embarrassed. Paula just giggles . . . and then tells everyone.

She comes to watch tapings of Full House, but we have to sneak her in, and she watches from under the bleachers so she doesn't

IF YOU WOULD HAVE TOLD ME   145

completely upstage us. She visits me on the road with The Beach Boys, and of course they love her.

I have exhausted my connections to get my dad a face-to-face with his favorite singer. No dice. Paula hits up her contacts, but we both get the same answer. "If Mr. Sinatra wants to meet you, you'll know."

A warm September breeze turns into a crisp evening chill in the open-air concert venue, the Pacific Amphitheater.

Comedian Don Rickles opens the show with his blistering act; he's the ultimate equal-opportunity insulter. He goes places very few entertainers dare. He even goes after Sinatra. "Make yourself comfortable, Frank. Hit somebody!" There's no race, creed, religion, gender, national origin, or socioeconomic group he won't skewer. He's laying out everyone in the audience.

He singles out an Asian woman in the crowd. "You over there, you look like a beaver eating a chair!"

He points to a Black gentleman and sings "Ol' Man River."

"And to you, the Mexican fella, here's some mud. Finish your hut!"

When his act is over, and the lights come on for intermission, I look around the very white, Republican Orange County crowd. There was no Asian woman, and no Black or Hispanic men. He was just pointing into the dark and doing his act. I realize he's a master of social wizardry. At the root of mocking things we're not supposed to make fun of, he's defusing them. Deflated by humor, the power of slurs and stereotypes is diminished. He delivers his punches with a flat expression, and just as everyone looks nervous, he laughs a little, and we all laugh with him. We laugh at each other, and then we laugh at ourselves.

Someone taps me on the shoulder. It's a sharp-dressed fellow named Tony O. "Mr. Sinatra will meet you now," he says casually. "Follow me, gang."

Paula and I gather up my mom and dad and follow Tony O. backstage.

Jilly Rizzo, Frank's right-hand goon for many years, stands about six foot three and is planted firmly in front of Frank's dressing room door with his arms crossed. He's sporting big square 1970s-style glasses, and I can tell those eyes don't miss a thing.

We wait patiently, and then the man himself, Frank Sinatra, enters the scene. He's decked out in a beautiful tuxedo, not a wrinkle in sight save a few lines of experience on his face. A red pocket square is neatly folded in his upper left breast pocket. His hairpiece, or divot as I call it, made by wiggist-to-the-stars Ziggy, is perfectly perched on his head. He's all business, but with a pleasant air about him. It's a tone I don't recognize yet: the seasoned performer in his zone. I'm still an excited puppy when I'm being introduced to fans, but Frank is here to work. He's polite meeting us, but his mind is on the show.

He graciously takes a few pictures with us, orchestrating the whole thing as if it's a professional shoot. Every picture will have his hands pointing like a conductor. He takes a shot with me and Paula, one with me alone, a picture with my mom, smiling from ear to ear, and we gather for a group shot. Everyone is in place but my dad. I give my father a "get your ass over here" look. Mr. Sinatra doesn't have all day.

My dad just stays back and nods. "I'm good."

I watch Frank Sinatra take in this exchange. He can interpret my dad's reluctance to be in his picture two ways: 1. Fuck you, Stamos's dad, you'll never get another chance like this in your life, Doo Be Doo Be Doo. Or 2. Stamos's dad is my kind of guy. He doesn't need a picture with me. Watching his son in this moment is enough to brag about for life. I've always thought of my dad as the coolest motherfucker in any room, even with Frank Sinatra in it, and that move proves me right.

My mom is another story. Loretta Stamos is a cross between Lucille Ball and Mother Teresa. Tonight, she's full-on Lucy. For years, she's been telling the same story about being in Las Vegas with my father on their honeymoon. She says she was waiting in the lounge while my dad was upstairs getting ready; they were going to see Don Rickles. Frank Sinatra, who was with Toots Shor, the famous restaurateur, slides up to her table and says, "May I please buy you a drink?"

I believe it. My mom has always been stunning. At twenty-one, she was radiant, redheaded, and rejecting. He asked to give her a kiss. She said no, but he did anyway. "How dare you! I'm a married woman, thank you very much!"

So after Mr. Sinatra is gracious enough to take photos with us, it's time to head back to our seats to watch the man himself in action. As I reach out to grab my mom's attention, I can't help but notice a look reminiscent of Lucy's antics. Her eyebrows subtly arched, and a sneaky grin plays on her lips, foretelling the shit she's about to stir.

"Now, mother . . ." I start, mimicking Ricky's tone. "It's time to head back to our seats."

"In just a minute," she brushes me off. "I need to tell Frank something." ("Frank," she calls him.)

As Mr. Sinatra makes his way toward the stage, my mom for some reason sees this as the perfect opportunity to recount her Vegas story and perhaps steal another kiss from the legendary singer.

She lunges toward him. "Frank, do you remember when you kissed me in Las—"

However, before she finishes her sentence, Jilly Rizzo goes into full mob mode and swiftly wedges himself between my mom and Frank. "That's enough, lady. It's showtime."

My mom is undeterred. "But in Vegas—"

"Yeah, yeah," he says, walking Sinatra onto the stage.

Then in true Loretta Stamos fashion she says, "He wasn't that good of a kisser anyway." Gotta love Loretta.

The thing that separates good performers from legends is their commitment to their craft every single time they perform. That's Sinatra. He's giving more than stars half his age. The way he owns a song and finesses a melody is unmatched. He is deeply human and honest. When he sings his timeless hits, I truly believe he has felt the same hurts and joys as the rest of us. That's connection. That's artistry. That's what moves an audience.

My father, not typically a wellspring of raw emotion, is undeniably touched by what we just saw. Our eyes meet, and we share an unspoken connection with mutual understanding. I don't remember ever sharing something like this with him before. As profound as it is, we both sense that lingering too long in this moment might tip it from beautiful to awkward. Thankfully, just in the nick of time, Don Rickles comes back out. As is customary, the old-school guys like to introduce celebrities that happen to be in the audience.

Don looks down at his three-by-five card and reads, "Ladies and gentlemen, tonight we have the real talent in the Stallone family, Frank. Frank Stallone, stand up and say hi."

He does. The crowd lets out a collective sigh; they were hoping to see Sly. Don shouts out a few more, Paula and another singer. I'm feeling good that I get bypassed. I'm already embarrassed at my mom nearly getting choked out by Jilly Rizzo. Best to lie low.

Don looks down at his card again and gets excited. "Oh boy! You'll looooove this guy!"

Oh shit, he's going to goof on me.

"Ladies and gentlemen, Tony Danza!" Ahhhh. Why is he

here? I know he loves Frank, but couldn't he come on another night? I hope he doesn't see me.

"And I saved the best for last," Don says, dripping with derision. "He's on a show called *Full House*, which by the way, I use as a night-light."

Don does a wild interpretation of what he thinks *Full House* is about. In his best British accent he says, *"Daddy, can I have some more apples?"* (I don't know what that meant.) "Here he is, a handsome kid, John Stamos!" He pronounces my name like the Greeks do.

Instead of standing up and waving, I sink down in my seat as low as possible. Maybe he'll just move on now and end the damn show. Nope. He does the Stamos-in-the-cheap-seats-smoking-grass number, and Frank does the smoke-one-for-me-Johnny rejoinder. My dad looks thrilled and bursts out laughing. That will be as close as I ever get to Frank, but Don Rickles will become one of my most important, unconventional friends for life.

18

KEEP MY NAME ALIVE

In the early 2000s, Don and I become close. It's a time when he is doing the Vegas circuit, and maybe a talk show here and there. He's flying under the radar of obscurity. Truthfully, most people think he's dead. Far from it. Don is sharp and on top of his game. People start to ask, "How are you friends with Don Rickles?" I say, "I just pay attention to him." Also, being a student of comedy, especially stand-up, I'm trying to crack the code of his particular kind of subversive genius. I think he likes having a kid around giving him the props he deserves.

Most young people don't know anything about his work. He has a moment playing Billy Sherbert opposite Robert De Niro in *Casino*, but it's a straight-man role. I want the world to know that he's not only still alive, but also that he's the funniest human being breathing on the planet.

I talk about doing the definitive documentary on him, and he just says, "Stand in line."

His son, Larry, has the same idea and teams up with John Landis in 2007 to produce *Mr. Warmth: The Don Rickles Project*. It's a wonderful showcase of his talent and wins a Primetime Emmy for Outstanding Variety, Music, or Comedy Special. Don also wins for individual performance. Everyone from Chris Rock to Robin Williams, to Martin Scorsese, to Bob Saget and me appears in it. From that moment until the day he dies, Don gets the accolades and respect he's earned. People finally get it. It's not just that he's funny, but that he's also a real softie, a guy who loves humanity and life. He really is Mr. Warmth minus the sarcasm.

YouTube is just becoming a thing, and I love showing Don Rickles some of his old performances. He'd never even seen them when he did them, so I pull up Johnny Carson's *Tonight Show* clips and his legendary appearances on the Dean Martin Roasts. It's incredible to watch him watch himself and laugh.

He turns to me and says, "I'm a funny son of a bitch!"

You are, Don. A whole new audience that otherwise would never see him is now diving down the Don Rickles YouTube rabbit hole and saying the same thing.

We become closer and closer. I make numerous trips to Vegas to see him. We yak on the phone for hours like a couple of gossipy schoolgirls. He seems a bit lonely at times. He's close to his family, his wonderful wife, Barbara, and kids, Mindy and Larry, but other than his best buddy, Bob Newhart, most of his old-timey friends are gone. He gets sentimental telling Sinatra stories.

There's something about my youthful energy that Don likes. He often says he's like a father to me. At events or celebrations, like his milestone wedding anniversary or big birthdays, he gets on the mic and talks about me way too much, almost to the point of annoying his own children. Mindy throws a dig at me here and there, and I don't blame her. It's uncomfortable at times. It's always different from the outside looking in. I'm a fan who becomes family, but they're his children, his blood.

When tragedy hits home, Don loses a little bit of his light.

Larry Rickles goes in for routine surgery at Cedars-Sinai, contracts pneumonia, and dies. He's only forty-one. It's the darkest time for the Rickles family. I call Don after the funeral, and he is as low as I've ever heard him.

"A kid is supposed to outlive his parents," he says, holding back tears.

It's a quick conversation. Don is old-school and doesn't talk much about his emotions or personal heartbreak. After that call, we never discuss Larry's untimely death again.

Instead of confronting the pain of loss, I try to distract Don into telling me stories of the past. He lights up talking about his wife and their great love story. Their union isn't glamorous like other showbiz marriages, but there is a deep adoring love that I've rarely seen in a couple. If you ask either of them how they are, they always say, "We're fine," as if they are one. That sticks with me. I want a connection that strong.

Don't get me wrong, they bicker with the best of them, but there's something sweet under their gentle ribbing. I spend many dinners between the two. Don quietly tells the waiter to bring him some cookies.

Barbara scolds him, "Don, you've had enough sugar today!"

Don turns to me. "John, what's she talking about? Did I order cookies?"

"Yes, Don, you did."

"Shut up," he'll say to me.

"Don, don't tell John to shut up!" Barbara will admonish.

"Don't tell me what to say to John. He's a big boy," Don responds.

This goes on, back and forth, until I stick him with the bill and head out.

I'm always pushing to get Don seen by a new audience. He was the original bad boy of comedy, so I try to hook him up with another friend I've cherished over the years, the great Howard Stern. I've been doing his radio show since the early 1990s, and I was also a guest on *The Howard Stern Show*, also known as the Channel 9 Variety Show. He's a loyal supporter and good friend, and he's the only other person I know as obsessed with Don Rickles as I am.

"There's no way you have a friendship with Don Rickles," Howard says.

Don was his main influence and the reason he became a comedian. He would watch Don on the *Mike Douglas Show* or *Merv Griffin* with his mom and realized that Don was the king. I try to get Don to do Howard's program, but he's not interested.

He says, "I don't want to go on and talk about who I'm schtupping and how I'm schtupping. That's all he talks about, schtupping!"

I promise him no schtupping talk, but he says it's too early for him anyway. I remain determined, and after years of trying, it finally happens.

Don finally trusts me that Howard has grown out of the Butt Bongo Fiesta dude and is now doing smart, deep, respectable interviews. In fact, he is hands down the best interviewer alive. Trust me Don, you will love him. I know it will be a big deal for Howard, his cohost Robin Quivers, and comedian Artie Lange. Artie loves Don and even worked with him in the Bob Saget film *Dirty Work*. They wrote him a bunch of insult lines and, of course, Don ignored them and did his own thing. He looked at Artie and said, "Look at you, you baby gorilla, why don't you work a zoo and stop bothering people!" He then shoved his face in Artie's big stomach. "Hello, ice cream! Having a good time in there?"

I thought it would be fun to surprise the gang. Gary Dell'Abate, Howard's longtime producer, helps me set up a ruse that I'm dating a new girl and want Howard and company to meet her and get their opinions. After an appearance on *Regis and Kathie Lee*, Don waits in the hallway as I walk in, unannounced, and tell Howard I want him to meet my new ladylove. Right on cue, Don Rickles walks into the studio. They go wild.

Robin can't believe it. She yells, "Oh my goodness! It's Don Rickles!" Howard stands out of respect, something he never does, and addresses Don as "Mr. Rickles."

Howard says, "Don Rickles is my hero!"

Don takes a look around the studio and deadpans his most unimpressed look. "The man works in a closet!"

Howard's been reading Don's book and finds it interesting that Don paints himself as a loser with women early on. Don says he doesn't know if Howard had that problem when he was a young man.

"Look at me!" Howard says.

Don looks him up and down and says, "Yeah, you look like a JEW-Zulu!"

They instantly bond over having to be funny to get girls. It's a fascinating insight, watching these two titans of comedy connect over their similar upbringings and how they wouldn't have survived if they hadn't found a way to make people laugh. I'm grateful to Howard for showing Don the respect he deserves. I knew he would. I also knew Don would enjoy the interview. And he does.

Don is definitely on the upswing. He's selling books and his star rises as Mr. Potato Head in the *Toy Story* movies. It's a character he loves because it makes him a hero to his grandkids. Tributes pop up all over the place. In 2013, Bob Saget and I fly out to be part of the Friars Club Lifetime Achievement Awards at the Grand Ballroom in New York's Waldorf-Astoria. Joan Rivers, Tony Bennett, and Bob Newhart show up to pay homage. A year later, Jerry Seinfeld hosts *One Night Only at the Apollo Theater with Jerry Seinfeld*. Again, a big-name night, with David Letterman, Tina Fey, Amy Poehler, Tracy Morgan, Robert De Niro, and many more filling the night with laughter and love for Don.

Now, when I go over to his house, he'll tell me Johnny Depp just called, or Robin Williams delivered a giant glass Tommy Gun filled with Don's favorite vodka.

"You know, I'm getting jealous of all these Johnny-Depp-Come-Latelys. Where were they when everyone thought you were dead?" I ask.

It just warms my heart to see him have this second wave of success. My obsession with comics and the craft of comedy doesn't go to waste when I'm spending time with the King of Comedy. One year he asks me what I want for my birthday. I ask that he join me to listen to the only actual recording of his act, an album he put out called *Hello Dummy!* He bitches and balks, but I make him sit and listen with me. He hadn't heard the act in years and gets a kick out of it.

I keep asking him, "Where'd that joke come from? How did you remember all the names? What made you . . . ?"

He stops me. "I'm just doing Rickles. Now shut up so I can hear myself."

He can read the phone book and make it funny. He never writes jokes, he just improvises. He doesn't have a team of writers writing jokes for him like Bob Hope or Jerry Lewis. Don doesn't like Jerry Lewis. In fact, in one of his legendary appearances on *Letterman*, Don does a bit where he impersonates Jerry singing the song "You'll Never Walk Alone" that Jerry would sing at the end of his telethons for Muscular Dystrophy. "*Walk on, walk on.*" Dave tries to move on but you could see Don take a beat. It's that moment that I talked about with Bob where you see the wheels turning: "Should I bail or double down?"

Guess what Don does? "You see, when that guy sings, the kids get worse."

Don's style is robust, and he can access a gag faster than anyone. After so many years, most of the time I know where he's going with a joke or ad lib. Occasionally, he throws a curveball that comes out of nowhere and floors me.

He made some impressive movies early on, *Run Silent, Run Deep* with Clark Gable and the Clint Eastwood–led *Kelly's Heroes*, but a sitcom, which everyone thought he would excel at, was not suited to his style of performing. He tries and fails with *The Don Rickles Show* twice and *CPO Sharkey*, where he plays a chief petty officer in the navy. You can't script this guy.

Sometimes he expresses regret to me that he didn't have more of a career as an actor. He watches me on *ER* every week and usually calls me after the show.

"How the hell do you remember all those lines?" he asks.

"It's like a muscle," I tell him. "You can do it if you really want to. It just takes practice."

I feel that with the proper role, Don he has an award-winning performance in him. Comedians sometimes make the best dramatic actors. I can see Don doing something emotional and heartbreaking. I hit up John Wells, who's running *ER*. Wells is one of the biggest and most respected writer/producers in the business. I ask if he'll write something special for Don.

"Can he act?" John asks. "We know he's funny, but how is he with drama? I heard he can't remember lines anymore."

"Who told you that?" I ask. "He learns faster than me."

John Wells holds back a laugh and says he'll work on something. He and his writing staff develop Don the role of a lifetime. I know a part like this is what Don has been looking for his whole career, but it won't be easy. The character starts off a lot like Don Rickles in the beginning, but the storyline gets deeper and deeper, becoming emotional and heartbreaking. The writing will do most of the work, and there are incredible actors on that show to surround him. All he has to do is show up. He does not. It's the first time I'm disappointed in him.

He got the script on a Wednesday, we had a table read on Friday, which he missed, but he had said he was ready to start Monday morning. His press agent, Paul Shefrin, called me Sunday night and said, "Don's out. He didn't like the role. Sorry."

"Sorry, Paul? Sorry?" I ask, pissed. "I worked my ass off to get him this, and now he's backing out the night before and all you can say is sorry?"

"Yup, sorry," he says, hanging up the phone.

John Wells and John Levey, head of casting, are not happy with me. They trusted me, and I didn't deliver. They scramble to figure out what to do and how to replace him. They cut the part way back and, at the last minute, get a grouchy old comedian named Jack Carter to take over for Don. It's a rough week.

I don't hear from Don the whole time we are shooting. He usually calls me at least two or three times a week for the hell of it, but I don't hear from him for two and a half weeks. I finally call him. He avoids any talk of ER and passing on the role. We are getting ready to end the call, and I have given up on getting an apology for what he did. I'm wondering if it was presumptuous and egotistical of me, thinking that I needed to do something good for the old man (and, of course, take credit for it).

He doesn't need me. I start to say goodbye, but he doesn't answer back. Silence.

"Hey kid, I really appreciate what you did. I didn't think the script was written very well. They were trying to write 'Rickles,' which wasn't funny," he says.

It isn't easy disagreeing with him, but we've always been straight with each other. "Don, that script was amazing. It was a beautiful part that would have been so good for you. Plus, those actors, they're the best in television—"

He interrupts me. "I've worked with Clark Gable, Clint Eastwood, Robert De Niro . . . come on!"

Okay. Got it. Love you, Don, have a nice . . .

In a soft, sad voice he says, "I'm sorry, John, the truth is there's no way I could remember all those lines. There are pages and pages of monologues. You know how bad I am with learning lines. I didn't want to embarrass you. Or myself. I'm sorry, kid."

Hearing that kind of fear and defeat in his voice kills me. That's not the Don I know.

"Don't be sorry, I get it. I love you."

The character on ER wasn't "Rickles," he was outside the box for Don. Maybe that's what scared him, that he couldn't just do a parody of himself. He was afraid to be vulnerable and take a chance at something that wasn't safe or comfortable. The man is in his eighties, maybe he doesn't need to take chances if he doesn't want to.

He risked a lot in his career, things nobody else could have pulled off. He made fun of presidents and every celebrity he ever came in contact with. He made mob jokes right to Sinatra's face. On national television, even. Who was I to convince him to do an edgy character on a thirteen-year-old hospital drama? That's being fearless? Hardly. He didn't need it. It was me who wanted it for him. If he feels safe just doing Rickles, so be it.

I ask him to do a guest spot in the pilot of a show I'm starring in called Grandfathered. I play a bachelor restaurateur (not exactly a stretch for me), and Don can do Rickles all day long and just have fun.

The scene takes place in the restaurant my character, Jimmy Martino, owns. He's just found out he's a grandfather. He's supposed to be babysitting the little girl while Gerald, played by my new favorite human, Josh Peck, goes on a date, but he's short-staffed and has no choice but to bring the kid to his restaurant that night and have his assistant keep an eye on her. Jimmy is running all over the place, and dining together that evening is a trio for the ages: Don Rickles, football star Deion Sanders, and the rapper Lil Wayne. One of the actresses is dating Lil and asked him to be in the scene. I guess Don is method acting because he's on his third glass of real vodka.

The director yells, "Action!" The camera pans to a three-shot of Don, Deion, and Lil Wayne.

Rickles opens his mouth. "Look, two Black guys and a little Jew sitting around all day so we can make Stamos a star!"

He turns to Lil Wayne. "I spoke to the warden. You're gonna work in the garden Friday."

As our jaws collectively hit the floor, Lil Wayne cracks a slight smile exposing his gold grill.

Don pats his pockets and says, "Oh shit, my wallet is missing."

I'm worried. The next sound we'll hear will either be gun-shots or laughter. Luckily, it's the latter, and everyone joins in. Lil Wayne has a good sense of humor about himself or he's too high to notice Don playfully eviscerating him. In many ways, they're both gangsters of their profession, so I think there's a mutual understanding. Everyone is having fun except me, who practically has to change my underwear three times that day.

Don forges on with his boisterous humor, but times change, and society becomes more conservative. We have countless con-versations at dinner about how people are less understanding when it comes to flinging barbs and slurs around the way Don has been doing it for sixty years.

Barbara says to Don, "Darling, you can't say the word 'fag' onstage. It's not accepted anymore. It's not right."

He'd protest and turn to me. "John, did I say that word tonight?"

"About ten times, Don, yes."

"Shut up." He'd bark, "It just *sounds* funny. It's a funny word."

"Not to some people," Barbara would say.

Don would just sit there, quietly thinking. Then he'd turn to me to justify or stick up for him.

I didn't, and that was that.

It's the thrill of a lifetime to do talk shows sitting next to the King. We hang out on *The Tonight Show* and *Kimmel* a few times. We all go to dinner afterward, and I try to bring people along that I know Don would like to hang with, like Garry Marshall and Bette Midler.

Barbara sometimes says, "Bring the young kids! We want to look toward the future, not the past."

Jimmy Kimmel invites Ryan Gosling, who adores Don. I'm the conductor of conversation at these dinners because I know what the guests want to hear. I know every one of Don's stories like the back of my hand, so I'll feed him the setup to a bit like it's organically part of the conversation. Although, sometimes it backfires.

"Shut up! I know my stories, I don't need you!" he'll bray in front of a large group of people, but always makes sure I'm sitting next to him. Barbara on one side, me on the other. He whispers little things to me throughout the night. He pinches my ear or kisses me on the cheek. He smells nice and dresses well, always the gentleman.

For my fiftieth birthday, I have a Rat Pack–themed party. Everyone I invite shows up. It's a little overwhelming and I'm moved by all the love in the room. I'm at a loss for words, so I start my speech by simply saying, "If you would have told me . . ."

It is a wonderful night that will make me smile every time I think of it. My friends share funny, heartfelt speeches. Bob Saget, of course, Garry Marshall, Jeff Ross, Mike Love, and after searing every single person in the room, Don sets his sights on me.

"From my heart, from my heart . . ." he starts. Now, nobody knows Don's schmuck-bait better than me. I'm expecting "From my heart . . . you're going nowhere, and I never liked you!" but there's none of that on this special night.

"From my heart, God has given this man a great deal of dignity, a great deal of love, and a style that God can never take from him. When he puts his arms around you, you know it's love. I love him and I love all of you who came here tonight to pay your respects to a gentleman that God will bless forever. Barbara and I have known John for a long time. We're married for forty-eight years. He always sits around with me, and we talk about girls, and marriage, and love. I try to be a friend, a second father to him. I tell him your time will come. Just be open and God will bless you as he's blessed my Barbara and me."

Years later, his hopes for me come true. I bring my wife, Caitlin, and her parents to an appearance I'm doing with Don on Jimmy Kimmel Live! Backstage, he's as charmed by her as everyone else. On the couch, I tell the "Smoke one for me, Johnny" story. Kimmel shows a picture of my date, Paula Abdul, with me and Frank Sinatra.

Don cuts in, "Why are you showing that picture? You got your beautiful gal backstage, dummy."

That makes Caitlin happy and me as well. He more than gives his blessing for Caitlin. I am so grateful he gets the chance to meet her. He also meets Bob Saget's girlfriend and future wife, Kelly, and we go to dinner at one of our favorite places, Taverna Tony. Don adores Kelly as well. Bob and I are almost like little kids showing off for dad. "We did it, Don!"

At another dinner, after a different spot on Kimmel, Jimmy

says on the q.t. to me, "I cut that joke Rickles said about Obama tonight." Don made some crack about President Obama being a personal friend of his. "He was over to the house yesterday, but the mop broke."

Jimmy doesn't want Don to come off as insensitive or unaware that those types of jokes are problematic in today's climate. The thing is, Don can't come off as insensitive because he isn't. He's above all the correctness because he's always used humor to tease out the cruelest, darkest, most mean-spirited aspects of society and make people face their own bigotry and hatred. Don wasn't making fun of President Obama; he was making fun of the racist asshole who would put an African American in a subservient category. Don was mocking racism by personifying the most desperate aspects of it. Those who don't get it are likely the butt of the joke. Don lampoons life itself, but his legacy will be one of love.

Whenever we'd part ways, Rickles would always say, "Keep my name alive out there, won't ya, kid?" I will, Don, I promise. Might even write a book one day with a whole chapter about you.

19

THESE ARE THE GOOD OLD DAYS
A DONKEY CALLED PEPPERMILL

As if being flanked by a gaggle of little girls on *Full House* isn't upstage-y enough, let's throw in some animals just to really make W. C. Fields do flip-flops in his grave. Why stop at just Comet? Bring on another dog, a parrot, a fish, a turtle, a rabbit, a horse, a deer or a doe, I can't tell, a pig, a chimp to spank me on the ass, a ferret, an ostrich (it's a puppet ostrich, but still), a fox, a skunk, an elephant, and two, count them, two friggin' donkeys.

One of the donkeys is distressingly endowed. His real name is Eeyore, his character's name is Shorty, but his junk is so substantial that Bob calls him Peppermill. Michelle and Kimmy get swindled into buying a donkey that they bring home. Of course, the hung burro tears the place up. There's a scene where Uncle Jesse stops the donkey's incessant braying by doing the only thing that will calm him down; he sings the *Three's Company* theme song to him all night long. So, there I am, serenading Peppermill, wondering which one of us is the real jackass.

I know I'm meant to do more with my talent than duet with a donkey. Every TV movie or afterschool special that has a hustler, convict, or prurient outcast draws me in. I jump at the chance to shed the goofy, Elvis-loving, hair-obsessed, one-dimensional character I feel I'm trapped in.

I play a sadistic pimp in an afterschool special called *Daughter of the Streets*, where a mother is distraught when her hooker daughter moves in with her pimp.

Back at *Full House*, Uncle Jesse is distraught when his unhappy niece moves into the garage with her New Kids on the Block poster.

In the TV movie *Captive*, I play a wannabe Native American who kidnaps a family and forces himself on the mother, played by Joanna Kerns from *Growing Pains*.

Back at *Full House*, I play a wannabe athlete with Kirk Cameron from *Growing Pains*, who eventually forces himself on all of us and ends up doing a guest spot on *Full House*.

In *Fatal Vows*, I play an abusive sociopath who leads a double life as a police officer.

Back at *Full House*, Uncle Jesse leads a double life as an Elvis impersonator.

I need to stop all that nonsense, settle down and settle in.

Assist don't resist.

There are young girls and boys watching, trying to figure out who they want to be when they grow up. As I commit more to the show, I realize I want this guy to be less surfacy. If the kids look up to Uncle Jesse, I need to give them something substantive to model.

I loved how the Fonz would snap his fingers to summon the ladies, but times have changed, and that tired narrative feels chauvinistic. So, Jeff and I decide to shed the playboy image and get Jesse into a real relationship. We set out to find the perfect Becky. She needs to be smart as a whip, challenging, and kind. We audition a few women, but Jeff has his mind set on Lori

Loughlin from day one. He remembers her from a film she did with C. Thomas Howell called *My Secret Admirer*. She's got a natural sophistication, seems brainy, and has a bright-eyed beauty that lights up the screen.

I recall her from the soap days. "Hey, didn't you forget to call my name out at the Emmys once?"

Back in the day we had a single, long-lost date at Disneyland where we made out at the Haunted Mansion. She can't remember the moment. Guess it wasn't as great for her as it was for me. Still, it's the first thing I think of when she walks in for the "chemistry read." That faded kiss ignites something, and the words on the page flow back and forth between us effortlessly.

"She's great, Jeff, but isn't she almost a little too sweet? I think Jesse would go for someone harder, edgier. Someone who can go toe-to-toe with him."

But I soon learn that her wholesome girl-next-door thing is her secret weapon. When she needs to put Jesse in his place, she not only goes toe-to-toe with him, she stomps, squashes, and puts her foot down on his biker boots in more ways than one. She has a duality that throws people off. She picks and chooses her battles and lets small things ride off her back but is a fierce protector of friends and family.

Lori Loughlin continues to be a cherished friend to this day. We've weathered storms together and stood by each other's sides despite life's hurdles. We've seen each other at our worst.

In March 2019, I get a strange text around 5:30 am from my good friend Roger Lodge. He asks if Lori is okay. I hit him back, "Why, what's up?" Something about a college scandal. I started googling, but there was very little I could find. I knew she was working in Canada, so I called to check on her.

"Hey, what's up?"

She says, "What's up with what?" like she had no idea what I was talking about.

"You okay? Roger said something about a college scandal with your daughters?"

"Oh that, yeah, I'm not sure," she answers so casually as if I just asked her if Nicky and Alex finished all their vegetables. "I have seen some emails lately from lawyers to Moss, but I stay out of it."

Before I can process her response, I notice an odd clicking sound on the phone line. When I asked her about it, she again adopts her laissez-faire tone. "Oh, they may be bugging my phone." CLICK—I hang up as fast as I can.

Then, switching on the news, the story breaks big time. I immediately text Lori, "Are you watching the news?"

"No, why?"

An FBI agent is announcing the largest college admissions scandal ever handled by the Department of Justice, involving bribes to prestigious colleges for falsified student acceptances.

"Turn on the TV Lori, now! There's a big press conference happening."

She asks, "What channel?"

I text back in all caps: "EVERY CHANNEL!"

I've witnessed moments where giving up could have been the easiest way out for Lori. She could have shifted the blame and let her family, marriage, and life crumble. But she didn't. I'm not sure I could have taken the hit she did with the resilience she showed. No matter how hard she was hit, how desperate everyone was to cancel her and throw her in with the pile of brutal criminals, she stood fast, protecting her daughters from the mud hurled at them day after day after day.

Still, she managed to get up every morning, then got down on her knees and prayed to keep her family together. She did the same every night. And in between, she mostly fought to stay alive.

Regardless of how dire the situation became, Lori's resolve and faith only strengthened.

She moved into the same neighborhood as me and Caitlin, which I found comforting as we could offer immediate support. Hours turned into lessons, discussions about life's highs and lows, good and evil, and the ultimate keyword—sacrifice.

In my Disney+ series *Big Shot*, I play Marvyn, a father to a teenage girl and a renowned college basketball coach. Despite his reputation and accolades, he is ousted, labeled a pariah for a Bobby Knight–style outburst.

He is a successful coach but a less successful father. However, over two seasons, he makes progress. A powerful monologue from David E. Kelley provides insight into Marvyn's journey as a dad. It starts with the standard struggles of parenting—time management, discipline—but ultimately, he discovers it's about sacrifice: prioritizing the needs of your child above your own. At the end of the day, you might not win a trophy or get a ring, but if done correctly, you'll have a more compassionate, intelligent, and loving version of yourself out there in the world. The essence of it all: Sacrifice.

Sacrifice is a loaded term, especially when it involves our children. How much is too much sacrifice for our kids?

We all stumble at times, with mistakes both small and large. However, the true measure of our recovery is accountability.

When it came time for her to face the consequences, I watched Lori embrace her responsibility, fulfill the legal requirements with her husband, and dust herself off with unwavering determination. What struck me most was her sheer grit and her ability to gather the pieces of her shattered world and rebuild.

Her unyielding devotion to her family is a testament to her

character. To watch her rise, time and again, was like witnessing a master class in resilience.

I am thankful that she continues to be a significant part of my life (and my neighbor).

When Lori's selected to guest star on *Full House*, she's only contracted for six episodes to try her out, but we click instantly, and the audience loves it. We have this fun mix of familiarity, sexual tension, and that feeling that "this can lead somewhere."

I'm also starting to really love the scenes with the Olsen twins. Right away, I know the relationship between Jesse and Michelle is an important one, but as the show develops, the connection grows.

I'm young, but I want kids someday, and these lovely little girls, so bouncy and bright, represent the best versions of future dreams. They allow me to consider fatherhood like a benched baseball catcher in a dugout, watching from afar without having to catch any curveballs.

I take them to Disneyland, I adore them, give 'em kisses on the tops of their heads, buy them a few crappy souvenirs, and then hand them back to their parents to do the hard work.

Their little sister, Lizzy, comes to visit them on the set, and she quickly becomes my new favorite Olsen. Not knowing, of course, that one day in the future the two of us would both have places in the Marvel Universe (her Scarlet Witch being a little more prominent than the Iron Man voice I do on Disney Plus's *Spidey and His Amazing Friends*).

For Becky and Jesse, it's a hop, skip, and jump from girlfriend to wife, to mother of our children, Nicky and Alex. Real-life twins Blake and Dylan Tuomy-Wilhoit star as the troublesome brothers. They are two little boys who are virtual clones of the Olsens. Big eyes, strawberry blond hair, and overblown adorableness. They don't really look like Jesse or Becky. Come to think of it, the three girls really don't resemble Danny one bit either. Hmmmm. I'm waiting for the episode where we find out that Joey is actually the father of all the kids, and Danny and I kill him.

With every season, the show continues to grow and gain momentum, regardless of the lack of press we receive.

Bob and I are still trying to work out our differences, but he gets another job that keeps him busy and off my ass. He's writing bits for a pre-YouTube show filled with pranks and dads getting hit in the testicles with Wiffle bats, called *America's Funniest Home Videos*.

The show is a smash, and I'm truly happy for him. He feels more confident and important. That eases the tension between the two of us slightly. Bob now has two hit shows.

That surprise success reveals an unexpected demand for unconventional video shows in America. Dave promptly takes advantage of this opportunity and debuts his own program, titled *America's Funniest People*.

Bob feels his show is not only the first, but also better than Dave's. I don't miss a chance to stir up shit between them.

"Now, Bob, your show is the original, but Dave has a cute cohost in Tawny Kitaen, and sometimes his jokes are funnier."

"I don't need a cohost," Bob asserts.

"Yeah, because no one wants to work with you," Dave says.

As the argument escalates, I sneak over to craft service and watch what I've set into motion while enjoying a turkey sandwich.

I try to spend more time with Bob, but our lifestyles are vastly different, and we have such distinct approaches to our work that we can't seem to connect on or off the set. If we could put our egos aside for one minute, we'd probably realize that our differences are what could help us achieve balance. It's beginning to feel like a lost cause, then life happens.

Bob's sister, Gay, is diagnosed with the debilitating disease scleroderma. It attacks the autoimmune system, inflames the skin, and shuts down essential organs. Bob spends his days raising money for research in the hopes of someday finding a cure. He directs the ABC movie For Hope, starring Dana Delany, to raise awareness for the cause.

At the same time, Dave Coulier's sister, Sharon, is diagnosed with cervical, ovarian, and uterine cancer. There is a connection among friends dealing with unimaginable circumstances, but also a loneliness because each situation is so unique and awful in its own way.

As all this is happening, doctors discover a tumor in my sister Janeen's brain. Bob, Dave, and I are no longer three guys who work on the same show; we are brothers worried about amazing women slipping away from us. Our sick and dying sisters define our grief, pain, sense of isolation, and deepening connection. Bob's sister doesn't make it and dies at age forty-seven.

He is heartbroken that she knew he was fighting for her, but that she doesn't live long enough to benefit from his efforts. A little part of Bob dies with her. Dave loses his sister as well. Janeen's diagnosis turns around, and to this day I thank God she's still here. She was misdiagnosed and did not have a tumor. Turns out it was the early stages of multiple sclerosis.

My family breathes a huge sigh of relief, but we are spiraling. You don't look at the possibility of the death of a loved one without being forever changed. Janeen is such an inspiration to me. She is the strongest-willed, hardest-headed one in the family. She knew this would never ruin her life or ours. Fiercely stubborn in her pursuit of finding a loving husband and having children one day, the same way our mother did, she barely speaks of her situation.

As advancements in research and medications become available, her MS never gets worse. Witnessing her resilience during this challenging period has left a lasting impression and continues to serve as a source of inspiration for me throughout the years. But even though I still have an amazing sibling to look up to, two guys that I'm becoming very close to have lost the beauty of two sisters, their hopes and dreams, their ideas, their humor, and their voices on the other end of the phone lines. What bonds us in grief, separates us in the losses that came for some, but not for others. Lori Loughlin is always around for support.

"Thank God I don't have a sister," she says.

Bob replies, "Yeah, Lori, but you are a sister."

All the fear, fighting for family, and frustration of loss has pummeled down some of our pettiness on the set. We're seeing not only what is important in our own relationships with each other, but also our relationships with the fans out there who are struggling with issues of life and death.

Bob is the earliest adopter of tech and gets a Mac. We all receive free subscriptions to AOL so we can connect with sick kids in the hospital. My mom stresses putting philanthropy first, and this brave new World Wide Web allows me to casually chat with a child a few hours after his cancer surgery. It's beautiful and humbling. I start to realize what our show means to kids holding on to life. They have to make sure not to laugh too hard or they'll pop their stitches. Critics don't get it, but those in critical care do.

On Thursdays, we pretape our show without a studio audience, but I always make sure to extend an invitation to special needs children and kids in wheelchairs. As our show gains popularity, more and more kids visit, and before we know it, the entire stage floor is packed with eager faces. They watch us shoot the show with excitement and are thrilled to meet the cast afterward. Seeing their joy touches our hearts.

In the same way my mom did with me, I emphasize to our cast, especially the younger ones, the importance of giving back and making a difference in the lives of these kids. It is a simple way for us to help them forget their struggles, even if just for a day. I explain that through our television show, we are visiting their homes and hospitals, providing companionship as they heal. I am proud that every member of our show becomes active in organizations like Starlight and Make-a-Wish, becoming beacons of light for millions of kids over the years.

At a Beach Boys concert in Ontario, Canada, at Boblo Island Amusement Park, Dave shows up with a young Canadian pop star from Ottawa. Now, during the encore we customarily bring up our guests and sing along with The Beach Boys classic "Barbara Ann." Dave loves doing this, and since he is trying to impress this new girl I invite her up as well. I don't know if she's talented or not. She's all hoop earrings and hairdo. It's a fun, forgettable moment. She asks me if I know anyone in the music business in the States who can help her out. I say some encouraging words and shrug it off.

Though Dave is really into her, he is recently divorced and feels he needs to be a full-time father to his son, Luke. He breaks up with the pop star and breaks her heart. One day as Dave is driving down Woodward Avenue in Detroit, he hears the coolest song on the radio. It's intense, brutal, familiar. It's his Canadian pop star ex-girlfriend, Alanis Morissette.

Dave drives to the nearest record store, buys the CD *Jagged Little Pill*, and pops it in the player in his car. As she belts out the first track on the CD, filling Dave's car with the emotional vocals, he pulls over, parks, and listens to the whole thing. He's stunned. He drives home and calls me. "You need to hear this," he says. "Remember the girl I took to Boblo Island? She's got a new album out, and there are some lyrics I think are about me."

He plays them over the phone. Powerful, hard, sharp, and real. As we both listen, he says solemnly, "My god, John, I must have really hurt that girl." He is going through each lyric with me, and his memories flood out. "Listen to this song 'Right Through You,' there's a line that goes 'your shake is like a fish.' I used to tell her to dead fish me, and we'd do this limp hand-shake. A lot of familiar stuff in here."

It's one of the most recognizable albums of the 1990s, an anthem for female anger and empowerment. If you would have told me the guy doing Popeye impressions on *Full House* was also Mr. Duplicity, the guy you hate to bug in the middle of dinner, I'd have laughed hard enough and long enough to service the show with enough canned laughter for five hundred episodes.

Somewhere between photo shoots, filming new titles, recording music for the show, late-night notes sessions, personal appearances, taking the girls to concerts and amusement parks, pool parties in my backyard with Bill Stamos at the grill, and working the charity circuit together, we often end up spending more time with each other than we do with our own families. What emerges on-screen, far from the glowering raised eyebrows of the critics, is something the fans understand: Bob, Dave, and I are becoming real brothers and the munchkins are our little girls.

It's right there in every episode and it's absolutely undeniable. We are family. When the season ends and we're supposed to go our separate ways, we stay connected, hang out, and can't wait to get back to our home away from home, a place where our hearts are as full as the house.

There's a time when we are pure, just by being born. We are

children. Then we blow it by growing up and fucking up. We are donkeys.

Eventually, we learn we have choices and find righteousness in choosing to be compassionate and caring. We are human.

Here's the thing, I finally truly get it. I understand why the show is so sweet, consoling, and loved. The children, the animals, and even these bumbling grown men trying to navigate a world of innocence and chaos remind people of the best of themselves.

Full House is the kind of hit that comes along once in a lifetime if you're lucky. I'm not talking about big ratings, lots of dough, or the way it becomes part of pop culture. It's more than a show, it's a family. It's everyone's family.

For a mom, dad, and their 2.3 children, it's their family.

For a widower who turns up the sound a little louder to stave off the silence of his loneliness, it's his family.

For the latchkey kid coming home to an empty house, it's her family.

This struggling little show I fought with every fiber of my being will become a highlight in my career. Full House turns out to be one of the most quintessentially important family shows of the twentieth century. On the surface, it's simple as hell. In the subtext, it turns the notion of the conventional family on its ear. Think about it. We didn't raise an eyebrow telling the story of three men living together in San Francisco raising kids. This was a show where the central character wasn't any single role, it was love.

We couldn't cast, write, or predict it. Then, against all expectations the stars align, and it was serendipity.

Eventually, when it touches my own heart, I get it.

The little kids that were supposed to be background noise, no more important than the furniture, grow up to become the kind of humans I hope to have one day.

They are precious, delightful, and bright. I step out of their light to let them shine. Candace, Jodie, and Andrea Barber, who plays the hilarious Kimmy Gibbler, steal my heart. As I watch them mug for the camera and casually clown through their scenes, I realize that children have a wholesomeness that translates in all mediums. They are gutsy and guileless. No fear. I will privately practice countless takes to nail a single scene where I'm acting "casual." These little ones will barely glance down at their scripts as they capture the hearts of a nation with a wink, nod, and folded arms. A stern rendering of a simple phrase can erupt the studio audience.

"How rude!"

Three decades later, I'm on the set for *Fuller House*. The studio is packed to the rafters on Stage 24 on the Warner Bros. lot. It's the same stage where we did the last two years of *Full House*. Friends, family, and fans from around the world show up to see the television reunion. There is no one onstage yet. The walls-on-wheels part to reveal the living room and kitchen set, replicated to look exactly as it did thirty years before. The set gets a ten-minute standing ovation. There's some laughing and crying. I join in.

Fuller House gets the same hard-knock reviews as *Full House*. Awful. I even show up on *Seth Meyers* to read them aloud. One compared our show to necrophilia. Come on, man. What kind of journalism is that? These intellectual critics who hate the show don't hurt me. They parrot what I already know to be facile, corny, and clichéd. I agree with them there, but here's what they miss: those scenes where sophistication yields to sweetness, the places where vulnerable kids and animals suddenly have all the power, those are the moments where the brain steps aside so the heart can feel something. The enduring popularity of the show is a testament to the power of universal human experiences; it's the warm comfort food of decency in a cold world of discord and division.

Fuller House never catches the same lightning in a bottle we captured with *Full House*, but it is a little love letter written on a Post-it note for the fans. And if it didn't touch your heart, no worries, it was never meant for you in the first place.

Bob Saget would joke, "We did *Full House, Fuller House,* next will be *Fullest House,* where I'll be in a nice urn above the fireplace." Of course, there could never be any version of the show without Bob.

GOD ONLY KNOWS

You've got to be a meth-smoking crack addict to marry someone because you fall in love. Love is fleeting. We live too long. After thirty years of marriage, "till death do us part" will be your best argument for assisted suicide. No wonder people are so disillusioned. They were sold a fairy tale.

That's my opening line from a pilot I did called I *Am Victor.* I play a divorce attorney who claims true love is for suckers but deep down inside he wants it with every fiber of his being. I am ready to get serious and settle down. We are not meant to be alone. Still, "till death do us part" sounds like a mighty long time. It's 1994, and I'm open to love. There's an angel on one shoulder and a Victoria's Secret Angel on the other.

Lori Loughlin and I are suddenly single at the same time. She's my Sandra Dee from *Grease,* the good girl with a kind heart who always makes me feel upbeat when I'm around her. She's one of the few women I have spent day after day with and still always look forward to seeing her again. I know what makes her laugh, we get each other, and we have the sort of true friendship that's supposed to be the foundation of a great, lasting relationship.

Then there's the Sandy-in-Black-Leather at the end of *Grease*. I meet a model at an after-party following a Victoria's Secret fashion show. Cue the cliché, but she's cool. She's a former gawky theater geek who shot up to five foot eleven, with bright blue eyes and a big smile. She started modeling in college and ended up on the cover of everything: the mythical *Cosmopolitan* of my childhood curiosities, *Elle*, *Glamour*, *GQ*, and the coveted *Sports Illustrated* swimsuit issue. Despite the fact that I show up to this after-party with Lori, I get Rebecca Romijn's number.

Lori has had my number the whole time. As each leggy beauty walks down the runway, she shoots me a knowing look and maintains a little smirk. She knows I'm not as ready to settle down as I feel. She's humoring me.

Lori or Rebecca? Rebecca or Lori? Am I going to sit in a swing forlorn at the drive-in wearing a motorcycle jacket warbling like John Travolta for Sandra Dee or am I putting on the letterman's sweater to enter the carnival in search of black patent leather stilettos with chills multiplying? Let's just say Rebecca's first call sounds a lot like "Tell me about it, Stud," and it's electrifying.

She's a free spirit and has a great time wherever we go. I like bringing out that big, bright smile.

We travel the world together, spend holidays with family, and grow closer and closer. The glam stuff gives way to an intimate relationship, the kind of comfort that feels like home. Less Victoria's Secret catalog lingerie and more topknot-and-sweats. She is my best friend; someone I genuinely care for.

After two years of dating, I propose to her on Christmas Eve, naked. It's a spontaneous moment, so I don't have a ring. She gets a cigar band around her finger. I'll later replace it with an emerald-cut, four-carat, Boucheron diamond, but I'll give it to a gal who says yes to a slip of paper pulled off a Montecristo.

My pals take me to Vegas for a bachelor party. Dave Coulier and Bob Saget narrate the bus tour on the way to the strip club. Despite their comedic predictions of a night of debauchery, Rebecca's father, Japp, is with us, and my dad is along for the ride, so it's a pretty tame night out with the boys. As it should be. We end up at The Palm at Caesars for a great dinner set up by my friend Roger Shiffman. Lots of laughter, lobster, lots of fun.

On September 19, 1998, we throw a tiny intimate wedding for about five hundred of our nearest and dearest at the Beverly Hills Hotel. Our minister asks me how I'm feeling. "I'm just happy to be nominated," I say.

Rebecca walks off a magazine cover and down the aisle. We're both nervous, but something clicks when we say our vows. We wrote them separately, but the sentiments we reveal are similar. I tell her about falling in love at first sight, the promise of not trying to change her, the encouragement of her dreams, my vow of fidelity, and the desire to always make her laugh. I also acknowledge she's a terrible cook and promise to cover the kitchen duties. I promise love.

Rebecca places my father's wedding ring (which he never wore, so he gave it to me, which I in turn never wore) on my finger. Before she speaks her vow, a low-flying paparazzi plane swoops over us, making a loud, long, gassy noise. I grab the mic and ask if that was Dave Coulier. The first big laugh of the day.

Rebecca promises not to change me, to allow me to grow without judgment, to devote herself to me while remaining independent, to be my best audience and best friend. She promises to love and cherish me forever. She promises not to cook. It feels amazing to hear your own thoughts and dreams mirrored back during one of the biggest moments of your life. I'm think-ing I got this right.

"Can I kiss her now?" I ask eagerly.

Inside at the reception, there are elegant Amazons from her world, Heidi Klum and Tyra Banks, and Rebecca's Dutch rela-tives, each taller than the next, eclipsing the models. The *Full House* family—Candace, Mary-Kate, Ashley, and Lori, Bob, and Dave—all show up to support me.

After a few speeches from the in-laws, I grab the mic and say, "Willy!" That's my dad's cue to come up and make one of his patented wedding speeches. He is a star on the mic and always captures a moment beautifully.

He welcomes everyone, welcomes Rebecca into our family, and says, "You know, my boy has made me proud in many, many ways, but I think the proudest day of all was when he chose me to be his best man. He truly is my best friend." I know it in my heart, but hearing him say it aloud is grounding.

He insists on my mother coming up to applause and intro-duces her as "the best woman a son and a husband could ever have." He's got that right.

My Beach Boys brothers are by my side, Mike, Al, Bruce, and even Brian Wilson. I'd always dreamed of having my first dance be "God Only Knows." Sadly, Carl passed away about seven months before, so a DJ will play the song. Paul McCartney called "God Only Knows" his all-time favorite song and "the greatest song ever written." As we walk onto the dance floor, the haunt-ing opening chords begin, and I sneak a glimpse at the man who wrote it, Brian Wilson.

A few years earlier, I was on tour with The Beach Boys and Brian was out doing a few shows. He had been through the Dr. Landy machine and was looking trim, happy, and inspired. He was a far cry from the genius who ballooned to more than three hundred pounds and didn't leave his bed for years. The controversial psychologist Eugene Landy had him on a twenty-four-hour therapy schedule and inserted himself into every aspect of Brian's life. Dr. Landy would eventually lose his license and exit with a restraining order.

An unforgettable Brian Wilson moment happened on that tour in Montreal. After a performance, most of the musicians headed up to their rooms, but Brian had a boogie-woogie rhythm stuck in his head and was determined to find a piano to work it into a song.

Jeffrey Foskett and I found a beautiful black Steinway in a banquet room, and along with Bruce Johnston, we all stood around the piano as Brian wrote a song right before our eyes. He played a groove reminiscent of "Shortnin' Bread" on the Beach Boys' L.A. (Light Album). He started assigning parts like I'd seen him do during the Pet Sounds sessions.

"Jeff, you sing 'Let's Rock.' Bruce, you sing, 'Rock, Roll, Rock'n and a Rollin'.' Stamos, you sing bass . . . sing Mike's part." He demonstrated the same lyrics and rhythm only much lower, "Rock, Roll, Rock'n and a Rollin'." He counted off and suddenly I was swept up into a true Beach Boys four-part harmony.

We sat and marveled. The old Brian was back. He launched into "You've Lost That Loving Feeling" but was interrupted by a big champagne burp, causing us all to laugh our asses off.

I guess my baritone Mike Love sound impressed him because he later has me go in the studio and sing the bass part on a song he was working on, "Spirit of Rock and Roll."

He played snippets of "Sail on Sailor," "Palisades Park," and "Little Honda," always going back to the song he was writing, "Rock, Roll, Rock'n and a Rollin'." He asked Bruce to sing "Disney Girls." He said he wanted to "dislodge from the earth."

Bruce could not sing the high part on the bridge, so Brian had to sing it for him. "Was I on that record?" Brian asked.

I can't imagine singing on so many classics that you can't remember if you sang on a song like "Disney Girls." He launched into "Rhapsody in Blue" and I melted away.

After he played "God Only Knows" right under my nose, I asked, "How long did it take you to write that song?"

Brian shrugged. "I don't know, I played it through a couple of times. The heavens opened up. I was God's instrument."

There I was, in my sleeveless Harley-Davidson shirt, in the presence of my musical hero, a true genius, telling me, the kid from Cypress, about how long it took him to write the greatest song ever written. If you would have told me I'd be sitting at the piano with Brian Wilson, as he plunked out "God Only Knows" . . .

And here I am, dancing my first dance at the Beverly Hills Hotel with my new bride to Carl's enigmatic voice, watching Brian sing along with his brother, mouthing the words. He looks sad.

"*I may not always love you.*" That's not a nice way to start a love song, I thought. It feels like I'm hearing the song for the first time, listening to the lyrics with a new intensity. They don't sound as hopeful or optimistic as I always thought they did.

"*If you should ever leave me. Though life would still go on believe me.*"

Does this foreshadow what's to come? God only knows.

We party so hard on our wedding night that we almost miss our flight to Greece the next morning. The door on the Boeing 787–9 is literally closing shut as we reach the gate. Sweaty and out of breath from running through the airport, we beg and plead and give our whole sob story. In a very rare move, the crew holds the flight for us, reopening the door, which delays takeoff time. As we walk on, we look less like a happy, freshly married couple and more like two people who had been up all night at a rave.

We land in Athens (still fully hung-way-over), take a boat to an island, and from a distance I can see a big rock with naked people jumping into the cobalt-blue Aegean Sea. This could be interesting. As we get closer, all the divers are men. The island of Mykonos is lovely, and this gay nude beach is just the first of our unclothed excursions.

After Greece, we hop to Necker Island, Richard Branson's private getaway. Rebecca is shooting the Sports Illustrated swim-suit issue there, so we arrive a few days early and fold it into the honeymoon. The theme of the magazine shoot is painted bodies, so after the bare buns of Mykonos, there are twenty international supermodels wearing front-facing body art, but they are completely naked from behind. Interesting way to start a marriage.

At dinnertime, I sit around with the execs who decide which model makes the cover of the magazine. I can tell they're excited to have a celebrity husband in the mix, and I make the most of it, passing around the wine liberally and talking up Rebecca as everyone gets tipsy.

"I might be sounding like a stage husband here, but my new bride should be on the cover. I mean, look at her, she's absolutely stunning, yet completely approachable. She's funny. Most girls that look like her aren't funny. Am I right?" They all nod. I got them in the palm of my hand. Then I go in for the kill. "Plus guys, she's a natural on talk shows, Jay Leno loves her. She'll be able to promote the hell out of the issue."

When the magazine comes out, guess who's on the cover? I'm not saying I had anything to do with it, but I was her hype-man the whole trip, and it's fun to see her success.

Models are starting to branch out and build brands. Cindy

Crawford has huge commercial contracts and hosting gigs. "That's what you should be doing. You're a natural," I tell Rebecca.

When Cindy leaves MTV's *House of Style*, I think Rebecca is perfect to take over the hosting gig. She auditions for the brass but doesn't impress.

"Were you funny?" I ask her. "Girls that look like you aren't considered funny. That's your secret weapon."

I have a few connections at MTV, make some calls, and request they give her another shot. We work on her audition, write some jokes, and tap into what makes her shine. Rebecca gets the gig and does a great job hosting the show.

Bob Saget is directing a black comedy with Norm Macdonald and Artie Lange called *Dirty Work*. I suggest Rebecca would be perfect for the role of Beautiful Bearded Lady. It's a small moment but another credit under her belt. Behind every good man is a good woman, and maybe behind every "It Girl" there's a "Not It" husband pulling a few strings. I tell myself that I've had a good run; now it's her turn.

I try to stay out of her light, and her career takes off. She plays herself in *Austin Powers: The Spy Who Shagged Me*, but it's a star-making turn as Mystique in *X-Men* that catapults her into the lucrative Marvel franchise. She plays a mutant; a nearly naked, blue, bombshell mutant. The film blasts through the box office, and she's slated for *X2* and *X-Men: The Last Stand*. She goes from a high-end catalog model to the big screen effortlessly. I'm proud of her.

I keep one foot in comedy, working with Garry Shandling in his groundbreaking comedy *The Larry Sanders Show*. I do a guest spot on *The Tracey Ullman Show*, and show up as a rake in some rom-coms. I have a hefty development deal at Warner Bros. and I'm meeting with writers around town to come up with the first John Stamos vehicle (yes, I'm talking about myself in the third person like Jerry Lewis). It's a lofty, cool position to meet talented folks and say, "Okay, wha'd'ya got for me?"

On a beautiful, but-aren't-they-all, day in L.A., the maître d' at The Ivy on Robertson seats me on the coveted outdoor patio. Behind the white picket fence, surrounded by roses, I sit on plush floral pillows under an umbrella with my sunglasses on as tour buses full of out-of-towners that are having fun stargazing drive by and gaze at me. Like Tom Cruise in *Risky Business*, I tip my glasses down a bit. Hello there. Sure, my wife is doing well, but damn it, I am, too. Cameras are clicking. Girls are screaming. I still got it.

Today I'm meeting with a fresh young writer. Doesn't really have much of a résumé, some show that I've never heard of called *Popular*. Before that, he was a gossip columnist for *Entertainment Weekly*. I'm told he's going to be the next big thing, so why not have a nice lunch on Warner Bros.' dime with the dude?

"Hello, John, I'm Ryan Murphy, nice to meet you," he says. Kid looks smart. Buzz cut, black-framed glasses, observant eyes.

After small talk and pleasantries, we order. I'm in the driver's seat here, so in a slightly arrogant tone I cut to the chase. "What ya got for me, Ryan? What's your idea for that soon-to-be-the-next-big-smash-TV-hit-starring-the-one-and-only-John-Stamos . . . that is if I like your idea." I'm kidding. I hope he gets that I'm playing Big Star in Sunglasses at The Ivy for a laugh. He does. He's got a laser-sharp sense of humor.

Ryan winds up. "Well, you play a male hooker. And you fuck the wife and the husband to help their marriage."

"I do what?" I say, trying not to spit out my eight-dollar glass of iced tea.

"You fuck the wife and husband, sort of like a sex therapist, but not alone. There's a cute blond guy and a cute Black guy who are also male hookers. You're a team. Sort of a service. You're like *Charlie's Angels* but hookers. Charlie's Hookers."

"Hookers. Charlie's Hookers."

The waiter slides appetizers onto the table. I'm thinking, *Oh man, I got to sit with this guy for another forty-five minutes?*

It's an out-there concept, but as he animates the characters and plot possibilities, the pitch is fascinating. Ryan Murphy is fascinating. I should jump at the chance to do a risqué show like this. I've been droning on about breaking away from the mulleted, Elvis-obsessed Uncle Jesse, and this is my chance. It could change my career. It could also crash and burn. Not sure America is ready to see their favorite uncle tangled up in a trisexual, pay-to-play throuple. "Check, please!"

I decide taking chances isn't in the cards for me right now and look for something that's more in my "wheelhouse," as they say. I jump into a project that Jim Leonard, another fine writer in the WB stable, creates for me called *Thieves*. I play a Cary Grant–type smooth criminal who specializes in the con game, sleight of hand, and crimes where he never gets his paws dirty. While casting my counterpart, I read with every actress in town. I'm fascinated by a fresh-faced, charismatic Eva Mendes. Good actress, beautiful, but one of the execs, who shall remain nameless ('cause he's dead), said she looked too "Mexican" and wouldn't let me cast her. We end up casting an Australian actress named Melissa George to play Rita, who specializes in ass kicking and taking no names as we team up to steal secrets for the FBI. I am sure this is my next big hit. It is the highest-testing pilot in ABC history. After seven episodes, that's exactly what it becomes: history.

I loved the show and I'm heartbroken that it gets canceled, but it just means I'll have more time to be the encouraging husband traveling around with my movie actress wife. My team is watching me pour a lot of creative energy and time into Rebecca's career, but they remain supportive, waiting for me to wake up and get back to my own thing.

I'm offered another script by Ryan Murphy, that will air on a brand-new network called FX. The show sounds daring and edgy. Exactly what I need. I pass on Charlie's Hookers, but I know Ryan is the real deal, and I should take this offer seriously. I let Rebecca read the script.

"It's demeaning to women," she says dismissively. I think there's more to the show, but we talk it out and I turn down Nip/Tuck.

Little by little, I start to second-guess my instincts, short sell my abilities, take fewer risks, and get lost in my marriage. I do, however, put some energy into the parties we're hosting on most weekends. She bounces back faster than I do.

21

I CAN!

I stay in touch with Jack Klugman, my OG old guy. I advise every young actor to roll with an entourage of crusty ol' gents willing to bust your chops. Jack doesn't care much for *Full House*. He says I'm a better actor and it's time to prove it. I appreciate the straight talk.

"Get to the theater!" Jack says with a voice that sounds like he's gargling gravel. "I can't just go do theater," I tell him. Plus, let's be real here, if anyone ever wanted me onstage, it would probably be for a musical. And let's just say my singing and dancing skills aren't exactly Tony Award material. Jack hammers me. "Doesn't always matter. It's about selling the song. You're an actor! The best musical theater people know how to sell the story within the song. I originated the role of Herbie in *Gypsy* with Ethel Merman. You ever hear me sing?"

"No, and can we please keep it that way?" I joke with him.

"The only real question is, can you hold the stage?"

What the hell does that mean?

I'm curious, but cautious. Like many of the things that life puts in your path, first you wink at an idea, then you wrestle with it a little, and soon it becomes a lifelong love. My first Broadway show is: *How to Succeed in Business Without Really Trying*. Also, what I call the start of my acting career.

It's 1995, and I get a call from my agent. "Listen, Matthew Broderick just won the Tony for *How to Succeed*, but he's leaving for five months to shoot a movie called *The Cable Guy* with Jim Carrey. He's coming back, but they're interested in you replacing him while he's gone."

The next words out of my mouth should be "Are you fucking crazy? I've never done anything like this before!" but instead I hear Jack Klugman's sandpaper voice, "Get to the theater!"

"I'm in!" I tell my agent.

"You'll have to audition," he says like it's a warning. "Only three weeks to prepare."

"I get it. Send me the material and I'll start working on it."

In my mind, I always believed that if I work hard enough, I can do anything. The acting and comedy chops required to play J. Pierrepont Finch come easily to me, the singing and dancing, not so much. I'll rent a dance studio, hire a teacher, and work day and night. I'll do the same with a singing coach. I've never been a great singer, and the thought of singing live feels very scary.

Des McAnuff, the play's award-winning director whose credits include *The Who's Tommy* and *Jersey Boys*, is a huge Broadway director and a nice man. He offers to work with me to prepare for my big audition that's scheduled for the following day. I'll need his help to stand up to the critical eye of Jo Loesser, widow of Broadway's premier composer, Frank Loesser, who cowrote *How to Succeed*, as well as *Guys and Dolls* and many other classic musicals.

On October 3, 1995, I head to Des's brownstone in the Village. As I arrive, Des, along with the rest of the world, is glued to the television. They're about to announce the verdict in the O. J. Simpson trial. It's all a blur: Marcia Clark's poodle perm nodding, clips of perpetual houseguest Kato Kaelin, Johnnie Cochran's smooth delivery holding a glove: "If it doesn't fit, you must acquit."

I hit play on the Walkman tape recorder I brought along for the piano tracks and start singing, *"How to apply for a job. How to—"*

"You're going to be great," Des says with his gaze fixed on The Juice. Is he even listening to me? I realize we're waiting on the verdict of the biggest trial of the twentieth century, with lives hanging in the balance and the very concept of justice on trial, but a little help on my audition would be nice, Des. I'm going to die in that audition tomorrow. It'll be bloodier than O.J.'s hands.

I go into the audition around 10:00 A.M. as prepared as I can be. I feel I'm finally sneaking up on that elusive fearlessness that I'd been trying to get back to for years.

I am in and out pretty fast. And to be honest, I couldn't tell if they were impressed or not; I was just happy there was no blood shed.

I sit by the phone for hours. And hours. I pace, I order lunch from room service. I get frustrated when the phone rings and it's my mother. "Yes, Mother," I say, as if she's called five times already (which she has).

She says, "Guess what? I just realized the address of your hotel is 151, those are my numbers. This is good luck."

Thank you, Mother.

I finish another room service meal and I'm ready to give up, go home and have my head examined, thinking I could be on Broadway. Then the phone rings. "Hi—"

"Hey John, it's Des, sorry I didn't call sooner."

I pipe in, "O.J. trial?"

"Yes, have you been watching? I can't believe—"

"Des, did I get the part?"

"Yes!" he says, like I knew this already. "I thought you knew this already." How?—"Anyway, everyone loved you. I wish you could have been a fly on the wall."

"I wish you could have called me eight hours earlier!"

Three weeks later to the day, I'm sitting in front of the vanity mirror in my dressing room. I did it. I can't believe I'm here. I stop and really take it all in. The flowers, telegrams, and well-wishers dropping by, telling me to break my legs. My hair is slicked back, not in a cool James Dean way, more like Jerry Lewis. I'm suited up in my baby blue window-washer's jumpsuit.

Over the tiny speaker I hear, "It's Saturday night on Broadway and this is your ten-minute call, ten minutes till places. And let's give a big warm welcome to Mr. Stamos tonight as he makes his Broadway debut." I can hear everyone applauding and screaming for me throughout the whole backstage area, echoing through the halls.

I start a new ritual: listening to Frank Sinatra's "Soliloquy" from *Carousel*. It's a master class in selling a song, with Ol' Blue Eyes fully immersing himself in each word, making it personal and telling the story as if it's his story. He channels every emotion and thought into the lyrics, and makes you believe what he believes, just like he did when I saw him perform live with my dad. Selling the song. That's exactly what I need to do.

I begin the show high in the sky, so five minutes before the overture starts, stagehands strap me into a metal window-washing platform. As the four thin metal cables begin to whir and pull me upward, I feel like I'm taking off on a spaceship. I'm slowly lifted a staggering hundred feet up and fifty feet over, completely out of sight from the audience below.

It's both exhilarating and nerve-wracking. But it also gets the adrenaline going, releasing serotonin. Give me that hit.

I can look right through the metal floor of the rig, way down to the stage, but I don't.

Since I'm a little closer to God, I pray.

My father couldn't make it to opening night but said he'd be with me up there when I start the show, nothing to be afraid of. Sure, easy for him, he's just here in spirit.

The overture starts and my heart begins to pound. This is it, first time on the Great White Way. And although it was never really a dream of mine, it should have been. It took a lot to get here. And regardless of what happens in the next few hours, I'm proud of myself. I close my eyes, take a deep breath, and . . . Oh shit.

The platform starts to lower, whatever nerves paralyze me melt away with an avalanche of applause from a loving audience.

It stops about halfway down, and as I open my book, the voice of Walter Cronkite booms throughout the theater as he explains, step by step, the rules that Finch must follow to succeed.

"Just have courage, and if you truly wish to be among the lucky golden few, you can."

Then Finch eagerly chimes in with,

I can!

And somehow, I do!

As my feet hit the ground, and I begin the opening song, that blast of adrenaline is better than any high I've ever experienced.

When doing television shows, movies, and concerts, the work is done at different times, in different locations all around the world. All the Broadway theaters are within about an eight-block radius, from Forty-Second Street to Fifty-Fourth Street. It's as if the entire neighborhood is synchronized to the same rhythm, with the curtains opening and the lights dimming simultaneously. There's a palpable sense of anticipation in the air as everyone is eagerly awaiting the performers, who have spent countless hours rehearsing and perfecting their craft, to take the stage with confidence and passion. Then right at 8:00 P.M., BAM! The collective energy has reached the end of its crescendo, and it's a spark so powerful, you'd have to be dead not to feel it. Our energy is contagious, and the audience feeds off it, and slings it right back at us. There ain't nothing else in the world like it. I'm starting to get hooked.

My dad finally makes it to New York to see the show and my mom tells me later it was the first time she ever saw him cry.

Jack Klugman comes and sits third-row center. I'm afraid to look at him, but when I do, he looks so proud. After the show he comes into my dressing room and gives me a big hug and a sloppy kiss on the cheek, then pinches them. "You were fantastic up there, my boy. You really held the stage!"

I go on for months, getting closer to the wonderful cast. Megan Mullally, who plays Rosemary and hasn't done *Will & Grace* yet, says I sweat like a stuck pig. Especially during our kissing scene. But in a nice way. I feel comfortable up there. All my years of doing sitcoms in front of a live audience, and hundreds of concerts with The Beach Boys, must have prepared me for this moment.

Eight shows a week, two on Wednesday and two on Saturday. I can't wait to get to the theater each day. I'm getting addicted to the laughs, lights, applause, and adulation. Also the respect that comes with taking a risk in doing live theater and succeeding. Getting good reviews, selling tickets, and, as Jack says, holding the stage.

Now that I've done Broadway, nothing will ever be scary again. Except for the fact that I have just said yes to the role of the Emcee in *Cabaret*.

22

LIFE IS A CABERNET

Rebecca and I share a love of theater. We like the old-fashioned musicals, stories about guys and dolls falling in love, falling apart, and singing their hearts out.

In the spring of 1999, we are in New York. We've just had a hearty brunch in Times Square and I'm thinking about a hearty nap.

We stroll by Studio 54.

I tell Rebecca, "They tried to revive this place in the 1980s? Total flop."

The disco nightclub is a shadow of its former self. It was once the eclectic center of New York's opulent nightlife, a serious celebrity playground, with regulars like Andy Warhol, Michael Jackson, Elizabeth Taylor, Diana Ross. Bianca Jagger once rode through the joint on horseback for her twenty-seventh birthday. I wish I'd thought of that for my twenty-seventh.

It has been transformed into a theater, Cabaret is playing there, and it's the hottest ticket in town.

"Oh, let's go," Rebecca says.

No, thanks. We like happy, peppy musicals, remember? Who wants to walk out out of a Broadway show depressed? And besides, it's too early in the day to process the rise of fascism, the evil of the Nazis, and the horror of the Holocaust. My childhood buddy Mike studied war and collected historical trinkets. He'd try to educate me about the era over the years, but it was too dark. I didn't understand war, what is it good for? Absolutely nothing.

Rebecca really wants to see it. "Fine, but good luck getting tickets," I shrug.

The show is sold out, of course, but we somehow score cancellation tickets on the spot for the 2:00 P.M. matinee.

It hardly looks like your traditional theater. The place has been transformed to look and feel like a real supper club, complete with black wood bistro chairs at small café tables with period-themed lamps on them. The red table lamps take the audience from the book scenes to the club by turning on whenever we're supposed to be in the Kit Kat Club.

Cool, immersive, but as the lights go down, I start dozing off.

Willkommen, bienvenue, welcome! / . . . Leave your troubles outside . . . / So, life is disappointing? Forget it! / In here life is beautiful . . . / The girls are beautiful . . . / Even the orchestra is beautiful!

The nine-piece ragtag band swells into a sleazy instrumental break, driven by the insistent bass drum, punctuating the strip-tease.

I'm fully awake now. I go from resting my head on Rebecca's shoulder to the edge of my bistro chair. *Cabaret* grabs me and doesn't let go.

All of it.

The seedy, seductive Kit Kat Club in Berlin, the American writer trying to tell his story amid the chaos, sultry Sally Bowles kicking up her heels, and the wild, wonderful Master of Ceremonies, who just welcomed us and begins to take us on a ride through Jazz Age naughtiness straight to hell.

By the time the final backdrop rises to reveal a white space with the ensemble standing within, I'm tearing up. It represents a gas chamber. The Master of Ceremonies has the last words: "Auf Wiedersehen . . . à bientôt," followed by a drumroll and cymbal crash. He then opens his jacket to reveal a Star of David and a pink triangle. The end.

Rebecca and I now have tears running down our faces. I bolt to my feet along with the rest of the audience. The standing ovation lasts five minutes.

I can barely walk after what I just saw. I am shaken. Alan Cumming had left the role and Michael C. Hall had taken over. He was excellent. Nothing like the guy he later played in *Six Feet Under*—a complete transformation.

A lot of the time, actors will see a movie, TV show, or a play and think to themselves, *I could do that.* In this case I thought, *I could never do that!* You will never see me on that stage in black culottes, sock suspenders with military boots, and painted-red nipples.

A year later, I'm on that very stage, singing for the musical director, Patrick Vaccariello. Directors Sam Mendes and Rob Marshall sign off on me, and the next thing I know someone's measuring my inseam for the culotte and suspender getup and fitting me for a groin harness codpiece thingy.

I'm not sure if I've ever had a panic attack, but when I found out I'd be the next Emcee, I definitely felt some sweaty, trembling palpitations.

J. Pierrepont Finch was a small stretch for me, I leaned mostly on Jerry Lewis for movement and rhythm. But the Emcee? Homosexuality, bisexuality, transsexuality, even bestiality (he has sex with goats) is all new territory. Darkness isn't part of my repertoire. Danger isn't in my bag of tricks. There are no cute smirks, hair flips, or double takes in this role.

And that's exactly why I should be doing it. I need to continue challenging myself. Win or lose, success or failure, I'm taking the artistic leap. That's my dad talking. He's only been gone a year, but his voice is still in my head. No boundaries, no holding back. Although, I'm not sure how he'd feel about this one. I imagine him sitting in Studio 54, one eyebrow raised, watching me flamboyantly mincing onstage, half naked, sparkly nipples, dry humping the girls and boys at the Kit Kat Club. I'm not sure my dad was ready to watch his son simulate sex acts and sing a torch song in a sequined dress and heels.

Maybe he would have understood. Early in my career, my first big press agent was a Greek guy named Greg Alliapoulos. Handsome dude with a big mustache and even bigger heart. He cared about me and my career as much as anyone did. I don't know if my parents had any preconceived notions about their son running around with an older gay man, but it didn't take long for them to trust and love him. (Of course, the fact that he was Greek didn't hurt.) He became family.

I had never judged people based on whom they loved. When a man hit on me, it was flattering, but I didn't fully understand it. One day I asked Greg about his attraction to men. "I don't really get it, Greg, you know, what do you see in guys?"

He looked at me like, "Are we really going there right now?"

"No . . . Yes."

I tried to kid around. "Hey, I grew up sheltered in Cypress. The gayest thing in town was the Catholic Church."

Greg laughed. "You know how you feel when you see a girl you're attracted to? That warm, tingly feeling inside?"

"Yup, I know that feeling very well."

Greg shrugged. "That's how I feel when I see a guy I'm attracted to."

. . . Okay. I stop and really take this analogy in. After a long beat, "I get it."

It may be an oversimplified answer, but I understood. Love is love. Be who you are. Be free.

Easy for me to say, I get to marry who I want, don't face employment and housing discrimination, never experienced health care inequities, and don't risk getting my head bashed in just for being myself in public. I have no idea how hard coming out can be in the face of challenges from family, religion, society, or whatever other forms of bigotry still exist.

I would go on to star in a movie my friends Neil Meron and Craig Zadan produced called *Wedding Wars*. My role was Shel, a gay party planner, who finds out my brother, played by macho Eric Dane of *Grey's Anatomy*, is behind the governor's speech against gay marriage. I go on strike and encourage the rest of the country to advocate for equal rights. A sweet little movie. It was one of the first films advocating for gay marriage before it was legal in all states. I'm proud to say I recently got ordained, and in my backyard I officiated the wedding of my dear friend Neil Meron. It was beautiful, and it was nice to really feel how far we've come.

Straight performers playing gay roles might be called out for appropriation, but at the time, it was important for mainstream actors—familiar faces—to bring issues of equality to Middle America. Sometimes you need to start in the heartland to change hearts.

Greg would have been proud of me.

On November 24, 1995, he died of AIDS.

A horrible disease. Another good one gone.

Devastating. He hid it from me for a long time, but I knew

he was sick. I visited him at home and in hospice. I brought Rebecca to meet him. I had always sought his counsel and blessing. He weighed in on every important decision in my life.

He wasn't himself toward the end. Gone was the wry grin and faux sarcasm. The drugs made him angry and depressed. Even when he didn't want me to come visit, I would. He was embarrassed, he didn't want anyone to see him sick. I hate that he felt that kind of shame. I want him to know I loved him.

When he passed away I couldn't attend his funeral because I was opening How to Succeed in Business. My mother was with me, but I told my father about the service in L.A. He didn't go. It was the first and last time I was ever disappointed in my dad. I learned Greg's Greek parents didn't go either. They were ashamed he was gay and died of AIDS. Shame on them. Shame on us all. He deserved a eulogy filled with love.

How the hell do I play this puppet master? He's a lovable, vulgar, exuberant, pansexual ringleader who becomes a victim of the rise of the Third Reich. I need to go to a perilous place to find my character's voice. My mother and I attend the grand opening of Disneyland Paris's new park, Walt Disney's Studio (no, that's not where I'm seeking racy, vulgar, creative inspiration . . . although . . .). Since we are already in Europe, I suggest we pop over to Berlin so I can do some real research. As I roam the streets, soaking up the history and studying the people, my sweet mom has a conversation with our concierge.

MOM: My son Johnny just got the lead in Cabaret. Have you heard of it?

CONCIERGE: Yes, Frau Stamos, I have. Everyone in Berlin has. How can I help you?

MOM: Johnny wants to do some research, that's why we're here. Can you tell us where the Kit Kat Club

is located? He wants to get right in the middle of it.
Spend some time with the people that go there. Take
some pictures, and ask a few questions.

CONCIERGE: That is not advisable. The Kit Kat Club is
outrageous and not recommended.

MOM: My son came all the way here to go to the Kit Kat
Club. How bad can it be?

CONCIERGE: It's not like you think, especially tonight.

MOM: We leave tomorrow. Can you please put us on the
list, or make a reservation? You don't know Mama
Stamos, we'll be fine.

The Kit Kat Club looks like a big warehouse from the outside. It's covered in graffiti and littered with advertisements. As
my mother and I stand in line to get in, a surly doorman looks
us up and down.

"You are not dressed properly. Please go back to your hotel,"
he instructs.

I'm in a suit and my mom is dressed in her usual elegant
pastels. The doors open as someone is leaving in a leather harness. We get a glimpse into the place. It's Caligula. Black light
paintings glow and electronic music pulsates. Most people are
naked. Boys in bondage masks, fishnet bodysuits, whips-n-
chains, genitals bound with ropes, and pale goths with black
lipstick smiles. Nobody wants to see their mom in latex with a
dog collar, so it's probably best to skip this part of my prep and
just read a book or two.

I get to New York and start my prep. I work out two to three
times a day to achieve that heroin chic look. Not exactly an easy
metamorphosis for a sun-n-fun, tan California kid with good
teeth, clear eyes, and a jovial disposition.

Makeup artist Monte Haught takes two hours before each

performance painting my skin pale and drawing track marks along my veins. He applies temporary tattoos. My eyes are heavily outlined in black to help create a piercing and almost hypnotic feel. My lips are red, drawing attention to my mouth, lending a sensual quality. And the pièce de résistance, red glittery nipples. All these elements create a look that is simultaneously unsettling and captivating.

I decide that I'm taking on the role to pay tribute to Greg; give him the eulogy he didn't get, the respect he was due, and that's when everything falls into place for me. That's when I completely trust the play, the directors, the other actors, wardrobe, makeup, and this seedy environment to take me where I need to go. I perform with complete abandon and know Greg is there to see me through.

"Honey, let's go see John Stamos in this fun musical. I wonder if he still has his mullet. I hope there's a baby in this show, he's so good with kids." Aw, the wife from Nebraska who wants to take her husband to see Uncle Jesse on Broadway. They paid good money for front-row seats, right up against the stage.

A drumroll starts the show. Then the familiar striptease notes begin and out I come.

Full drag, long leather coat, with the requisite bow tie, glamour makeup, and replacing the mullet, a mohawk.

Willkommen, bienvenue, welcome!

Leave your troubles outside.

So, life is disappointing? Forget it!

In here life is beautiful!

Then I proceed to grab, slap, prod, and rub the girls and the boys as it suits me. In turn, they grab, slap, prod, and rub each other, *also* as it suits me.

Mrs. Nebraska's jaw hits the table. Mr. Nebraska sits with a scowl, his arms crossed. Like that's some sort of defense move to keep me away. Fat chance. I slink past, make overtures, and blow in his ear. He looks like he wants to deck me. I shake my ass. He starts putting his coat on.

Back onstage, I ad-lib in a German accent as I point to the vagina of one of the Kit Kat girls. "*Stop bending down like that. Already dis week vee are losing a table, three bottles of champagne, and a waiter up der!*"

That's it. He's done. He gets up and drags his wife out with him. And that's when I know I'm doing my job and servicing this play. They walked out not because I was bad, but because I was good. Too good.

Word on the street is I'm a must-see Emcee and people would not only not walk out, but come back again and again.

As I rack up eight shows a week, my exhibitionistic inventiveness goes deeper, darker, and more and more debauched. There's a moment at the end of act one where the Emcee lifts his long black leather coat, just high enough to reveal a bright red swastika tattoo that Monte hand paints on my right ass cheek.

I have to leave the offending image on during the week so Monte can just freshen it up before each performance. I regularly get massages throughout the run of the show because eight performances a week is tough on my body. My regular guy knows about the show, but when he has to go out of town, he sends in a replacement for the session. He doesn't tell the new masseuse about my role in the musical. I forget about the tattoo until I turn over. Turns out the guy is Jewish.

"Umm, pay no attention to that symbol that represents hate, violence, and persecution of your people. It's for my role, I'm playing, sort of, well, a gay Nazi." I just stop babbling and offer him two free tickets to the show.

Before act two begins, the Emcee comes out for a completely spontaneous ad-libbed audience participation moment. I make a few jokes to the people in the balcony.

"Hello, poor people!" Then I dance with unsuspecting audience members. I look for a good-natured woman ready to play along and I drag her onstage. I ask her name, where she's from, and plant my face in her bosom. Then I grab a man and slow dance with him (he always tries to lead). I take over, twirl him back toward his seat, and coquettishly stick out my ass. "Come see me some time, the BACK DOOR is always open!" But I'm finding it harder and harder to pull a guy onstage. I get it. If they dare take my hand and allow me to drag them up there, they know I'm going to embarrass them, in a loving way, of course.

One day when Sam Mendes is in the theater I tell him about the issue I'm having, and he gives me the fix: "Don't look them in the eye. Just grab a hand and pull. No eye contact."

Got it, grab and pull. It works every time.

Except once.

I do the bit with the girl, then go to grab some sucker's hand with no eye contact. He doesn't budge. Oh, okay, we've got a tough guy over here. I pull harder, and he resists. It becomes a tug-of-war, and he's winning. He pulls me close and whispers in my ear, "I don't have legs." I look down and see his prosthetics nearby. Damn you, Sam Mendes! Twelve hundred audience members are wondering what the hell is going on. Think fast, Stamos.

I ask if I can sit in his lap and just sway back and forth. "It would be an honor," he says. I give him a lap dance, a big hug, and it's on with the show!

There's a very heavy moment in the play that's still giving me trouble. I tell Sam about the challenge I'm having with the number "If You Could See Her." It's a vaudeville novelty act where the Emcee denounces bigotry by singing about a forbidden love. It's an indictment of how people judge others on race, religion, sexual orientation, and appearances. I am dancing with a woman wearing a gorilla mask as I sing about how no one will approve of our love and ask why can't they leave us alone.

But if you could see her through my eyes—then, the Emcee grabs her hairy face and changes his lighthearted tone—she wouldn't look Jewish . . . at all.

It's supposed to be chilling, but instead folks are chuckling along with a Nazi sympathizer suggesting falling for a Jewish woman is like dating an ape.

"So, it's messed up," I tell Sam. "When I get to the anti-Semitic shit, everyone laughs."

Sam nods and explains, "They laugh because they're uncomfortable. Those aren't ha-ha laughs. They're worried that for a split second, they may have shared a sentiment with a Nazi."

I get it, and any hesitation I have with the material goes away. Be uncomfortable. Be very uncomfortable.

It's great when friends and family come see me in the show.

As the Emcee slithers through the audience, sometimes I'll catch their faces in the crowd: Howard Stern, Hugh Jackman, Mike Love. Before they can take a sip, I swoop in and down their fourteen-dollar drinks.

The Olsen twins are all grown up and have moved to NYC to begin building their multimillion-dollar fashion and entertainment businesses. It's pretty weird having adult Michelles sitting there in stereo watching me play someone so different from their beloved Uncle Jesse, but they get it. We share a mutual pride for how far we've all come.

As I settle in for my two-hour makeup session, I sip a bottle of red wine, a cabernet sauvignon, and figure out how to make it last the whole show. This is not a recommended acting method, but it does help me, especially early on, to drop my inhibitions and abandon any fear.

I try to time it out so that my last swallow comes right before I walk out and hit my mark in fuck-me pumps and a satin dress to belt out my final torch song, "I Don't Care Much." It's a hauntingly beautiful ballad, but it takes a little liquid courage to get through it.

Each night, Cabaret ends with the same low drumroll. I drop my leather coat and I'm wearing a prison outfit. My badges reveal I'm a Jewish homosexual headed for the gas chamber. There's an audible gasp from the audience. The lights come up. Some people are crying as they rise to applaud longer and louder than I've ever experienced after a performance. I end up selling the most tickets out of any Emcee, other than the original, during that Broadway run.

The emotional tenor of the show requires release after-hours. The cast works hard, and the debauchery onstage spills out into the street. We drink it up, sweat it out, and put ourselves back together for the next performance.

Alcoholism is genetic. Hereditary. My parents both enjoyed imbibing regularly. They functioned well and never considered stopping.

Proclivities can lie dormant within for a while, but I'm pushing my luck, drinking a bottle of wine every performance (including matinees). I can stop if I want. I've got this under control. I'm fine. Although it feels like I might be awakening a sleeping monster.

I can say farewell to Cabaret, but can't cut loose the cabernet chromosome.

23

ANTONIO: A RICH, CREAMY SPANISH SOUP

My friends at the Roundabout Theatre Company call with an interesting proposal. Sydney Beers, general manager and executive producer there, who has been so good to me, gives me a choice of leading roles. "Neil Patrick Harris is leaving *Cabaret*, so you can return to being the Emcee, you were my all-time favorite by the way, or take over Antonio Banderas's role of Guido in *Nine*. David Leveaux, who's directing, and Antonio think you'd be a wonderful replacement."

Rebecca had done the film *Femme Fatale* with Antonio Banderas in Paris. It was directed by Brian De Palma. Big movie. I'm happy for her, but also down on myself. I can't even get a pilot made. Trying to keep your cool while watching your wife on the set simulate a lesbian sex scene in a bathroom or give an erotic lap dance to a handsome Spanish superstar is like attempting to balance on a wobbly tightrope of sanity. We're still connected, but things are starting to fray a little.

I had seen *Nine* already because Rebecca wanted to support

her friend by checking out the "previews" before the opening of the play. I always go to a preview with an open mind, but I was shocked at how shabby it was. Antonio is dynamic on-screen, but his voice wasn't very strong and his English occasionally incomprehensible. He still had some charisma, but the overall effect was kind of a mess. I knew we'd go backstage after, but wasn't sure what to say. "Uh, great costumes."

I had a fleeting fear I'd be asked to replace him when he went back to Hollywood to make more movies and remember thinking, *Don't do it. Say no. This is an awful musical. Whatever you do, do NOT do this show.*

So, of course, a year later I'm saying yes. I've done *Cabaret*. I loved it, but it's no longer a challenge.

Sydney Beers is thrilled I'm taking the role. "Johnny, you'll be great!"

I land at JFK to start my three-week rehearsal process. I ask the driver, "Can you just drop me off at the theater?" I want to see the show before I start the following day. I've let the producers know I'm going to swing by. Sometimes you don't want to watch the actor you're replacing. You want to start fresh with your own interpretation. In this case, I'm pretty sure I don't want to cop anything Antonio is doing, I'd just like to get a feel for the whole production again.

The driver turns left from Broadway onto West Forty-Ninth. The street is so crowded we can't get to the theater. The whole block looks like it's cordoned off for a crime scene or a parade.

"Jeez, what's going on tonight? Is the president in town?" I ask.

My limo driver looks wistfully out of the window. "Antonio," he says, like he's describing a rich, creamy Spanish soup. "The show has been sold out for six months. I hear he's leaving soon. Good luck to the poor bastard who has to replace him. There's no one like Antonio, I don't know how—"

I interrupt him. "All right, all right, pull over here, pal. I'll walk the rest of the way."

A nice kid meets me at the side door of the theater and guides me past the crowds. The place is packed to the rafters.

"What's going on here?" I ask. "They givin' away free tickets?"

He just looks at me funny. He takes me over to the stairs to sit and watch. "Sorry, Mr. Stamos, there's not one seat available. This is where they asked me to seat you."

I'm not fancy. I'm fine with the stairs. I'll be taking notes and doing prep anyway.

"Rumor is you're taking over for Antonio," the young usher says.

"Me? No." It hasn't been announced yet, so I can't let on. Plus, I don't want it to get out that I'm at the show tonight, it's not cool to make the last guy feel bad. I'm younger, more experienced in theater, and probably going to crush his numbers. Gotta lie low.

The usher says, "Oh, thank God! I'm a big fan of your work so I'd hate to see you take a nosedive in this. I mean, you're a good actor and all but Antonio . . ."

Why does everyone say his name like it's hot buttered ecstasy?

Onstage, church bells ring, an overture of a cappella female voices begins, and there, at a big round table, in shadow, is Antonio Banderas. The place erupts in screams and applause. Antonio is the mythical, egotistical film director Guido Contini in the midst of a midlife crisis. He's singing his ass off. *Guido, Guido, ME ME ME! I want to be Proust! Or the Marquis de Sade . . .* He's brilliant. He's funny. He's charming. He doesn't miss a beat, a joke, a dramatic moment. By the end of his performance, I say his name like every other fan seduced by his talent. I open my lips slightly, pull them back breathlessly, lifting my tongue toward the roof of my mouth and ending in an orgasmic O face: *Antonio*.

Everyone explodes out of their seats, and tears are flowing. The audience weeps because they are moved by his magnificence. I weep 'cause I'm the poor bastard who has to replace him.

I can't do what he just did. No way. What the fuck was I thinking?

We meet backstage and he hugs me, drenched in sweat. "Johnny Boy, you are going to be fantastic in this role!"

"I can't follow that! You were incredible!"

He just smiles, still awash in applause. "You'll be fine! If you need anything, I'm here for you."

Fine? Did he just say the word "fine"? I hate that word. And with one more sweaty hug, I'm displaced like another adoring fan. I wander into the hallway and end up chatting with the stage manager. I can hear Antonio screaming on the phone at someone.

The stage manager looks both ways and confesses, "Probably talking to his wife, Melanie. They fight like cats and dogs. She's playing Roxie in *Chicago* across the street and getting love letters for reviews. Drives him crazy, and she knows it. Then he gets her back by telling her all the girls in the cast are flirting with him. They go on and on. Sometimes we can't get him out of his dressing room. He'll hide under the desk!"

I must look alarmed because he pats me on the shoulder. "But you're going to be just fine." Fine, there it is again. Not great, not fantastic, fine.

I hear whimpering from Antonio's room. I start to go back but stop when I hear his voice shout out, "This role is cursed! It's cursed!"

Fine. Fuck me.

Rumors are flying around about *Nine*. The rest of the cast is female. Guido and his playmates. Twenty-two women of all shapes and sizes, each one more talented and beautiful than the next. It's a role that can mess with your head and marriage.

It's demanding, with a complicated operatic score. I immediately start putting in my hours. Composer Maury Yeston is kind and patient. I fly out my singing coach, Eric Vetro. He's the greatest vocal coach alive and a dear friend. If he can't get me ready to sing these songs, no one can. Guido only leaves the stage once throughout the entire show. He never stops pushing the story forward with dialogue and song. There's not much dancing, but a lot of expressive movement. I get comfortable with the music and moves but can't connect with Guido's mental collapse. His breakdown.

Under the pressure to create a new cinematic masterpiece, Guido must face the ultimate decision of life and death. He's a guy who looks into the abyss as relationship pressures and career anxieties drive him to the brink of desperation. In the end, he will push away every good woman in his life. He will be alone, on his knees, with a gun to his temple.

No matter how hard I try to access that hopeless, bottomless pit of despair eight times a week, I just can't. I have too much light in my eyes. At forty, I still look and act like I'm in my twenties. In the old adage of art imitating life, there's one place Guido and I find connection. I'm not putting enough energy into my own relationship. I slowly start to give up on Rebecca.

I spend too much time with fellow cast members. Forget a phone call here, a check-in there. As the show starts to lose direction, I lose faith in myself. I let outside noise seep into my skull. I become afraid to leave my dressing room and spend some time under that desk like Antonio did, feeling cursed.

I give up on me, giving the paying public permission to give up on me as well. Word gets out that I can't handle the role. The first time I miss an easy note in a song, I get rattled and almost will myself to miss it again the next night. I'm practically having panic attacks in the first ten minutes of the show, so I turn to my old *Cabaret* trick: a bottle of red.

I'm a few years older and not in the same physical shape, so the drinking doesn't help me through a performance, it helps me out of one. I call in sick one night and have my understudy, Paul Schoeffler, take over the show. I have a sore throat. Sore-ish. Not too sore to keep me from grabbing a slice at John's Pizzeria down the street from my apartment.

It's a cold night, and I'm feeling exhausted and a little worthless. I'm wearing a hat and a big coat so no one recognizes me. It's nice to be somewhere warm, dark, and anonymous. I just need to sit alone and eat a few feelings with extra cheese.

"Hey, John," I hear.

"Uh, yes?" I say, simulating an extra scratchy voice just in case. It's a couple all decked out for a night on the town.

"Hey, we just saw *Nine*," the guy says. "We came all the way from Jersey to see you. . . ."

I stutter and stammer like Bob Newhart. "I . . . I . . . I'm so sorry. I'm sick. Just woke up. I'm starving and there's no one around to grab me food." I'm adding a performative little cough and bullshitting. I feel guilty.

"I'm so sorry I wasn't there for you guys tonight, I'll get you tickets to the next show," I offer.

"No, don't apologize, your understudy was amazing! We couldn't believe how good he was. That's a tough role, well, you know that. No, we don't need to see it again, but thank you. Please tell your understudy how much we loved him!"

Make my pizza to go.

The show closes early, and word on the street and in my head is that it's my fault.

I'm depressed. It was a failure. I go home feeling a little older and despondent. There is more pain in defeat than I could have imagined. No one died here, unless you count my ego. It's ironic that the moment I tank the show, I become the perfect Guido.

24

NEGOTIATE MY BALLS

As I'm lifting Rebecca up, I'm losing myself. While we have great friends in common, she's bringing in a new crop that throw shade, name-drop, and try to outdo one another with obscure references. She makes it clear that I'm the TV guy and she's the newly minted film star. Toxic friends in her ears concur. She implies, sometimes subtly and sometimes openly, that I'm not smart enough for her and her entourage of ass-kissers. Somewhere deep inside, I start to believe it.

Years go by with ups and downs. We party and get healthy when we need to be. But through all that, there's zero talk about having kids and starting a family. This was always our plan. Our dream. It feels as though she doesn't share that dream with me anymore.

Rebecca doesn't notice me slipping away and I don't notice myself adrift. She's busy with her career and new friends. We're trying new things and growing, but not together. It's easy to be busy, calendared to the hilt, rushing around, and plugged into various projects. It's harder to make time for each other, slow down, disconnect from the chaos of the world, and make eye contact again. I don't talk openly about my feelings of emasculation, and she doesn't share what's in her heart.

I keep thinking, *This is a phase. We'll both find ourselves and come back together, start a family, get back on track.*

It doesn't happen, we stop happening together, and something cruel and calculating creeps into the pleasant patter of the day. She smiles at me a little less, doesn't look me in the eyes over dinner, takes phone calls in the other room. Whispers behind doors. She makes a trip to the store seem clandestine.

Betrayal starts as a sinking feeling in your stomach, grows into a suspicion that clouds your every thought, and by the time you find out the truth, it's uniquely horrible at first but also expected, like you've been waiting for something bad to happen. There's nothing more to say. There's a point of no return, and what felt like a phase is now her phasing me out for good.

It seems like the right call in the bright light of day, when my head is on straight and I'm thinking logically. At night, when everything clouds over, I'm totally confused. In the darkest hour, the schmuck who proposed, the clown who'd do anything to make her laugh, and the husband planning for the future all sit up torturing me with "what-ifs." The guy who promised her and himself "forever," just like in the Beach Boys song, now sees that forever might not last the night.

March 17, 2003, we separate secretly.

"Separate? What does that mean? We date other people?" I ask.

"It means whatever you think it means," she says.

It means pure hell for me. I head to New York to shoot a shitty small-budget indie movie, and God only knows what she's doing. She makes it clear that a separation means no contact. It's a strange, fucked-up "what the hell is happening" type

of heartbreak that up to this point I've never felt. I wasn't prepared for this one.

I muddle through a few months in New York, finish the
movie, and hang out with friends. I've got nowhere to call home;
I'm lost and trying to get through the days while I figure out my
next move. I'm sitting on my bed at the Rihga Royal Hotel, my
home away from life, when, out of the blue, Rebecca calls.

"Hi, I thought we weren't supposed to communicate with
each other?" I say with a tinge of optimism mixed with false
bravado.

"I'm calling to get your opinion on something." *Oh no, here it
comes. On what law firm to use for our divorce?* I think to myself.

"In our bedroom, I was thinking of . . ."

She's calling to get my input on a remodel she wants to do to
our house, as if we will be living there together again. Does this
mean there's still hope?

She shows up in New York soon after and declares she's
decided to take me back. Has she gotten whatever it was out of
her system during our couple months of separation? Does she
realize no one measures up to me? That she can't live without
me? Who knows, but who am I to question it? I'm overjoyed
and can't wait to get back to the way things were. The way we
were.

Not so fast, hotshot. Rebecca has a list of, not demands, but
thoughts on how things should change. How I should change.
She's now the one in charge, and I feel like I've forgotten what I
wanted out of this marriage. Just to be happy?

We give it another go. We river raft with our old crew, the
"Circle Flirts," something that was an annual outing, but this
time there are some new rafters, Rebecca's newfound besties.

We travel to Holland to celebrate her father's birthday. After,
we fly to Kuwait to join the USO tour "Project Salute 2003,"

which pays tribute to the men and women of the U.S. and Coalition armed forces. It was an eventful trip but took place early on, before soldiers started stepping on land mines.

We're off to Japan, but first we celebrate my fortieth birthday with family and friends at the Grand Californian Hotel at Disneyland, where Rebecca gifts me a Dumbo. The ride vehicle has a goofy grin, rumpled hat, ruffled collar, and endearing upturned eyes. I'm smitten with the adorable little bastard.

It's easy to make a relationship work when you're busy, luxury travel, fancy gifts, all while plugged into various projects. Rebecca shoots movies with Robert De Niro and John Travolta, I shoot a few phone commercials.

As a favor to me, she carves out a weekend to accompany me for a change, to my premiere at SXSW. It's an underwhelming opening of an underwhelming movie, a small sex comedy called *Knots* that I shot during our split in New York. "Rebecca, John, over here. Rebecca!" One lousy paparazzo yells out, "Rebecca, let me get a single of just you." I step aside. These will be the last pictures ever taken of the two of us together. It's one of our best performances, acting like we are happy and still in love.

I realize I can't live up to the man she wants me to be, this guy she has in mind, someone closer to her father. She's done, and I'm tired of not being the apple of her eye.

I'm doing a table read of a new pilot I'm shooting for ABC, *Jake in Progress*. I call Rebecca to tell her how excited I am about how the reading went. She is apathetic at best.

I take a long pause. "I'm not coming home," I say. I'm waiting for her to tell me to please come back, don't leave. I'm waiting for her to say let's work this out. But after an equally long pause, she just says, "Okay."

The minister at our wedding said when two people fall in love, they want to shout it out to the world. When two people fall out of love, it's almost like they have nothing left to say to each other.

Soon after, a publicist makes the standard Hollywood breakup statement to the press: "The split is amicable, and they have asked that the media please respect their privacy regarding this situation during this difficult time." Blah-blah-blah. A bland, legal boilerplate is all the poetry left from a ten-year relationship.

I'm heartbroken and feel like a failure. I thought I'd be the dad of three kids by now and grow old with Rebecca. I'd spent a lot of time being single and a good amount of time being married. I like marriage. I want that soulmate by my side through thick and thin, happy and dark times, for better and for worse. This is thin, dark, and the worst.

A week before our mediation process, she comes over to see the beach house I'm renting. Her new little puppy, Better (obnoxious name for a dog) takes a shit on my welcome mat. She cleans it up and offers to come back and help me decorate. She never does. I asked her if we can at least go to lunch sometime.

"Yes, but if you talk about the past, I'll get up and leave," she says.

That lunch never happens.

I never knew I could be so angry and hate-filled toward another human being, much less one I had been dedicated to for a decade.

On June 1, 2004, I'm sitting at one end of a long table in our business management office, and she's at the other. Mediation. Our "people" take the inside seats, being as bipartisan as they can. I try to stay calm and cool. I don't want to let on how angry I am. My therapist clues me in to the fact that anger, at its core, is hurt. I'm hurting pretty bad.

I have that sinking feeling in my stomach, fear mixed with pure dread. I've also downed about a half dozen beers. I've always followed my gut and usually been right, but today the only intuition I have is that I need to be close to a toilet in case I have to pee.

We go through all the requisite unpleasantries of mediation: you get the house, I get the Dumbo. There's a solid prenup, but Rebecca made decent dough during our marriage, so she'll be fine. We're cruising through a list of depressingly standardized legal mumbo-jumbo and are about to wrap up.

Steve Campeas, our business manager, says, "Okay, last order of business. According to your prenuptial agreement, Rebecca, because of all the joint taxes John has paid out over the last few years, you owe him a large sum of money."

I'm a bit shocked, it's a lot.

"But," Steve continues, "to be fair, she should probably only pay about half, so—"

I explode. All that pent-up rage and sadness I've been stuffing rises to the surface, "Fair? Fair? Fuck fair! You wanna know what she did to me?"

Steve tries to calm my ass down. He speaks in a sort of mono-tone rhythm that is sometimes soothing but not today.

"Now, John, this is a negotiation—" he begins.

"Negotiate my balls!" I shout.

Everyone gets quiet. Even the moderator, who I'm sure has heard worse, looks taken aback. Out of the corner of my eye, I see my personal business manager, sweet Micki Supple, a woman I've worked with since the beginning of my career, looking at me with such sadness. I feel horrible about using that kind of language and losing my cool in front of her. I have a lot of respect for Micki. I've trusted her with every cent I've ever made in my career. I look back at her a little defeated, and she gives me a subtle wink and nod. She understands what I'm going through.

She's been in the weeds with me during this relationship and knows the gut-punch I took. She's letting me express myself, however messily, in this moment.

"Give him everything I owe him," Rebecca says.

I want to yell out that she owes me the last ten years of my life, dreams, goals, and plans for a fairy-tale future. I don't say a word. That's when you know something is over. There's no fight left, just resignation.

It's done. We both look across the table at each other for the first time with sadness in our eyes. That's all the truth and vulnerability I'm going to give her. There is a chance to say something profound or to finish on a high note, but I don't. I default to business.

"So, I want to be the one who files for divorce," I say. "The press is already shading the split as 'Rebecca Romijn, movie star, superstar, has finally dumped the ex-teen idol destined for dinner theater starring in *The Odd Couple* opposite Scott Baio. The tabloids are slanting things like you're leaving me; like you're the dumper and I'm the dumpee. At least give me this, Rebecca. I file and the headlines will read, 'John Stamos files for divorce!'"

She sighs. "Yeah, fine, you can do the filing."

"I will!" I assert, with what little power and control I have left in this moment.

I don't really feel she owes me anything more than an apology. I guess I owe her one, too. But we don't say a word. I walk over and give her a hug. We spill tears. We had promised each other that we would spend some time together after today, but we don't. This will be the last time I ever see her. We will not cross paths again, we will not run into each other at events. This is the end.

I try to move on, but for a long time, way too long, I harbor more and more blame and anger toward her. I certainly can't blame myself. No way. Drinking helps me feel like I'm right.

Let's have a toast . . . to me! I wasn't a perfect husband but I'm a good guy. One more round! Look at me! She was lucky to have me! I made her career! I'll be back, baby, and when I am, I'll forget your name. Pop the cork, pour the wine, sit in that self-righteousness.

This split is testing my limitations. How much punishment in booze, reckless behavior, and self-loathing can I take? I'm sturdy but pushing my luck. I'm squandering goodwill and losing control. Up, down, sideways, heartbroken all night. No grace, no gratitude.

I feel busted up beyond repair—a failure to those I love and a failure to myself. It's a public divorce that knocks the wind out of me, dents my pride, and leaves me feeling lost and soulless. I had started to give up on myself in the marriage, and after the divorce, I make sure to finish what I started.

Still, there's something in me that knows if I ever intend to get married again, I'll have to do a lot of work on myself. My therapist makes that clear.

"The only reward for hard work," my therapist will assert time and time again, "is MORE work!"

But instead of getting to work, I'm getting loaded, getting in my car, and getting a DUI that sends me to rehab. It's in my moment of greatest shame that I let go and forgive Rebecca and myself.

I'm sitting in a rehabilitation facility in Utah with a counselor who works there acting as my sponsor. He's working the twelve steps of recovery with me. The fourth step in AA requires us to make a "searching and fearless moral inventory of ourselves." He says, "Make a column and start by writing a list of resentments gathered up over the years."

Resentments? This part is easy. I'm writing at warp speed, trying to document all the shitty stuff my ex-wife did to me.

"I've got this!" I say, flourishing my pencil as I write out how she single-handedly ruined our marriage and my life. I go on and on. I put my pencil down and think for a moment. Pick it up and keep jotting. She did this, she did that. I'm filling pages and feeling semi-vindicated.

My sponsor looks at my screed. "Good," he says. "You get it all out?"

"Yes, sir!" I say with a satisfied look on my smug face.

He challenges me, "Now, in another column, I'd like you to write down what part you played in these resentments."

Huh?

"What are you talking about?" I say. "I mean she—"

He interrupts me. "Yeah, I get it, but even if you have one percent, or ten percent of a part in all that, I want you to write it down."

As I start to write, I realize it is a lot more than one or ten percent. I was responsible for the demise of our relationship more than I want to believe. I need to push out all the bullshit and fess up. I haven't been able to confess to my family, friends, or the world, but it's time to come clean to myself. It cuts to the core but it's the only way out; the only way to rebuild and grow.

Anything less than truth is paralysis. If you want to cram the ugly reality down your throat, just be ready for it to seep out of your pores in other ways. It can present itself as disease, destruction of future relationships, or disappointing those we love.

I want to say: "It was all for the best and thank God I got away from that wretched person. If I would have stayed she would have burned down my life and left me for dead." But that's not the truth. We simply didn't make it. No good guys, no bad guys. I wished it could have worked out, but without this great loss, there would have been no chance for greater love, a family, a new fairy tale.

After walking away from a relationship that lasts a decade,

I want to impart some profound wisdom or cautionary advice, but mostly I just learned to hold on to who I am. No matter how much you love another person, don't forget to love yourself. No matter how much you want another person to succeed, don't sell yourself out. For women, it's about keeping your independence and empowerment in any relationship. For men, I don't know, compromise wherever you can but don't negotiate every aspect of life. Keep your balls.

25

THE BIG D

I rent a bachelor beach house in Malibu for the summer. It is an old nautical place jutting over the ocean. I decorate it with whatever furniture I have in storage. Not sure if maroon leather couches, handwoven Indian rugs, art deco prints of Sinatra, Marilyn, and Brando fit the maritime motif, but it works for me.

Depending on the tide, the break is far enough out to reveal a sandy beach where my young nieces and nephew catch sand crabs, or it soars so high that the waves crash under the house, shaking everything like an earthquake.

I grow my beard, fish off the deck, and breathe in the ocean air. I pull up a halibut or mackerel, gut it, marinate, throw it on the grill, and eat dinner watching the sunset. My mom, my sisters and their families, agents, managers, old friends, new friends, everyone comes around. They want me to be okay.

Bob and I are now both single and we're spending a lot more time together as well. Our relationship is shifting from being good friends to being the brothers we both wished we had.

When Bob gets out there and really starts dating, I'm right

by his side. I am his Cyrano, his wingman, his fashion consultant and emotional support animal before that's even a thing. Then, it's his turn to get me through my impending big D. No matter how many times a husband and wife go to Disneyland together, happy endings aren't guaranteed. This is where Bob jumps in with something like, "*You don't want to get a hand job on 'It's a Small World,' that fucking song will ruin the mood. 'Big Thunder' is better.*" When dealing with tragedy in his own life, he often pivots to inappropriate humor, the kind of jokes where you cringe and say, "Whoa, too soon, man," but he knows how to pull back when he needs to. I am hurting, and Bob knows it.

Bob rallies the *Full House* crew to come hang. He makes sure we all stay close. He knows how important it will turn out to be. I can't think of one sitcom where the cast is closer than family, supports each other, and spends an embarrassing amount of time together like ours. Bob is the glue.

We usually meet up over at Taverna Tony, my favorite Greek hangout in Malibu.

Imagine walking up the stone steps under a vine-covered archway, blue and white washing over you as if you're in Santorini, and you see a gigantic table with the entire cast of *Full House* laughing their asses off while chowing down on saganaki, spanakopita, and lamb.

For dessert Tony brings out karpuzi, fresh watermelon with the Greek pronunciation "car-pussy." Put a name like that in front of a crew like ours after a few bottles of our favorite red wine, Megas Oenos, and you're guaranteed a good twenty-five minutes of car-pussy jokes. "This is the only car you don't want to be described as roomy." If it looks like we are having the time of our lives and truly enjoying each other, we are.

Afterward, we all head back to my pad down the street, hit the deck, and dance the night away under the stars. I have my baby grand Steinway piano delivered for some great sing-alongs. There are a few nights when I am afraid that it is going to finally make the flimsy, salt-air-weathered floor give way and we'll all bust through to the ocean below singing a Beach Boys song.

No one dares to drive home, so it always turns into one big slumber party, with everyone scrambling for a place to crash. There's a master and one guest room. The girls grab the guest room, Dave hits the couch, and Bob?

Now, it isn't the first time Bob and I sleep in the same bed together (on and off TV). We never wake up in each other's arms but definitely know the smell of each other's morning breath.

"Bob, your breath smells like a piece of shit took a shit in your mouth," I say.

Bob loves that joke.

In the morning, Bob sneaks one of the Olsen twins down to the beach and into a waiting car to avoid the paparazzi. He still feels like a father figure to the girls, no matter how old or rich they become. The rest of us wake up slowly, grab a coffee or a beer, and enjoy the last lazy days of summer.

That August, Bob invites me to go to the premiere of his movie The Aristocrats, a vaudevillian homage to the filthiest joke of all time. The documentary features a who's who of great comedians. My man, Don Rickles, with Chris Rock, George Carlin, Jeffrey Ross, Robin Williams, Carrie Fisher, and Sarah Silverman among the list of luminaries. It's vile, transgressive, and covers just about every taboo in society. Bob is so proud to be named in the same breath as these stars, and he ends up stealing the whole movie.

I'm trying to concentrate on the plot but I'm slightly baked. I'm not much of a pot smoker, it just makes me sleepy. It's 7:00 P.M. at a party: "Who gave Stamos weed? He's sound asleep in the corner."

Someone at the premiere has me smoke a joint with them.

Might be my good pal Matt Stone, of *South Park* fame, but maybe I'm typecasting here. Bob goes to the front of the theater where the director is introducing some of the comics, and I get seated next to Sarah Silverman. I have a big crush on her, but she wouldn't know because I'm trying to negotiate the narcoleptic fog of weed while watching my best friend tell a joke about incest, bestiality, and diarrhea.

Bob's scene is exploding on-screen. I can see him lift off into a stream of consciousness that sets him apart from most, almost Robin Williams–like. He's flying by the seat of his pants, letting something otherworldly take control. As he gets sicker and sicker with the material, he remains wide-eyed, cheerful, and guileless. He never actually gets to the punchline, but apparently didn't need to, judging by the reactions of his fellow comedians. They are all doubling over and wiping away tears. I love seeing Bob shine.

Throughout the years, Bob and I become a team: the poor man's Rickles and Newhart. We throw each other legendary birthday parties. We support each other's charities. I bring him into my Super Bowl yogurt spots. We do talk shows together and magazine shoots. I love the cuddle video we do for CollegeHumor that becomes a classic.

One of my favorite bits is in his act when he does a song for the encore entitled "Danny Tanner Was Not Gay," sung to the Backstreet Boys' hit "I Want It That Way." There's a line in the bridge where he sings, "*After eight years with them, in a house with two men, they were my second family. The last show shed a tear. Then Stamos grabbed at my rear. And uncle Jesse was inside of meeeeee....*" That's my cue to casually stroll out from backstage, walk up to him, and shake my head in disgust. Then I bust out Bob's famous line from *Half Baked* with Dave Chappelle—"*I seen him!*"—and then we finish the song together.

The crowd goes wild.

26

SHITTING THE BED

DEAR SON —

WHAT DO YOU HAVE?

HEALTH
LOVE OF A BEAUTIFUL WIFE
LOVE OF FAMILY
LOVE OF FRIENDS
TALENT
YOUTH
EXTRA ORDINARY GOOD LOOKS
CELEBRITY
WEALTH
A CUTE FANNY

WHAT DON'T YOU HAVE?

E. R.

BIG F'N DEAL!

LOVE YOU,
MOM

After five years of playing Doctor Doug Ross on ER, George Clooney thinks he can make a go of it in the movies. Can you believe the balls on this kid? When he leaves ER, producers are looking for a replacement and I'm thinking, *Hey, who better than me? Right? A no-brainer.*

I'd taken meetings with John Wells, the show's cocreator and showrunner in the past. He's a titan of television and someone I've always wanted to work with. This is my shot. Enough time has passed from *Full House*, I have Broadway cred under my belt, and I'm beginning to be taken somewhat seriously.

I am so ready when interest heats up in me playing a new doctor on the upcoming season of the still-very-hot medical drama.

Everyone at the studio, who happen to be my friends at Warner Bros. and the NBC execs, are all good with casting me in the role of Dave Malucci, Italian tough guy and paramedic whose temperamental attitude gets in the way of his talent as a future doctor. I get him. This is mine.

Well . . . almost mine.

There's a small speed bump I have to deal with, a meet and greet with John Wells and a few writer/producer types. My longtime bulldog manager, Danny Sussman, presents it to me as more of a formality.

"Pappy, just go in there and do your thing. They already love you. This is yours to lose," he assures me. We call each other Pappy, I'm not sure why.

Mine to lose? What does that mean? I thought they wanted me.

Danny waves off my fears. "They do! They just want to meet up and talk a little bit first. Might have you read a scene or two. No big deal."

"Read?" I ask.

"Yeah. You pick whatever scene you want. They're asking everyone to read."

Everyone? I thought this was my role. The role that will catapult me to a Clooney-level career. We both started out in goofy sitcoms. We're both funny and self-deprecating. Hell, I was doing this first. I practically paved the way for guys like him and now I have to audition to replace him?

Fine, they want me to read, I'll read. I'm good at auditioning. Haven't done it in a while, but no sweat, I got this. I have the whole thing planned out in my mind already.

I'll go play doctor for two or three seasons, then parlay myself into movies. Probably start off with something lighter, a romantic comedy with a twist, like *Out of Sight* with Clooney and Jennifer Lopez. Might skip the Batman bit, since I'm still not that athletic. Let's see what the Coen brothers throw together for me. I love those guys.

Slow down, Doc. The train to Clooneyville is about to take a detour.

It's a hot day. Warner Bros. Studios is located deep in the San Fernando Valley, where the sun takes out its revenge on humanity.

I cruise onto the lot a little early, park, and read through the script one more time.

The medical jargon is a little tricky, but I'll be fine.

"Grab the sphygmomanometer. Diagnosis: xerostomia, onychocryptosis, and hippopomonstrosequipedalophobia." In English, grab the blood pressure cuff, the dude's got dry mouth, an ingrown toenail, and a fear of long words.

As I walk across the lot, I say hello to the guard at the gate and chat up folks I know from working there for so long.

A crew member shouts out, "Hey, Stamos! What are you doing here?"

"Meeting John Wells for a gig on ER," I say.

"You'd be perfect! Look forward to seeing you. We miss you around here."

As I get closer to the offices, I spot at least a dozen Italian or Greek tough guys, who kind of resemble me, pacing as they read their lines aloud.

They stop and look up at me. I give a meek wave. "Hi, fellas."

I get the feeling they all sense this role is already mine, and they're asking themselves why are they even wasting their time reading today. *Of course John Stamos is going to get this.*

I'm grateful when I see Jinny Jong, a smart advocate and friend, who used to be my manager's assistant. She's now working for John Wells and on her way to running John Wells Productions. She grabs me and pulls me away from the gaggle of Stamos clones and puts me into another room.

"Hang here, away from those guys," she says. "I have to run and fetch John his Diet Coke. He can't do anything without it."

Nerves are beginning to kick in. I call out to Jin, "Hey, this is going to be easy, right?"

"Totally, you got this. You're going to be fine."

Fine? I don't like that word. It's the linguistic equivalent of beige.

Now my heart starts pounding. It's okay. This is natural, this is good. It'd be crazy if I didn't have a few nerves.

The sweltering Valley heat seeps into the little office I'm in. I feel my face. Drenched. I duck into a bathroom and look in the mirror. I'm Albert Brooks in *Broadcast News*, re-creating the scene where he makes his television debut, dripping with sweat. I try to dry off, but the dispenser is out of paper towels. Haven't I made Warner Bros. enough money to stock some damned paper towels? I ball up a wad of toilet paper and start to dab. As I keep patting, I notice the thin paper sticking to my face. I look like a victim of a shaving accident gone horribly awry.

A woman barges in. "Hey, Uncle Jesse, what are you doing in here?"

I wanted to say, "What the fuck does it look like I'm doing in here?" but before I have a chance to respond, she says, "This is the *women's* bathroom."

"Oh shit, I'm so sorry. I'll be right out!"

"You're really sweaty," she says. Am I? Really?

I spot an air dryer and point the blower toward my face. Not sure why I thought hot air would help.

Jinny knocks gently. "J, you ready?"

"In a minute!" I call out desperately. I'm wearing a black T-shirt, how are the sweat rings around my pits so noticeable?

"Everyone's waiting," she says, sounding apologetic.

I walk out, to see Jinny holding John's Diet Coke wrapped in cellophane. She's laughing at me.

"You know, that's the women's—"

"I know that, of course I know that, why would you think I didn't know that?"

She leads me down a hall, and I try to act cool.

I tell her, "You know Danny, your old boss, pitched this to me as a simple meeting with Wells and maybe another producer." I walk into a room and see over twenty people crammed together.

I try to make a joke. "Hi, I'm reading for the roll of Doctor Hyperhidrosis." Crickets. Crickets.

I shake John Wells's hand with my schvitzing paw. He discreetly wipes my sweat off on his slacks, trying not to embarrass me. "See, hyperhidrosis, uncontrollable hand sweat." Okay . . .

There's Peter Roth, head of Warner Bros. TV, about six producers from ER, same number of writers, legendary director Jonathan Kaplan, the head of talent at NBC, John Levey, head of casting for all John Wells productions, secretaries, and assistants. The most people I've ever seen at any audition in my life. All serious drama folk.

Again, I try to lighten the mood. "Are we waiting for more people? I notice no one from craft service is here yet."

These bastards are stoic.

Levey asks, "What scene have you selected?"

"Uh, right. Scene 21A, page forty-two," I say, rummaging through my papers.

"What? You must have an old script." Levey sighs. "Here, read scene 21B. It's highlighted and basically the same."

Sure, a bunch of highlighted words I've never seen before.

John Wells plays Good Cop. "Don't worry about the words, you don't have to be word perfect. Just do your thing."

Well, if my thing is sweating, barfing, pissing, and defecating all over your shoes, clothes, and Diet Coke wrapped in cellophane, John, no problem.

My hands start shaking so badly that the words on the page become blurry. And that's the way they are coming out of my mouth.

"Here, let me start over," I say. Each time I do it gets worse. I probably sound like I'm having a stroke.

"And scene."

I even stumble over a "thank-you" before slipping out so fast I feel like I'm rushing down a water slide. I get to my car redfaced and disheveled.

I probably should have driven myself straight to the real ER for dehydration, but I decide to head home, brush off what happened, and take an optimistic approach.

As I walk through my door and out of the heat, I go through scenarios that could have a happy ending. *It's unanimous, I nailed it, and I start Monday. Or they want me to come back for a chemistry read.*

Or . . .

"You shit the bed!"

I hear a tiny voice coming out of the answering machine speaker. I leap to pick it up. It's John Levey.

"Hey, Levey, how did I do?"

"You shit the bed!" he says again.

I'd never heard that term before. "I'm sorry," I say, a little defeated, "but it was hot in there and—"

Cutting me off, he says, "Better luck next time." He hangs up.

The positive voices in my head have drowned in flop-sweat and the negativity in the darkest recesses of my mind speaks up.

You suck, Stamos! You're not the actor you think you are. Time to give it up, Hair Boy. Go back to sitcom-land where you belong. The same voices that tell me how much I suck have added *You shit the bed* to their repertoire.

It's easy to hold on to something so profoundly that it weighs on you until it becomes a detriment to moving forward. The more you replay it in your mind, the worse it gets, and you bury the shame somewhere deep.

I will avoid John Wells at all costs. I don't know how to face him, apologize, or deal with the embarrassment. I repress bad feelings pretty well, but when I'm in a low state or things are just a little too quiet, I wallow in the humiliation.

"When one door closes, another one opens?" If it's the door to the women's restroom again, not exactly the kind of opportunity I'm hoping for.

"Everything happens for a reason?" Yeah, because clearly there's a cosmic plan in place that involves a bed, and me shitting it.

Fast-forward a few years. September of 2006, I'm on the back lot of Warner Bros. I've been hired—without auditioning, by the way—to play Dr. Tony Gates, a regular on ER.

The episode is called "Two Ships." Two airplanes collide and crash in downtown Chicago, and my character is badly injured when a burning building explodes as I rush in bravely to save a woman.

I'm nowhere near as destroyed as I was after that first audition a few years ago, but still battered, bloodied, and lying on a gurney when John Wells comes by to welcome me.

I'm instantly apologizing; I haven't seen him since Sweat-Fest '04. "John, I've been meaning to apologize for my horrible audition a while back . . ."

John says, "What are you talking about?"

Oh damn. Why did I mention it? He probably didn't remember, but now he will and fire my ass.

"Oh, you're talking about when you came in for the Malucci character?" he asked. "Yeah, we sort of knew it might not work before you even walked into the room. The second you showed up our thoughts were confirmed. You were too much like George. Same energy, swagger, charisma. George had just left, so before you even opened your mouth, I decided it wouldn't be fair to put that kind of pressure on you. Thank God you were available now."

I'm smiling, although it's hard to tell with all the fake blood on my face.

In an interview for my E! True Hollywood Story, Wells says, "We were looking for people that were underestimated, and I think John is greatly underestimated for his acting ability. I've been wanting to work with him for years."

Not everything that hurts is an emergency. Sometimes we need to test our pain threshold to see how well we heal. I know I'll be indebted to that man for the rest of my life. There are so many good people on this show. The actors, crew, writers, directors, and doctors who help me achieve the authenticity I need to be convincing in this role.

I walk around the hospital set and can't believe I'm here. This is my shot. I'm not the same guy who walked into that audition years ago, thinking I'd use the show for a little exposure and toss it for the first film that comes along. I'm no longer on the Clooney track. I'm showing up as Stamos. He's good enough.

I take in the rows and rows of hospital beds set up for fake patients coming in and out of the emergency room. I think to myself, *Do not shit these beds.*

I spend the next four years doing the best television I've ever done.

Every day is a learning experience, watching some of the most talented people on television at the top of their game. Maura Tierney, Linda Cardellini, Scott Grimes, Parminder Nagra, Goran Visnjic, Mekhi Phifer: a new crew as solid as their predecessors.

Initially, they call me the NFG—the New F'n' Guy. I learn later that they were worried I'd show up with my bag of sitcom tricks and not give the character enough dramatic weight. I do my best, and they envelop me into the gang.

The show is going into its thirteenth season, and while it's still doing fine, the ratings and audience enthusiasm wane a little. NBC decides to do the unthinkable and take ER off the air for a brief hiatus, but after three weeks of what can only be described as a stunning ratings performance, the network reconsiders and goes from an order of twenty-two original episodes to twenty-four or twenty-five. The ratings increase significantly, and the show is once more firmly number one in its time slot.

Kevin Reilly, head of NBC, says, "Stamos has given the show the additional boost it needed."

Entertainment Weekly reports:

If there's such a disease as triskaidekaphobia (the fear of the number 13), ER seems to have discovered a cure: John Stamos. . . . NBC's decision to cast the heartthrob as cocky med stud Tony Gates has injected so much new life into the drama, now in its 13th season, that speculation is swirling about a—gulp!— 15th go-around for the series.

Tony Gates is pretty much everything I'm not. He comes in

hot where I tend to be more relaxed. He's an impulsive maverick where I usually weigh pros and cons before leaping. He's a take-charge kind of guy who's been through the Persian Gulf War and braved the streets as an emergency paramedic. My biggest battles are internal. He has a troubled past where I've been loved and nurtured since the day I was born. He starts off at the bottom of the ER totem pole . . . okay, maybe we have a little in common.

27

BURN

Around the middle of the thirteenth season, Maura, Linda, and I are all in strange emotional places. I'm recently single and still feeling the aftershocks of divorce. Same with Maura. Linda is coming off a tough breakup. We drown our sorrows a little but also talk about wanting to experience new things, meet new people, do things we've never done before.

"Hey, my brother is getting married at Burning Man. Let's all go!" Linda says one day.

On August 31, 2007, me, Maura, Linda, and 6,500 other people will descend upon a seven-mile-square patch of Nevada's Black Rock Desert. The Mad Max–style festival promises radical inclusion, radical gifting, radical self-reliance, and radical self-expression. We can handle that.

We pick up a fully loaded motor home in Reno and head out to the desert in search of the meaning of life and a horse with no name, or whatever.

On the ride, I'm bloviating about all of us being too famous. "We've got to disguise ourselves. Except for the naked folks, everyone is in crazy costumes anyway, so we need to blend in."

It would be wild if word got out that the cast of ER was there. People seem to think we're real doctors and we don't need overheated, dehydrated burners coming to our RV for medical attention. I certainly don't want to be signing autographs all day and night, so I sport full face paint in the spirit of Braveheart. Hide my hair in a bowler hat, throw on a white tank top with a leather kilt, and finish off the look with combat boots. This is my first time at Burning Man, and I want to experience it through the eyes of a normal, nonfamous person.

After about an hour of achieving total anonymity, with no one looking at me, no preferential treatment, and no pretty girls coming over to flirt, I'm hating it.

My friends are laughing. "Oh, poor Johnny can't meet girls if he's not recognized!"

The cat is out of the bag. I have zero game without the fame. Who cares? That's not why we came. We are all getting over losses that remind us too much of who we've been at our lowest points. It's time to slide out of the skin we're in and become someone else for a few days. We step onto the playa and step out of our comfort zones.

We're cruising bikes through the desert. There's nothing to see for miles until you come upon a soaring structure that seems to move through the heat waves in the distance. Ride closer and it's an incredible art installation. Three giant people, hundreds of feet tall, praying to an oil tank. There's something you don't see every day.

Ride on a little farther, a massive Mack truck bent into the shape of a large S with topless women climbing all over it. This place is like the Disney electrical parade, with a few more drugs and 100 percent more nudity.

We go to a hand-built ornate temple and write down our wishes for the year. We all pen some private note about letting lost love go and opening our hearts to what the world has in store for us. We stick them in the walls to be ignited on the eve of the Burn.

The trip is planned for three nights, but after night two, Maura gets antsy. She and her friend Julie want to split. We plead with them to wait another day and go home with us as planned, but she wants to leave now. She hitches a ride from a guy camped next to us who's heading out in a Honda. He looks like a guy who would be named something like Swanny. His name is Swanny.

The Burn is the event's biggest night, where they torch a giant wooden man in effigy. I take a nap that afternoon, and when it's time to make the trek to the middle of the playa, I'm sound asleep, which is code for passed out.

Unable to wake me, my crew heads out but leaves a detailed map of how to meet them in front of The Man. It reads: "Our camp is at 9 o'clock, Estuary, so go down to the Arctic, make a left at 7 o'clock, right on Kelp Forest till you hit 3 o'clock and Coral, look for Intertitle Reef and we'll be right to the left of that. Burn Time!"

Burn this. No phones, no GPS, not even a compass. After a lifelong battle with traditional maps, I'm required to be a cartographer of pure fuckery.

The burners have a funny tradition where they switch all the dopey street signs making it impossible to get anywhere. Estuary is now where the Kelp Forest was, the Kelp Forest is now Green Rock something, ha, ha, ha.

Now I'm fully lost, but there's a girl about a hundred yards in front of me in nothing but a G-string exposing a perfectly shaped butt. I figure she's heading toward the Burn, so I focus on her swaying ass like it's a divining rod. Show me the way.

She's moving quickly and I'm clomping behind her in my clunky army boots. We walk long enough that I begin to think she's just a mirage in the desert, but we stride the length of the esplanade and finally end up in front of The Man.

I'm out of breath and wishing I wore sensible shoes. I catch up with her and start to introduce myself. She turns around, and it's a dude. A dude with a great ass. "Hey there," I say. I get a knowing, *wait a minute hey aren't you the guy* smile in return.

It's the first and only time I get recognized at the Burn.

I return to ER feeling I've experienced something incredibly unique, something I've never seen or done. Also seen that, done that, never need to do it again. A little of my ambition might have gone up in flames during the big burn. I'm still inhabiting Tony Gates, but not with the same intensity as when I started the show.

A true pro has to stay intense. Hard work begets more hard work.

That lesson is lost on me right now.

Mike Love, the man who cowrote the soundtrack of my life and provided a dream come true a thousand times and more.

Me and Jeffrey Foskett, the man who introduced me to my heroes.

The Beach Boys sing "Kokomo" in the Tanner living room.

My handsome brother, Bob.

Bob and Ashley Olsen, cheering me up at the beach house in Malibu.

Me, Mary-Kate, Ashley, and Minnie at Disneyland. It was a special treat to take them there for their first visit.

I loved any chance I got to spend time with the kids off the set.

Me and Candace at the George Michael concert.

A visit from Lizzie Olsen, who now goes by the name of Elizabeth and is a superstar in the Marvel Universe. If you would have told me . . .

The Boys.

Bob would run out and grab my buns when we were being introduced before the show.

Our final curtain call in 1995. Ended too soon.

James Earl Jones gave me legitimacy as an actor—and a blow-up doll for my birthday.

How to succeed on Broadway while really, really trying.

Don comes to opening night of *Bye Bye Birdie* and saves the day.

Sweethearts and swastikas on those crazy *Cabaret* nights.

Monte Haught making sure the symbol of hate is drawn on straight.

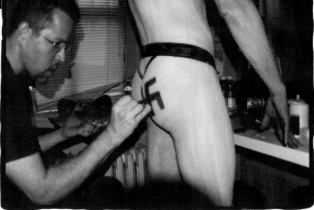

Mary-Kate and Ashley backstage at *Cabaret*.

Howard Stern and me: reformed playboys and lifelong Rickles fans.

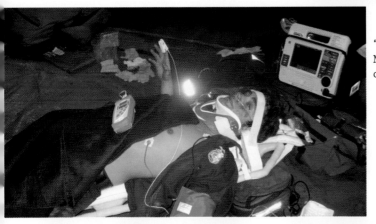

"Oh, hi, *John Wells*." My very first day on the job.

Sam (Linda Cardellini) and Tony hard at work saving lives, and looking very serious.

The ER cast goes from saving lives on TV to saving our own spirits at Burning Man.

Rickles, Brad Grey, Phil Stutz (my therapist), Bob, and Johnny Knoxville trying to recover from Rickles's toast.

My whole life I wanted to be on a Garry Marshall–type show. If you would have told me he would turn out to be my godfather in showbiz, my mentor, and my dear friend back when I was in the audience for a taping of *Happy Days* . . .

Looking on with respect and love.

The day I met Caitlin on the set of *Law & Order: SVU.* "*Let's take a picture. You want me to text it to you?*" What a ruse.

"*Go on and ask the girl!*"
Proposal at Disneyland in the Animation Building.

Not only is he a member of one of the greatest bands in rock-n-roll history, not only did he cowrite some of the most iconic songs ever written, but Mike's also an ordained minister who married Caitlin and me at the Little Brown Church in the Valley.

Our first dance in our backyard. Jeffrey Foskett sang "Darlin'," one of Caitlin's favorites.

My loves, my life.

Bob, Kelly, Caitlin, and me. The last picture I took with Bob at Nobu in Malibu.

28

BLUNDER DOWN UNDER

I promise myself that I will not drink at work. Not during the day while out to lunch, not in my trailer, no drinking at work. And if I do, I promise to march myself right into an AA meeting and take it seriously. I break the first promise and don't keep the second.

I have a few friends in the program who see trouble on my horizon. Your own kind can spot you a mile away. Dewey Bunnell from the band America is a good friend. Met him when America was touring with The Beach Boys. He invited me to a few meetings, as did Doug Fieger from one of my favorite groups, The Knack.

We became friends over the years. I'd have great jam sessions at my house and Doug loved to hang, play music, and impress the girls when he'd bust out his number one hit song, "My Sharona." I started to notice that he and Dewey would always leave early, while I stayed up and partied all night. Then back to work early the next day and around lunch, have a little hair of the dog.

Who would have thought rock stars would have to coax a

happy-go-lucky actor into a church basement for bad coffee and twelve steps. Doug eases me into the idea of sobriety by taking me to a men's meeting for musicians. He thinks I'll be inspired seeing artists I respect tell their stories. I'm not. I have a tough time articulating my problem, or even admitting I have one. I don't understand the lingo. They're speaking a foreign language of serenity, sanity, admissions, and amends, and I'm totally lost.

A legendary rock star guy gets up and talks about losing everything. How his kids found him in a dumpster with a needle hanging out of his arm. How am I supposed to follow that? "I drank a light beer in my Star Wagon trailer at work the other day, amen."

I bail on the AA meet and greets and convince myself that I have it under control.

Warner Bros. asks me to go on a promotional tour in Australia. Hell, yeah! Australia is my favorite place on the planet. I always say I plan to retire there and start my own shrimp farm.

I jump at the chance.

I have a trip planned to go to Greece with Bob Saget, so I'll just head to Australia afterward and fly my best friend, Mike Owen, there to meet me. He's always wanted to go.

In an effort to get back the passion I had when I started, I stop drinking for a while. I want to return to ER sharp and focused for the new season. But, here I am with Bob in Greece, my father's homeland, and I'm feeling sentimental and missing him. Why not lift a glass of ouzo to toast the most significant Greek I would ever know? And why stop at one, right? I mean, the man was a great Greek!

And just like that, I'm drinking again.

I make a deal with myself, I'm only boozing it up in Europe, but won't touch a drop in Hong Kong, where I'm making a two-day pit stop before heading to Australia. And I will definitely not hooch it up in Australia. I have a lot of work to do.

After a wonderful week in Greece slamming the sauce, I say goodbye to Bob and the bottle, and board a plane for Hong Kong. The drinks I have on the plane don't count because I'm in in the air, over international waters, so. Of course, when I get to China, I become weepy remembering how much my dad loved going to the Chinese restaurant by our house, so I'm topping off chow mein with a sake bomber, or five.

Time to head to Sydney. It's my fourth time zone in just a few weeks. I'm met by Mike at the airport. He's excited to experience Australia for the first time. A group of press reps that work for Warner's Australia are so excited to host me. They accommodate my every whim and will go over all the key talking points promoting ER with me.

The light outside looks like early afternoon, but I barely know what time of day or year it is. I'm jet-lagged and dragged. All I want to do is rest up before the big press day tomorrow. My pleasant, helpful handlers have done their research and read somewhere that I said my favorite fish-and-chips place in the world is Doyles. They set up a big welcome dinner there for me. Couldn't say no to that. Or to the beer. And after about four hours of being fish-and-chipped and beer-battered, I beg for a bed.

"It's only four P.M. here," Mike says, talking me out of sleeping. "We need to go out on the town and stay awake to get acclimated." Sounds reasonable.

"One drink," Mike says.

Fat chance, as we get swept up by the overly hospitable Aussies. One drink turns into one o'clock in the morning which turns into, "Hey, who drank all the booze from my minibar?"

I sleep about eighteen minutes before the alarm goes off. I have a round of interviews first thing in the hotel lobby. It should be easy to run a comb through my hair and amble down the stairs, but it hurts to even open my eyes. I drink seventeen shots of espresso in my room and two miniature vodkas I snag from Mike's minibar.

When I don't show up downstairs for show-and-tell, the PR pros knock my door. No answer. They start to worry and head to Mike's room.

"Do you know where Mr. Stay-moss is?" That's how they pronounce my name. Mike has a key to my room down the hall, he opens it, and finds me asleep.

He plies me with more expresso, and I beg him for another itty-bitty bottle of Absolut. I'm propped up in front of the press and ready to take questions. Absolutely.

The first journalist is a nice guy. He tells me what a huge fan he is. His daughters love me. I take a few pictures with him, sign autographs for his kids, and apologize for being a little out of it.

"We flew in yesterday and I'm really—" I start.

"No need to apologize, mate, this is Australia! We don't judge here," he says. Then he takes a sharp turn and berates my appearance for twenty minutes.

"What's the matter, mate, can't afford socks?" I look down at my sockless ankles. This is going to be a long day. He should be happy I've got pants on.

The more interviews I do, the more I feel I might pass out. Mike is nearby in the lobby when the press reps rush over and ask him, "Mike, what's the matter with Stay-moss? He's drunk and a bit out of it. Quick, take these to him!" They hand Mike two Bloody Marys.

"You want me to give him more alcohol?"

I finally get to my room and pass out. Only a few hours of rest before the piercing telephone rings.

"What?!?" I yell out, one-quarter angry, three-quarters groggy.

A distraught Loretta Stamos is calling me. The interview went out over the wire and my "mate" apparently hammered me for being drunk. My mother is concerned. "Do we need to come get you, Johnny? Are you okay?"

"Yes, Mom. I'm just super jet-lagged. I'll call you later. Love you."

"I love you more," she says. I can hear she's still worried.

In my inebriated, crooked thinking, I am furious at the journalist for freaking out my mom. I know how I'll get him back. I'm going on the popular *Kerri-Anne* show, and it seems logical in the moment that I will inform the world that the reason the insulting journalist is embittered is directly related to his minuscule manhood. It's almost as if nature's cruel joke has bestowed upon him not only a lack of journalistic integrity but also an embarrassingly inadequate appendage.

I show up at the studio, and champagne and OJ await me in my dressing room. I don't remember having this in my rider, but, hey, don't want to be rude. Mike pours us some mimosas, easy on the OJ. By the time I'm sitting across from a well-coifed, leopard-clad Kerri-Anne, I'm drunk on top of drunk. She's articulate, probing, and sensationally serious for a chat host. I look like a character from a Tom Waits song: wasted, wounded, rumpled, and ribald. I start the interview by giving a shoutout to vodka.

"I'm just getting over jet lag," I say to excuse my bearing.

Then, I launch into a routine, calling out the journalist for commenting on "my fatigue" and level small-penis accusations as the crowd titters. I've got dick jokes.

Kerri-Anne scolds me, "You obviously don't take criticism well."

Whoa. I try to lighten the mood, talking about my love for Australia, but she's persisting. "Why would you let someone get under your skin?"

I try to run out the clock by rambling about the Aussie people and The Beach Boys. The interview concludes with us cuddling awkwardly together on the couch talking about death.

"What a great way to end an interview," I slur. "You know Elvis died on a toilet. He was fat. Let's see, who else died? My career after coming to Australia?"

Luckily, my career is fine. My publicist makes a "John-was-on-Ambien" statement before I can weigh in. I want to say I was drunk, I was wrong, and I am sorry. I should take responsibility for my mistakes and show effort to improve. Not sure how long the goodwill I've accumulated in the business will hold up.

I keep it together and finish my time on ER strong. I'm no longer the New F'n' Guy, I'm an old gunslinger hanging up his spurs (or, in this case, a fake doctor hanging up his steth) and letting Tony Gates ride off into the sunset.

29

BYE BYE BOB'S KNEE

Just as ER is ending, I get a call from my pal Sydney Beers from the Roundabout Theatre Company, and she says, "How'd you like to come back to Broadway?" And before I can say I'm not interested in replacing anyone again, she blurts out, "We want you to play Albert in Bye Bye Birdie. It hasn't been done on Broadway since Dick Van Dyke. You'd re-originate the role."

"I'm in!" I've always wanted to play Albert Peterson, and I idolize Dick Van Dyke. Who doesn't?

It's a fun group of people, a mix of fresh faces and Broadway virtuosos. I am particularly excited to work with someone I've been a fan of forever, the great Bill Irwin. Paul Lynde pioneered the role of Mr. MacAfee, but Bill contorts the character into his own with bendy, stretchy, Gumby-like moves. He's a genius of physical comedy and facial expressions and a very nice human as well.

Gina Gershon plays the character Rosie. She's a character herself. Super fun, eccentric, and playful. I'm a huge fan of her movie Showgirls, in the sense that it's the second-worst movie ever made, with *Never Too Young to Die* taking the gold medal of cinematic catastrophe. I know every line and goofy dance move, so it's not above me during rehearsals to emulate that feathering of jazz hands in front of my face, all while melodiously singing, "Put On a Happy Face." Gina's a good sport, and we're building some solid chemistry.

I'll always bow to a master of his craft, so I call Dick Van Dyke for some pointers. He asks questions instead of offering tips and I share places where the play feels creaky. Behind his supportive words, there's a sadness. He's feeling blue and apologizes that he can't be there opening night. He has recently lost his wife and the pain is evident in his voice. I just listen. I thank him for his time, offer my condolences for his considerable loss, and he's the one to lighten the mood by ending on a high note.

"Have fun!" he says.

"I will," I tell him. "I'll be fine."

His voice gets stern. "Fine? You will not be fine. I hate that word. You'll be better than fine. Be yourself!" I love this guy!

I fly home for a few days to receive a star on the Hollywood Walk of Fame. If you would have told me when I was a kid, leaping from star to star, daydreaming about the future, that my own name would join the legion of legends in the biz, I'd never have believed it. To make the moment even more amazing, it's right next to Dick Van Dyke's star, who's next to his own idol, Stan Laurel.

When I get back to *Birdie*, I'm infused with a little more confidence. That star may seem like a silly thing, but it's a symbol of staying power and survival. It reminds me that even if I don't light up the world every night, I can still shine.

Opening night. Flooding in among the critics and journalists is a who's who of Broadway. I get a rousing reception as Albert Peterson makes his grand entrance on a conveyor belt. He's on the phone, dealing with the news that his star, Conrad Birdie, has been drafted into the army.

Everything is going along swimmingly until the mighty locomotive makes its grand entrance into the fictional town of Sweet Apple, Ohio. It is a sight to see, an enormous and impressive piece of stage machinery that had been running like a well-oiled machine during previews all week. But on opening night, the behemoth chugs out about halfway and then screeches to a halt with a cacophony of ear-splitting metal-on-metal grinding noises. And then, silence. The curtain falls, leaving us all hanging for a painfully awkward five minutes.

"Psst, Stamos, the train died. Get out there and stall for time," the stage manager begs.

Technicians are swinging tools like mad behind me and I'm winging it before twelve hundred or so confused theatergoers. It's hard to break character and suddenly start improvising. After a few lackluster bits, I hear a familiar voice from the darkened audience, a voice dripping with sarcasm and love.

"Are they gonna fix the train, or is this going to be a weekend?"

I laugh with relief. "Ladies and gentlemen, Mr. Don Rickles." The crowd goes wild.

"Get a haircut, Stamos!"

Then another member of my posse saddles up to save the day. "Hey, handsome, is it over? I have to pee."

"Hey, it's Mr. Bob Saget in the house," I call out above the cheering crowd. "Come on up here and help a brother out!"

Bob runs down the aisle, tries to leap onstage in a single bound, but smashes his knee so hard I swear I hear it crack. He has so much adrenaline flowing that he barely notices. We don't have a handheld microphone, so he leans into the stage mic rigged to my forehead and says, "I'm really glad your crotch isn't mic'd."

Gina comes out. Please say the stage is fixed. I look at her with pleading eyes and she shakes her head like, Nope, keep vamping. She whips out an old poster of me, some glory shot from the teen idol days.

"I finally saw Full House for the first time at the dentist's office," she says. "What was that about?"

Bob replies, "Oh, it's basically just like Brokeback Mountain—but as a sitcom."

Thank you, Bobby.

Rubber-bodied Bill Irwin performs a little classic clowning. He pops his head out from the bottom of the dropped curtain, starts to climb out, and pantomimes himself getting yanked back in. Mr. Noodles, ladies and gentlemen.

"When do I get my money back?" Rickles heckles.

The stage is finally fixed, the curtain goes up, and Saget is in pain but stays for the whole show to support his brother. The next day he goes to the hospital with a busted-up knee and discovers he needs surgery.

The show is getting mixed reviews, but I've been on both the precious and poison end of the critic's pen, so I avoid reading too much press and focus on tweaking what I can from show to show. One writer says I dance and sing with "disarming esprit," so I think a little of the fun I'm having on this production shines through.

I'm really loving getting to know Bill Irwin. He's as kind as he is talented. I first saw him perform with his comedy partner David Shiner in their hit show Fool Moon. I was transfixed. The guy takes vaudeville standards to a whole new level; a contortionist kook.

After a solid performance one night, Bill and I are still a little hopped-up. "You want to hang out?" Bill asks. "I'm meeting a friend at a bar down the street."

We walk into the bar and his friend, Robin Williams, is surrounded by people, but he's not holding court like I expected. He looks a little meek and retiring in the group, the listener rather than the performer.

"You guys were so brilliant in *Waiting for Godot*," I tell Bill.

When Robin sees Bill, he bolts up and rushes over. They embrace and Bill says, "You know John Stamos, right?"

"Yeah, how you doing, Captain?" he says, shaking my hand.

"Good, man," I say. "You probably don't remember this, but I met you years ago at a taping of *Happy Days* before you did Mork. I got an autograph from you that said, 'Dear money, send Mom.'"

He lets out his big, unmistakable laugh. He really finds it funny, and a light goes on behind his eyes. But not for long. He slowly slips away, leaving Bill and me staring at each other. Quite different from his stage persona, he seems introverted and alone.

I say bye bye to *Birdie* and feel somewhat redeemed for *Nine*, but still don't capture the satisfaction of playing the Emcee in *Cabaret*.

30

CURTAIN CALL

I get a call from Danny, my manager (by the way, the greatest manager on the planet). "Pappy, I got a good one for you. How'd you like to play opposite the greatest living actor, two-time Tony winner James Earl Jones?"

"What?" I say.

Danny says, "Hold on, I'm not finished, kid." He goes on to say I'll also be working with the matriarch of the theater, five-time Tony Award winner Angela Lansbury. Danny starts rattling off her credits: National Velvet, The Manchurian Candidate, Murder, She Wrote. I tell him she'll always be Mrs. Potts from Beauty and the Beast to me. What's the gig?

Gore Vidal's three-act play The Best Man. It's a political potboiler set during the 1960 presidential primaries pitting a principled secretary of state against a populist candidate who will do everything he can to hide his own corruption. Oddly enough, I'm not cast as the good guy. I'm the slick, cold-blooded, right-wing, backbiting Senator Joseph Cantwell. Time to get ruthless.

My pal Matt Stone is presenting at the Tonys and needs a date. As we walk in, the first person I see is my new costar James Earl Jones. Someone introduces us, saying, "James, this is John Stamos, he's your new Cantwell in *The Best Man*."

James asks if I'm going to be able to go toe-to-toe with his character. "You think you're tough enough, young man, to go toe-to-toe at Arty Hockstader?"

I grab his hand and clench my teeth menacingly. I take a breath and I take a chance. "Fuck you, old man, when I hit that stage you won't know what hit you!"

He slowly smiles that enormous Cheshire Cat grin of his and says, "Looking forward to it, my boy!"

Matt looks at me aghast. "Dude, you just said 'fuck you' to Darth Vader."

"I did?" We both get a good laugh out of that one. It's cool being at the Tonys with these guys. I can't help but think that just a few years ago he and Trey Parker were mainly known as the irreverent, foul-mouthed troublemakers behind the hilarious yet vulgar *South Park*. However, after their musical *The Book of Mormon* earns an impressive nine Tony Awards the year before, Stone and Parker have now ascended to the ranks of theatrical royalty, walking among the snarky, highbrow theater critics and elites with ease.

The Book of Mormon is one of the most respected, highest-grossing musicals of all time.

I couldn't be prouder of their success, but I'm also relieved they opted for a different fashion choice than the infamous dresses they donned at the 2000 Oscars—the same frocks worn by Gwyneth Paltrow and Jennifer Lopez the year before, while tripping balls on acid. My buddies.

Back in '97, when *South Park* debuted and it was all the rage, someone asked if I had an older brother named Richard.

"Ummm, no, why do you ask?"

In the second episode of *South Park*, titled "Big Gay Al's Big Gay Boat Ride," John Stamos's older brother, Richard, was introduced. I was the first celeb they goofed on, what an honor.

My animated older brother Richard was hired as the halftime-show singer for a football game between the South Park Cows and the Middle Park Cowboys. Jimbo Kern and Ned Gerblanski convince people to bet on South Park by planting explosives on the mascot. It's to be detonated when Richard tries to hit the notoriously high F note in the song "Lovin' You" by Minnie Riperton. He fails, causing Mr. Garrison to quip, "Well, I guess we know where all the talent went in that family."

I asked Matt and Trey why the hell they used me, or my fake brother, in their show.

"You were the first celebrity we saw when we came to Hollywood," Matt said.

Apparently, I barged past a secretary in the William Morris Agency lobby, where the guys were waiting on the couch. The secretary yelled, "Hold on, Mr. Stamos, you can't just barge in without me calling first!"

"Oh yeah?" I said. "Fuckin' watch me!"

Trey and I may both geek out over Disney and musical theater, but that's pretty much where our similarities end. He's a creative genius who's operating on a whole different level.

They came to see me in *Cabaret*. Matt says, "Dude, Trey hates everything and loved you. That's like getting a standing ovation from a statue." Matt and I connect on a more down-to-earth level and become good friends.

As I start rehearsals for *The Best Man*, I'm honing suck-ass, bullshitting, morally bankrupt Senator Joe Cantwell, who presents himself as the "people's candidate." I got that part down. His win-at-all-costs self-righteousness is his fatal flaw.

He's empty inside, lacking empathy and love. Plus, he isn't really as smart, rich, or affluent as he tries to appear. I need help to convey his backstory. When talking with me about his theater experiences, Jack Klugman would generously share small strategies and methods that he'd use to better embody his characters. He would come up with little techniques even if they were intimate and personalized, meant only for him. So, I tear a hole in my sock and stick my big toe through it, feeling the pleather bottom of the shoe. It reminds me that Cantwell has a hole in his sock like the hole in his soul.

I start studying political figures and fuse together two that help me create the character. I take some of the smoothness of presentation from John Edwards (not to mention his perfectly pomaded helmet hair) and add a dash of Rick Perry's southern swagger and pompousness. I've avoided discussing religion and politics for the majority of my career. It's fine for fellow actors to do so, but I recognize that people dislike being force-fed our viewpoints. Additionally, why risk alienating half of my fan base? Although, sometimes even by performing a counterpoint to your beliefs, you end up taking a stand.

This play walks a fine line, but I'm drawn to Vidal's sense of satire.

John Larroquette, who plays my nemesis, William Russell, a President Clinton type, is a bit of an enigma to me. He's smart, but not one for small talk or chitchat, especially about topics that don't interest him. I can't help but feel a bit intimidated, so we never really get close. Despite this, I've learned to respect and even like John, though I still can't quite figure him out.

In contrast, James Earl Jones is a "what you see is what you get" kind of man. He's a big, beautiful, generous spirit, both on and off the stage. It's impossible not to be drawn in by his warm personality and infectious charm. And what an honor to be in his presence.

Every night before the show, Corey Brill, a fellow actor and friend, leads us in a vocal warmup. Now, I get it for musicals, but for a nonsinging role? But when James Earl Jones—one of the most iconic voices of all time—is getting into it with goofy exercises like "Red leather, yellow leather . . . ," you better believe I'm right there with him. It's a sight to see this towering legend dressed in a black T-shirt, khakis held up by suspenders, and big ol' sneakers, bending, stretching, yawning, and grunting right along with the rest of us.

Corey sometimes tries to trick James into saying the singular phrase he doesn't want to say from a lil' space picture he did.

COREY: "*The lips, the teeth, the tip of the tongue.*"
EVERYBODY: "*The lips, the teeth, the tip of the tongue.*"
COREY: "*Ta tee, Ta taa, Ta too, Tutu.*"
EVERYONE: "*Ta tee, Ta taa, Ta too, Tutu.*"
COREY: "*Luke, I am your father.*"
EVERYONE, EXCEPT JAMES EARL JONES: "*Luke, I am your father.*"

At the end of our exercises, Corey usually breaks out his ukulele and I'll grab my guitar for a few tunes. James will sing a folk song like "Streets of Laredo." He loves singing.

Kristin Davis, from *Sex and the City* fame, plays my doting wife in the show. She brings her newly adopted child to rehearsals, and James beams as he holds the beautiful baby girl while softly singing in her ear. I never take these moments for granted. I never want to forget them. Joyous.

I call James Big Daddy and he calls me Little John. His eyes are like laser beams. There's nothing phony or fake about this man. He's a force of nature in his seventies, with stamina that puts the rest of us to shame. When he steps onstage, he becomes the epicenter of every scene with a gravitas that's undeniable. James is an "in the moment" actor, fully immersed in the present. Impossible not to get sucked into it. He makes everyone around him better.

One night, in the middle of a scene, James suddenly starts stomping like he's auditioning for a Riverdance sequel. His size-thirteen feet are coming down on the stage like he's trying to put out a fire.

I can't tell if he's lost his mind or if this is some next-level method acting. When we finally get offstage, I have to know what's going on.

"What the hell was that all about, Big Daddy? Did you have a rock in your shoe or something?"

He looks at me dead serious and says, "Nah, man. Tsetse flies. They got onstage and I had to squash 'em. Those little buggers carry diseases, did you know that?"

No, I did not, James.

The director gives me a stern warning. "If James goes up, under no circumstances do you feed him his lines. Even if it feels like eternity."

"Got it," I say.

But what do I do when it actually happens? I totally cave and give him his line like a desperate game show contestant.

James isn't too pleased about being treated like a lost toddler and proceeds to scold me right there onstage, still in character. It's like getting chewed out by Mufasa himself, but with less mane and more disappointment.

On other nights, right in the middle of a scene, midline, he'll stop and start laughing that resounding deep James Earl Jones laugh that sends shock waves through the first few rows of the audience. It'll happen at the most unexpected moments, moments in which no sane person would even think about laughing. It's thrilling and terrifying but oddly masterly. I don't question his process.

My old pal from *General Hospital* Demi Moore drops by to check out a performance. She watches James intently, as most actors do. Backstage, I introduce her to James, and in her syrupy, scratchy voice, she says to him, "I think I know why you break into laughter from time to time onstage, Mr. Jones."

I'm thinking, *Don't talk to Mr. Jones about his process!*

He looks amused. "Oh? Do tell, young lady."

"It gives you time to think of your next line. I do that, too," Demi says.

James lets out a laugh louder and more joyful than onstage. "You got me, young lady!" He turns to me. "She's something else." Oh yeah, James, she is.

I stand next to him during the curtain call. I hold his large hand and we bow together. Under his breath, so only I can hear as we fold in half, he'll say something like, "There's some pretty girls in the third row."

He so gracious and kind when I bring guests to meet him in his dressing room after the show. Especially the ladies. He loves the ladies.

Far from living up to his legendary persona, he has a wild sense of humor. For my birthday he gives me a plaque of a majestic bald eagle soaring in front of an American flag and a blow-up doll.

Every once in a while, as the curtain drops after a show, James says, "Little John, let's go work on that moment in the Hockstader and Cantwell scene in the living room set."

Once the audience leaves and the theater is empty, I meet James Earl Jones onstage, and we'll focus on a specific moment or two. But I can never quite tell if he's trying to help fix something in my performance or if he just loves acting and wants to keep digging at the scene to make it the best it can be. Either way, his passion and dedication are clear. He never lets up, always giving everything he's got every time he steps on that stage.

The night before the show is closing, he wants to rehearse. He has one more shot at it and wants to get it right. That unwavering commitment is what separates the greats from the merely good. The thing I continue to see while working with these greats is what my therapist continues to pound into me:

Your reward for hard work, more work.

As the final curtain falls on our run, I'm filled with a sense of accomplishment and pride unlike anything I've felt before.

I've finally become the kind of actor that Jack Klugman always knew I could be, someone who can hold the stage and bring complex, weighty characters to life. I know that this experience has changed me forever, and I'm excited to see where my newfound passion and respect for the craft will take me next.

I run into James as I head out. Since the show is closing, it's probably the last real conversation I'll have with him. I want to express my gratitude for his mentorship. For so long, I've been searching for that professional validation and personal growth that we all crave. It's a lesson I've been trying to learn with my therapist: to mature, to take things seriously. And in this moment, with James by my side, I feel like I'm finally getting there.

We walk across the stage. Red, white, and blue posters from the set hang in the shadows. The crew takes down a sign reading CANTWELL FOR PRESIDENT. American dreams dismantled.

I put my hand on James's shoulder. "Big Daddy, I can never thank you enough for this chance to redefine myself and break free from the limitations of people's perception of me."

He puts his hand on my shoulder and says, "It's been my pleasure."

We open the door to hundreds of fans.

"Hey, Uncle Jesse, we love you! Uncle Jesse, say 'Have mercy!' Please?"

My heart sinks. I'm ashamed of my own naivete in thinking that anything has truly changed. Minutes ago, I was blabbering about my highbrow legitimacy to James Earl Jones. I'm too embarrassed to look at him. The fading lights of Broadway mock me as I slink away.

Then someone shouts at James, "Hey, Darth Vader! Can you say 'Luke, I am your father' into my phone?"

I look at him, and he looks at me, shrugging his shoulders. He lets out one last big, beautiful laugh, and I can't help laughing with him.

It's a cliché to try to talk about life in the same breath as the theater. Shakespeare has already nailed it, writing, "All the world's a stage, and all the men and women merely players." Sinatra sang of facing "the final curtain" in "My Way."

In the theater, you are born, find family, act out, and die night after night.

J. Pierrepont Finch in *How to Succeed in Business Without Really Trying* reminds me that when you're down, you're not out. One day you're washing windows and the next you're on the other side of the glass, enjoying a penthouse view.

The Emcee from *Cabaret* teaches me to explore and embrace the complexities and contradictions within, to feel liberated from the constraints of societal norms, and to be empowered to express my truest self.

Guido in *Nine* teaches me there's a fair amount of humility in a little humiliation, so before you put a gun to your head, consider there's another script somewhere out there waiting just for you.

Bye Bye Birdie's Albert Peterson teaches me that when gray skies abound, chances are they're going to clear up. Cycles, like the seasons.

I won't take away a damned thing from my shallow senator in The Best Man, but James Earl Jones shows me that no matter the situation, sometimes we need to laugh out loud to buy enough time to remember our lines, to remember who we are inside.

Garry Marshall is the one who calls me with the news that Robin Williams has hanged himself.

Garry's busted up and sounds so sad. He's giving me advice, but I think he's really talking to himself. "Don't get depressed. Whatever you do. Call me. Call your mother. Promise me you won't get depressed."

"I won't, Garry," I promise. "I love you."

I think about the autograph Robin signed for me when I was a kid. He was bigger than life. I remember chatting with him in a bar somewhere near Broadway. He faded into the crowd. You never know where someone is in a scene; you can't second-guess their motives or process.

It's hard to imagine those who are so alive no longer being part of the show.

Theater is life and life is theater.

There's nothing better than a curtain call where the audience keeps applauding and you're drawn back to the stage for your ovation. There's nothing worse than a curtain call because it's the end.

31

THE REAL BEST MAN

Dear J

A. First I want to thank you for the opportunity to have a great trip & a view of Europe. Without you we surely wouldn't have done it.

B. You made me so proud those three weeks, that my chest is about 60 in. Your hard work and handling of all the people around you is fantastic. You are truly head & shoulders above everyone there.

C. Life isn't very long and a man doesn't have many great moments. But you have given me many.

Thanks
I love you
Dad.

After visiting me on the set of a movie called Born to Ride in former Yugoslavia, my dad wrote a note and faxed it to me when he got home.

I don't recall receiving the fax, but I'll never forget the day I found the original letter. Years later, as he lay dying in our home, I went rummaging around in his room, looking for a keepsake, piece of jewelry, an old watch, something that would remind me of him. I open a drawer, and under some shirts, I spot the bottom of a letter. *"Thanks. I love you, Dad."*

I get what I came for, something to remember him by.

In a Rolex world, he was a Timex guy. When the dough rolled in, I tried to buy my dad a new car. Cadillac. He loved them, and when the new Caddy convertible came out, I wanted him to be rolling through the neighborhood with the top down. The proud son of a gun wouldn't take it. He stuck with the El Camino. Every four or five years, he'd put a new 350 Chevy engine in, pop on a new tire or two, spray on a fresh coat of paint, and roll for another thousand miles. Not one bone in his body sought to impress anyone with things.

He would rather spend his money on family vacations, save for my sisters to go to college, or put away a nest egg so my mom would never have to work a day in her life.

He rarely spends any money on himself, and if he loses at the track, he considers it a charitable contribution to the fine thoroughbreds at Los Alamitos Race Course.

As a kid, I loved going to the track with him. I became quite the entrepreneur (or scam artist, however you want to look at it). While my dad was in the stands screaming at jockeys and horses, I found a way to make my own cash without waiting for some large animal to cross the finish line before the rest of the large animals. I'd hang around at the exit and grab programs from patrons who were leaving early, then sell them for fifty cents (roughly half price) to the people coming in late. I'd make about five bucks a night, just enough to pay the old-school general admission rate at Disneyland.

After the last race, we'd load into his El Camino, and I would put my head on his lap and doze off. My dad absentmindedly stroking my hair as we drove to our house on Carob Street is a memory I'll cherish forever.

The only smell more synonymous with my dad other than smokes and Aramis cologne was Chinese food. Once a week, he'd gather up a group of us to meet at a Chinese restaurant. Sometimes there would be twenty-five people crammed around the table, and everyone got to pick one dish. The more people, the happier my dad would be. We'd all be laughing, telling stories, and cracking open cookies to share our fortunes. Not sure who started it, but it became a tradition to read the fortune cookie then add "in bed." Like, "People rise to your expectations *in bed.*" I don't need to hear my robust aunt read, "Every exit is an entrance to new experiences, *in bed.*"

And if you were a regular and didn't show up, my dad would be pissed. He'd take names and follow up to make sure the delinquent diner had a damned good excuse. Not only did he want friends and family to connect regularly, but with fewer people, there were also fewer different dishes, which meant the more it would cost per person.

The ritual occurred Tuesday nights, but when *Full House* took over that time slot, no matter how much my dad pretended not to like it, he moved the sacred Chinese dinner to Wednesdays so he could watch every episode of his kid's show.

Things were simpler then. No cell phones, no screens. We'd just sit around actually talking to each other. If the kids got restless, one of the adults, usually me, would cruise them through the restaurant to check out the decorative dragons or lobster tank.

When the bill came, my dad would tally it up and always include a big tip. He understood servers need every penny. When

I'd start to pull out cash, my dad would shake his head and wave me off.

"I'll get the little ones, you get the big ones," he'd say, smiling and proud.

There is a picture of me, my dad in the middle, and my Papuli (Greek for grandfather) on the other side. Dad would say, "I'm the poor guy in the middle of two rich guys."

Hardly, Dad, you were richer than all of us in the most important ways.

On New Year's Eve 2000, my parents are in Las Vegas when my dad has a heart attack. He can't be resuscitated. He falls into a coma that lasts six months. We bring him home, and he peacefully passes away with all of us surrounding his bedside.

"Tonight's specials are cake and cock . . . and we're out of cake!"

That's Bob's opening joke at my father's funeral. I asked him to host the reception at Assumption of the Blessed Virgin Mary.

"Any Jews here?" Bob jokes. He's on a roll. "I'm a Jew. I've been circumcised nine times. Try the calamari!"

It's much-needed levity on a hard day.

I see a look I've never seen before on my mother's face. Such sadness. The only man she has ever loved has been taken, and there's not a goddamned thing I can do about it. Gosh darn, I mean. My mother never used the Lord's name in vain and I wasn't allowed either.

There are two things my dad requested before he passed: he asked to be cremated, and wanted a big, fat, Greek Orthodox funeral.

We learn that he missed a few ceremonial details, like the fact that the Greek Orthodox Church will not perform last rites without a body in the casket.

The priest freaks out when I tell him my dad's wishes. No

body in a casket, no Orthodox ceremony. So begins a righteous racket of donating money to the church to palliate the situation. We scramble to get a suitable casket in time, of course the most expensive was the only one available. After the service we'll have my dad cremated. I grease the priest, he looks the other way.

I smell the incense they waft in your face during the service. I'm feeling a little disconnected from the faith of my upbringing.

Gilded gates, Verdi marble floors, rows of chandeliers, and baroque portraits of the saints with eyes that follow me around like the busts in the Haunted Mansion at Disneyland. I was always afraid of places where your sins shine, but salvation seems imminent. Repent, rinse, repeat.

My dad was only sixty-five when he passed, so he had tons of friends still kicking; a lot are missing the hell out of him. Close to a thousand people show up.

One of the most valued traits I got from my father was the way he treated everyone equally. It didn't matter if someone was a dishwasher at one of his burger joints or the executive producer on one of my shows. Today at his service, Raul, the busboy from the Yellow Basket, is sitting next to a big-time Hollywood producer. Both weep just as hard.

During a three-hour-long service, in Greek, mind you, my sisters feel invisible as Father Hand-out-opoulos somehow misses the fact that they're actually part of our family story. He's mentioning way too many times how proud my father was of me, as if I'm the golden only child. They've endured a lot of that over the years. They're saints and shrug it off most of the time. They know how much they mean to me and how they've contributed to my success. They're my biggest fans and the most supportive sisters a brother could have. I'd be nothing without them.

Through our tears, we express gratitude for our father's years of guidance and goodness, his example. His headstone reads: *he roared like a lion but was as gentle as a lamb.*

I cut together a highlight reel of William Stamos's greatest hits, and he comes back to life on monitors throughout the reception hall. There he is, making proud and funny speeches at all three of his kids' weddings. Cut to a scene of him looking handsome in an army uniform for a small part I gave him in a movie. There's a beautiful section of his love story with my mom: they're dancing, he tries to dip her, he drops her. As Sinatra sings "My Way" there are pictures of my dad just living his life, and not in a shy way. Regrets? He had none.

32

I LOVE YOU MORE

I wish you
could see
yourself through
my eyes ~
you'd see your
warmth, caring,
passion and loving
ways. Our hearts
will never be far
apart from one
another.

My mom called our humble home on Carob the Castle of Comfort. I'm sleeping in my childhood bedroom. It's safe, warm, and nonjudgmental; a place where I close my eyes and all the innocence that has slipped away from me comes rushing back. The happiest place on earth.

My mother's faith was deep and indomitable. To this day, I know no one else with a stronger belief in God and His love for us than my mother.

My life has been lived within these walls, my sisters' stories hang in the doorways, holidays have been celebrated in the living room, my friends playing guitars and singing Christmas carols all night long. I remember running down the stairs to see what Santa had brought. We would have dinner every night at the kitchen table together, and my sisters and I put on little shows for our parents after we'd eat. We made up silly songs, "Birdie, Birdie in a Tree," our mom loved that one.

She also loved Las Vegas. If the track was my dad's happy place, then strolling casinos full of pinging slots and felt tables piled high with chips was her great joy. She didn't live extravagantly. She cut coupons, saved plastic bags, hawked deals, and loved the 99 cent store. She was always frugal but never cheap. However, when she set foot onto the Vegas Strip, all bets were off.

She wasn't a high roller, but she was a long roller, and the no-clocks-in-the-casino trick kept her pulling for pennies until the sun rose. Most VIP managers, pit bosses, and cocktail waitresses knew Loretta Stamos. She made people feel good. She would look everyone in the eye, truly listen as they spoke, and recognize what made them unique.

Forget flaws, social status, or style, she shone a light on what made someone special, mined for gold in each heart, and people felt radiant around her. I could always tell where she had been gambling even after she moved on to another machine because there was a loving energy she left behind (as well as postcard pictures of me that she carried in her purse to give away).

My mom took my dad's death very hard. We all did, but my dad was the love of her life, and she just couldn't get over the fact that she lost him at the age of sixty-five. As much as none of us want to admit it, we all know she will join him soon.

Hello my
SON SHINE
Can't wait to see
you
wake me if
you can
Like the rest of
the world
I love you
But I love you
even more!
Mom XOXOXOXO

I come back and visit her as often as I can. I return to my castle of comfort on Carob Street almost every weekend. We really need each other. I would say it's an equally healthy, codependent, and maybe at times too-close relationship.

I can't help but wonder if my attachment to her is preventing me from finding a partner who I can build a life and family with. As much as my mother provides me with comfort and stability, I know that there is another kind of love and fulfillment that I am missing. She really wants that for me as well, but I'm not sure how I'll find a bride and start a family if I'm spending every weekend at home. By this time, my cool "boy cave" my parents had decked out for me was now converted back to a garage filled with boxes of old memories I figured she'd throw out someday (I'm so glad she didn't). So I'd sleep in my mom's office/guest room with wall-to-wall posters of me throughout the ages. It's kind of hard to impress a future wife in a shrine to oneself. "Mom, can you turn down *Wheel of Fortune?* I'm trying to make a baby!"

In an *Extra* interview, my mother and I are both in cowboy

hats and jeans. I'm promoting the charity she started, the Vanguard Cancer Foundation, and her "Denim and Diamonds" event to raise money and awareness. She started it in the name of her brother, who passed away from the horrible disease. She is going on and on about what a great father I'm going to be one day and tells the reporter, "He's going to name his son Bill, after his father, right, Johnny?" No pressure there, Ma.

The next few days and months are a strange schizophrenic time of pitching shows during the day and returning to her bedside at night. I'm working on a concept with Dan Fogelman of This Is Us fame and Danny Chun from The Office. It's called Grandfathered. I'm also sitting, silently watching the person I love most in the world wither away.

My mom wants to see me every weekend and is so sad when I have to leave. I'm overwhelmed with guilt when I pull out of the driveway. What a beautiful feeling knowing that each time there is an accomplishment to share, our family gathers together: my sisters' graduations, engagement parties, weddings. My mother is the center of all celebrations. When I drive away, the world gets bigger, more disorienting, and I find myself a little lost. Each time I get closer to home, I feel better.

I hop onto the 101 and call her to tell her how many minutes away I am. On the 5 right off the freeway, I pass the old familiar medical complex they use in the General Hospital titles, and when I hit the 605 South, get off on Del Amo and pass Duke's, one of my dad's joints, I feel content knowing I am close to the healing magic of my mother's hugs.

When anyone would leave our home—me, my sisters, friends, or relatives—my mother had a ritual where she would stand on the lawn and wave goodbye until the car turned onto Crescent Street and drove out of sight. I'd always roll down my window, buckle up, and tell her I loved her.

"I love you more," she'd say. I felt I was leaving her for good each time.

As a child growing up in that house, I had limited understanding of the concept of death. I always thought of it as something temporary or reversible. As I got older, I developed a false sense of invincibility and believed that if anything went wrong with my parents, even their health, I'd find a way to fix it.

My mom dies on September 22, 2014. We get her home just in time. We knew she wouldn't want to die in a hospital, and it was time for her to go.

We barely make it. The hospice nurse beats us to the house and sets up for our mom's departure. My sisters and their kids circle around her, get her comfortable, and surround her in love. We take turns holding her hand, saying our goodbyes, and thanking her over and over. We cry a lot. She knows she's loved; she knows we can't live without her; she knows what an amazing mother she has been to each of us individually.

She dies knowing this. We should all go knowing just this much.

My mother's lucky number was 51. Not sure why. It's one of those things I wished I would have asked her about. The numbers 51 and 15 were her casino cries. "Five one, baby, one five!"

As they wheel her to the ambulance in a private moment, just before they lift her in, I kiss her cheek 51 times.

I am struck by all the things left unfinished. I wish I could have given her everything she wanted for me: a happy marriage, a little grandchild named Bill.

Just as she used to stand on the lawn waving as I'd leave after those long weekends, I join my sisters, brother-in-law Bobby, and nieces and nephew outside as we watch the ambulance drive away. We are all waving goodbye, and just before it makes a right on Crescent and starts to drive out of sight, we yell out, "We love you more."

It takes my sisters and me a long time to sell the house, not only for sentimental reasons, but also because it made the houses on that show *Hoarders* look clutter-free.

Someone else will buy our house. Maybe another little boy will run down the stairs to see what Santa brought him. Those still feel like my stairs, my living room, my memories. I hope he gets everything we got in the Castle of Comfort.

I let go of my crutch, haven, and home sweet home. My parents have died in this house. The memories still linger in every corner of the place, but the love is gone. We were the love. My mom, my dad, my sisters, and me. The house at 8462 Carob Street still stands, but for me, it is gone forever.

Those little letters of wisdom in pretty penmanship were always waiting for me and my sisters to find at the perfect moment when a revelation from beyond can save your soul. Walking back into her Castle of Comfort when she isn't there to comfort me, I open a cabinet. There's the final note she knew I needed to get through the rest of my life.

> Dear
> Jon—
>
> Life is an occassion... Rise to it.
> Don't be sad because I died..
> be happy because I lived!
> I had a
> Wonderful
> Life

And thanks to you and Dad, so did I. I love you more.

33

BANG

Knock, knock, knock. A young woman in only a bra and panties opens the door to find two detectives, Stabler and Fin. Stabler protectively places his finger to his lips, signaling her to stay silent. In the same motion, he reveals his badge, which he has discreetly tucked in the palm of his hand.

As they step over the threshold, the detectives enter a candlelit room, a small table adorned with two glasses of champagne, a plate of ripe strawberries, and tempting chocolate. Muy romántico.

From behind the closed bathroom door, a voice exclaims, "Get ready, Stacy, 'cause I'm going to rock your world!"

Fin doesn't hold back his disgust, barking out, "Especially when she finds out she's pregnant."

They kick open the door, interrupting Ken Turner in the act of poking holes in a condom while wearing his reading glasses. The detectives quickly confiscate the tampered condom and take Ken into custody, his hands cuffed behind his back, on charges of endangering the welfare of a child and an illegal adoption. As they lead him away, Fin turns to the woman and holds up the damning evidence, a condom package riddled with holes.

She won't be Ken's victim today, but the actress playing her, Caitlin McHugh, might not get rid of me so easily.

When you meet the woman who will be the love of your life, your future wife, the mother of your child, it's like getting shot through the heart. You see her, BANG! She smiles, BANG! And if she opens her mouth and she's smart, funny, and kind, BANG, BANG, BANG!

"The episode is called 'Bang.' You'll love this part. They wrote it with you in mind."

I'm on the phone with my manager, Danny Sussman. He's trying to convince me to do a guest spot on *Law & Order: Special Victims Unit*. I'm not really interested. But for some reason Danny is pushing this one.

"Listen, I just got off the phone with the head honcho over at *SVU*, *Law and Order*, and he said you were literally the only person they want for this. You're perfect."

"Okay, okay, you're selling me. So, who's this Ken Turner character?" I ask.

"He's a reproductive abuser with an urge to father as many children as possible, even if the mothers of his spawn aren't in on it. He's so egotistical that he wants to spread his progeny far and wide and will stop at nothing to get what he wants," Danny shares cheerfully.

"Cool, a narcissistic, quasi-rapist, deadbeat dad with a dick of steel and a soul of darkness," I deadpan before shouting, "WHAT THE FUCK?"

"You've been wanting to play an asshole for a while now," Danny says. "Here's your chance."

When I get the script, I flip to the climax, where the detectives and the women I've swindled discover that I've fathered more kids than anyone imagined. "Twenty children? Oh no. It's not twenty . . . it's forty-seven. You only checked the United States. Look around Europe . . . I have forty-seven children and I love each and every one of them."

It's disgusting and delicious. I'm in.

"I'm Caitlin."

Caitlin is a model and actress, so duh, she's beautiful. Long, flowing dark hair; flawless skin with adorable freckles. But there's something else there, a light behind her dark eyes. Her smile is warm and welcoming, not just pretty and pleasing. She's graceful but goofy, too. She isn't easily impressed but not standoffish. You hear of people being called magnetic, but until you feel that pull that almost yanks you out of your shoes, it's hard to describe.

"Hi, I'm John." Yeah, um, so I'm going to marry you, have a baby with you, and spend the rest of my life with you.

She's confident and smart, that's obvious, but she has a natural humility that draws others in. Her heritage is Irish and Filipino. Mine's Irish and Greek. There's some common ground on the Emerald Isle and then two exotic elements checking each other out. I want to ask her on a date, talk about the future, and convince her to run away with me.

I head over to hair and makeup to get touched up, and Caitlin is there, getting her hair done. The stylist is pulling a brush through her long hair, and it falls around her face perfectly. God, she's beautiful. Stay cool, Stamos. You've got this.

"I'm getting married right here at Chelsea Pier," Caitlin tells the stylist. "See over there?" She's pointing to a wedding venue we can all see out of the window. She talks about her fiancé, an Italian restaurateur, man-about-town.

My heart drops, and without even making eye contact I say, "Don't get married."

Shit, why did I say that? What an asshole. It sounds like the kind of thing a guy who's been burned, bitter, and divorced might say, joking around, of course. I'm not the kind of creep who hits on married or engaged women, so I can let go of the idea of any sort of relationship and concentrate on playing Ken Turner. If I was a dick like him, I'd move in right away but, ya know, I'm not.

I'm wallowing in a little nice-guys-finish-last self-pity. I mean, here is one of the most naturally beautiful women I've ever seen, and she's going to get all dolled up in white and marry someone else. I hate this man with no name and face.

On the set, I strategize how a sick, sadistic cretin would poke holes in condoms to impregnate unwitting women.

"So, obviously I'd do it behind the bathroom door," I say. "Could someone grab me a pair of prop reading glasses, please? It's precision work, finding the right place to poke, so this guy needs to be really focused."

I can hear Caitlin talking to a crew member.

"Living in New York, I really miss Disneyland. I grew up near there and it's my favorite place in the world. You could say I'm a bit of a Disney geek," she says a little sadly.

Oh, come on, Universe, this is unfair. I can't let that go.

I saunter over. "Did you say you like Disneyland?"

In between takes we connect over our love of all things Disney. Disney talk and musical theater. Turns out she loves musical theater, too. I try to impress her with some of my Broadway creds.

"So, yeah, I was in *Cabaret*, and I played Albert in *Bye Bye Birdie*. Then I was also in the revival of . . ." Man, what am I doing? This is pathetic.

She seems mildly intrigued but definitely not a fangirl. I

need to drop all the "I did this and I did that" bullshit. I can tell she's genuine and interested in a friendship. Now I'm really smitten.

I take a few photographs on the set with the director and crew members. "Oh, hey, Caitlin, let's grab a picture."

I snap a shot of us together, and she likes it.

"You want me to text it to you?" I ask.

"Sure." What a ruse.

I suggest we stay in touch. As friends. I enter her in my phone as The Girl from SVU, which is still the way it is today.

I'm keeping in touch, but each text feels weighted by my desire to be more than friends, and there is this distance between us: she's in New York, I'm in L.A.; she's engaged, I'm shit out of luck.

I guess her fiancé only buys into "it's just my 'probably gay friend' John Stamos" for so long. I get a text reading: "We can't text anymore, it's making my fiancé uncomfortable."

Okay, fair.

I want to tell her, "Leave that guy. He's controlling. He doesn't believe in you like he should. You deserve someone who trusts you unconditionally." But let's face it, the guy is right. He should be uncomfortable because I'm crushing on his woman, and there is a thin line of decency, dignity, and that damned Loretta Stamos morality keeping me from going for it.

And with that, I have five and a half years trying to get over the woman who quite possibly might be the one. Five and a half long years.

I open the heavy door of Stage 26 on the Warner Bros. lot, where we shot the original Full House, but tonight we're taping Fuller House, the reboot I'm exec producing. We always have a studio audience to augment the canned laughter. I look up in the bleachers, and there she is, in the front row of the audience. She's wearing a bright red sweater and checkered skirt. That smile.

I almost don't believe it's her.

I'm in a better place than I was five years ago. I'm feeling semi-cocky. I'm producing Netflix's biggest family show, producing and starring in *Grandfathered* on Fox, and I'm freshly sober. There's an extra bounce in my step.

I cruise up to her, get real close, and ask, "Hey now, what are you doing here? You're stalking me, aren't you?"

"Don't flatter yourself," she says, laughing. "I'm here to see my friend Kimberley Drummond, she's playing the Jamaican veterinarian on the show."

Right. Then, in my best executive producer voice I say, "Why, yes she is. And she's doing a fine job." I give a thumbs-up to an actor on the set.

"That's not her. That's the girl who plays Kimmy Gibbler," she says. I can tell she's amused.

I know that. Quickly changing the subject, I point to the dude sitting next to her. "And this must be your husband?"

"Oh no, I'm divorced, this is just a boyfriend."

He looks at her. "Just?"

Game on!

I stalk her on Instagram; really get to know her. Nice pictures. She's at Comic-Con with the boyfriend. Let it go for a few weeks.

Check again. Walking her dog with the boyfriend. Okay, cool. Let it ride this weekend. Pop back on. She's at Disneyland . . . with the boyfriend. Damn, that one burns. Not sure how much more of this I can take.

It's time to unfollow her and stop torturing myself. Next thing you know there will be a picture of the two of them in Hawaiian shirts cuddling at a Beach Boys concert. Must delete.

But before I do, I check one more time, like little Charlie Bucket from *Willy Wonka* unwrapping another bar of chocolate, looking for that golden ticket but ready to be dejected again.

There's a pretty picture of Caitlin with her dog. Alone, with her dog. No boyfriend. Pulling back a corner of the wrapper and there shines a piece of gold.

I've got the golden ticket: a single Caitlin.

This time, no flirting, no texting games, no waiting around. I move immediately. "Do you want to go to Disney World with me?" That's it. That's the ask.

"Yes."

I was trying to impress her by pulling the Club Fame card. John Stamos in the Mouse House. I usually wear a hat and dark glasses, to become relatively incognito.

So once in EPCOT, I lose the glasses and start making eye contact with people in an effort to be recognized. Hmmm, not happening.

It's the hat. I have famous hair, that's why I'm not being rec-ognized. I whip off the hat, and it starts to work. One by one, people recognize me, and more and more follow. That move is called "feeding the pigeons." I would be humble. "Oh, wow, just a sec. Gotta take a few shots with my fans." Check me out, Caitlin. I'm a charming celebrity.

Since we were in the Experimental Prototype Community of Tomorrow, Caitlin calls the move of gratuitously flossing one's fame EPCOTing. When she sees me trying to get recognized or letting a room know that John Stamos has arrived, she calls me out. "Enough EPCOTing!" I think that's the moment I fell in love with her.

Disney was magical, but I need to bring the romance. So for our second date, I take her to a funeral.

First Lady Nancy Reagan made a list of whom she wanted at her funeral before she died, and I'm on it. I guess I made an impression at The Beach Boys Fourth of July concert, and later when we performed at the Reagan library. During the service, love letters that she and her husband, the former president, wrote to each other were read, and it was incredibly touching. Especially because of who I was sitting next to.

This feels different from dating. We're bonding. I want to tell her all the big stuff I'm planning in the future, but also the little mundane things that happen every day. I want to hear about her recent photoshoot, her dog Lilo's antics, and learn more about her family. I want to listen to her dreams and figure out how to make them come true.

She wants to travel. So, we travel. And travel well together. She's super low-maintenance, appreciative, and easy to make happy.

We got that covered. But here's a true test for us. Try this at home if you will:

Write and direct a short film with your partner as the star. If you can make it through the process without feeling like ripping out every hair on your head while screaming into a pillow, the chemistry works. If you can handle disagreements over "artistic vision" without her wanting to stage a coup or launch a full-scale revolution for making her do fifty takes, you've got cooperation. If the nervous eye twitch you develop while directing goes away, you've got chemistry, and it's time to put a ring on it.

For a long time I believe that I need to be with someone who has a bigger, more exciting life than mine to elevate me, a power couple always in the press, always on the go.

I am wrong.

What I need is someone to eat off the same plate with me. Someone who makes me comfortable enough to be silly, someone I can dance poorly around, someone who gets it when I cry at commercials. I also need someone honest enough to tell me I have food in my teeth or too much product in my hair.

I want someone who kisses me as if it's the last scene of a romantic movie and we're on a bridge with a perfect sunset behind us, even though we're just in line at the grocery store. After all those years of teen magazines asking some form of the question "What Does John Stamos Want in a Girl?" I think it's simpler than anyone could have imagined.

I decide to do something I've never done in a relationship: give it everything I've got. No shortcuts or half-measures, never letting up on constant commitment. If for some reason it doesn't work out, at least I'll know I'm capable of doing all that next time.

There will be no next time. This is it.

After six months of dating, I ask Caitlin to move in. Then, after a week of living together, I drop the baby bomb.

"So, do you want kids someday?" I ask.

We are swimming and splashing around in my old-school, kidney-shaped pool overlooking sparkling L.A. I've seen these panoramic views almost every night, but when you're considering changing your life in a big way, everything seems new and different. It's like the whole city is with me, waiting for an answer. I imagine it's the last thing she expects to hear. I swim closer and get quiet. She looks down, thinking. That's Caitlin, composed, thoughtful, and careful before she speaks. I know however she responds, it will be the fully considered truth.

"I'd love to be a mother," she says with a little smile. Music to my ears. I had put that dream aside for so long, maybe even let it go, but suddenly this tradition I've come from, this family that made me, has a chance to grow. I'm amazed at the woman open to making that happen.

The producer and planner in me goes all in. "And have you thought about a timeline?" Damn, Stamos, way to bust out the calendar and spreadsheets during this romantic moment.

She looks amused. "How about six months to a year?" she asks.

I dip under the water with the biggest smile on my face. It's a wonder I'm not drowning. Hey, with that kind of timeline, we're a few months behind, so we better get started.

Be careful what you throw out into the universe because once you shout your intentions to the sky, the world starts to spin your dreams into reality.

I get a chance to return to Greece for a program called *Who Do You Think You Are?* Caitlin comes along. It's a genealogy documentary that traces the guest star's ancestry. Family has always been a foundation in my life, so in this moment filled with exciting unknowns, I'm really interested in looking backward.

And while we're here, it occurs to me that the motherland is the perfect place to conceive a child.

"I have a few 'oops' moments on this trip," I tell Caitlin. One in a hotel overlooking the Acropolis. Another in a little mountainous town in Crete (as Greek mythology would have it, the birthplace of Zeus). "Why not try for a Greek God?" I suggest.

Caitlin thinks it is a little too soon, but I pull receipts. "Didn't you say six months to a year? If we get pregnant now, that's right in the middle of your timeline."

She looks at me like I'm speaking Greek.

"Remember that day in the pool?" I say.

"What I said was, I'd be ready to start trying to get pregnant . . . not actually give birth . . . trying . . . " she says.

Ah-ha. Quick word of advice: when family planning, keep your head above water.

34

THE ODYSSEY

In the spirit of the Greek classics, I present *The Odyssey: Stamos's Sperm*.

Despite a rather enjoyable spate of trying, we are having some fertility issues. After a year of good times without pregnancy test lines, we're both a little worried. Caitlin sees specialists and herbalists. She gets standardized tests, drinks aromatic teas, does bloodwork, and has her belly poked with acupuncture needles.

I'm told "no hot baths." Easy.

Caitlin is young and healthy, so maybe it's me slowing things down. It's not like I'm in my twenties (or thirties or forties). Time for me to get my little swimmers checked out. Maybe their freestyle crawl ain't makin' it the full length of the pool.

I'd have to say that in my sordid, colorful life, I've done just about everything. Twice. But I've never jerked off in a cup. (Although there was this one party . . .) So I'm pretty nervous going to the fertility clinic. Caitlin drives me and wants to come in.

"No way!" I say. She starts laughing at me. Is she enjoying

this a little? My anxiety levels are through the roof, and I don't even have anxiety.

"Come on," she says. "All you have to do is jerk off in a cup."

Easy for her to say. How big is the cup? What if I'm not a good aim? You know how bad I am at sports.

"Just hurry up, you goofball."

I walk into a standard, antiseptic office. Talk about zero atmosphere. There are around seven men standing by to stroke one off for science. Everyone looks somber. My natural instinct in a situation like this is to start cracking jokes.

I sit next to an older gentleman. "Come here often?" Crickets.

A nurse waiting in the doorway deadpans, "Hilarious, Mr. Stamos, right this way."

Don't they know my alias, Sy Sperling, Founder of the Hair Club for Men? Damn. Of all the times to shout my name out, the Jack Shack lounge of Sperm Central isn't the place.

"No relation!" I yell out. No one cares.

"Let me take you back here, where it's more private," the young nurse says.

"Who cares, my cover's already blown."

The nurse leads me into a small, sterile room and gives me the rundown.

"Okay, here's your cup," she says practically. "Please write your name and date of birth here." She points to a large glass jug filled with little packets of something. They look like condiments you'd get with a to-go order. I hope they're not. "And there's lube over there if you need it."

Um, great.

"Don't need it, but thanks," I say, thinking it makes me sound studlier.

"If you want something to watch, we have cable, Netflix, Showtime, and Cinemax (uhh, don't you mean Skinamax?). Also, there are DVDs in the drawer. To use the player, turn on the TV with this remote. Then, with this other remote, go to input four . . . or three . . . no, it's four. When you're done, put the lid on the cup, make sure it's screwed on tight because they can be tricky, then drop it in the paper bag and bring it out to me. Oh, and make sure you try to get enough in there to fill up to this line," she says in a spunky way (pun intended).

Jeez, that's a lot, but, I got this. I think.

She hands me the remote control and a man has to wonder how many hairy palms have held that same device after handling "Junior."

"Okay, have fun," she says. She leaves the room, and I'm totally confused. Just to be sure the little packets are not condiments, I open one up and it gets all over my hands. Yup, lube. I try labeling the cup with the jaunty little sperm pen she leaves behind. I've got lube fingers and mess up the J before I drop the cup. Damn it. Can they hear me? Nah, this place must be soundproofed.

"Beyoncé is having twins? No way!" I hear the nurse and receptionist gossiping about Queen Bey like they're standing right next to me.

All right, let's get this done.

Maybe a little porn? Nah.

I don't need no stinkin' porn. I have a good imagination. Think of Caitlin. Beautiful but also hot. Nice. Everything is starting to work. Success is right around the corner, then from the outside watercooler, "Have you watched *Game of Thrones* this season? Cersei has sex with her twin brother, Jamie. Gross, right?"

Yes, that's gross, I think to myself. You know what else is gross, not soundproofing these jack closets! Talk about a boner killer. All right, time for a little light porn.

I flip on the TV and dig into the DVD drawer: *Shaving Ryan's Privates?* No. *Romancing the Bone?* No. *Sleeping Booty?* Sacrilege.

I look up to the television and, I shit you not, it's on Netflix, and the *Fuller House* landing page appears. Oh my god, this can't be happening.

Here's the deal, if I'm going to jerk off to myself, it ain't gonna be to old, tired Jesse from *Fuller House*. It's going to be to young, hot Jesse from *Full House*.

Somehow, I get through it. I fill the cup, put the lid on, sign it, hand in my homework.

As I walk out, I can't help myself. I say, "That's the last time I'm coming here!"

It turns out I don't have to go back. My boys are okay.

I'm on the road with The Beach Boys a lot during this time, so while I'm banging drumsticks, Caitlin is home peeing on pregnancy sticks. I check in to see how it's going, and she is shrugging it off. I can tell she's a little disappointed when it doesn't work out, but that's a place where a man needs to shut his mouth and just support, stand by, and love his partner. Her body will do the work, the heavy lifting. That's her space. Trying to make a baby isn't exactly a chore on my end. I get the good deal here. I honor what she will go through giving life. This is on her terms, her time.

It's beyond my comprehension. Any man who thinks he has a say over a woman's body is a fool. Even if we don't conceive in Greece, the act of making life is something out of mythology; it's ancient, beautiful, and beyond words. I don't press her on the matter. What will be, will be.

In one perfect moment, every daydream and night dream will merge. My mother and father will look down on their future progeny from the heavens like archaic gods (or, you know, like Zeus and his wife in the final scenes of *Xanadu*).

Caitlin jumps on a plane to meet me in Vegas on tour. I'm coming from somewhere else and my own flight has been delayed. I land late, and as I'm driving toward the Bellagio, the three words that stress me out beyond belief are repeating in my head: showtime upon arrival.

She pulls into the hotel before I make it. Mike Love and his loving bride, Jacquelyne, whom Caitlin has gotten very close to by this point, are arriving at the same time she is. Jackie takes one look at Caitlin and says, "You're pregnant!" They hug and cry together.

When I finally get to the hotel, I'm rushing like crazy to get ready for the show. I run to my room. No Caitlin. I shower in two minutes and cram my ass into a pair of leather pants while drying my hair.

"Where are you?" I text Caitlin.

"I'm with the Loves," she texts back.

"I have to leave soon," I write.

"Okay, stay there. I'll be right up."

I wait for ten minutes and need to get going.

Then I hear Caitlin opening the door.

"I'm going to be late!" I yell out.

"Me, too," she says. That goes right over my head.

She gives me a warm hug and kiss and hands me a gift bag. I set it on the table, thank her, and start to head out the door.

"Can you please open that now?" she asks eagerly.

"What part of 'I have to leave for the show, I'm going to be—'"

"Open it now! Please. It's important."

"Okay." I rip open the package, and it's some bath bombs. Seriously?

Caitlin points to the card and I read, "Sweet Cakes, Life is sweet, sometimes salty, bitter or even sour. No matter what life's flavor, I like eating with you. Though I might need a bigger portion because I'm eating for two. You're going to be a great daddy and now you can take a bath."

I'm caught off guard. Here I am, rushing around ready to rock like some teenager in leather pants, and this is the ultimate adulting moment of my life. I'm beyond that place of wishing, hoping, getting checked out, waiting for results, and stressing about it. I'm giving in to whatever happens, that place of letting go. That always seems to be when you find success, fall in love, or even create life. I'm going to be a dad. Recognizing that fertility challenges can sometimes take more than two to tango, we ultimately did end up needing some medical assistance to conceive. We are incredibly thankful to our doctor who skillfully employed intrauterine insemination (IUI) to assist in the arrival of our precious baby.

Everything moving so fast is now in slow motion and I am crying with happiness. I know I will always cry thinking about this moment. Hell, I'll break down at the damned mall if I see a bath bomb display.

I'm looking forward to whatever kid comes my way but in the dubious era of gender reveal parties, where dummies are blowing shit up just to announce the genitals of an unborn baby, Caitlin has the perfect plan. She gives our OB-GYN a gift box with two "Have Mercy" onesies featuring a silhouette of my mullet. One is blue, one pink. She asks the doctor to put the one that represents the outcome of the ultrasound in the box and promises not to sneak a look until we are together.

I'm on the road during her tests, so when she comes to LAX to pick me up, she's dying to know. We sit in the car in the airport parking lot, take a deep breath, and open the box. Blue onesie.

"Should we name him Billy?" Caitlin asks. I can't believe it. I can't. She knows it's my dream to name a little boy after my dad. She's a kind, generous soul.

Airplanes fly overhead. Everyone is coming home or going away. We are somewhere in between. We are feeling alive and awake in the moment. I don't want to leave this place or this person. I want to sit for a spell and feel the excitement, the joy, a touch of fear, a deep well of gratitude. I've wanted a family my whole life, but it always felt out of reach. Some of that was circumstance and some of it was me.

I think about one of the oldest attractions in Fantasyland at Disneyland: Peter Pan's Flight. It has been part of the park since opening day in the 1950s. Peter Pan, the boy who never grows up, shouts, "Come on, everybody! Here we go!" You hop on a pirate ship, Tinker Bell sprinkles pixie dust, and you fly off to Neverland, avoiding the snapping crocodiles below.

That's how I feel. Peter Pan, at the eleventh hour, is becoming a man. And here we go.

35

Disney Girl

On October 22, 2017, I am accompanying a pregnant Caitlin through Disneyland. The temperature is a record high for October, and I can tell Caitlin is feeling hot and uncomfortable. The Animation Building will provide the most relief from the sweltering heat, and I want to get there fast. I forget to factor in that Caitlin is walking and eating for two. She needs to use the restroom every four minutes and keeps stopping for snacks. Pee, popcorn. Pee, macarons. Pee, Dole Whip.

My heart is pounding and I'm sweating bullets from the scorching heat.

"Are you okay?" she asks.

"I'm fine. I'm just hot and bothered."

"You're acting strange."

"For wanting to get my pregnant gal out of the heat?"

I grab her hand as we arrive at the entrance of the Animation Building.

"So sorry, Mr. Stamos, we're closed due to technical issues," says a nervous cast member.

"Are you kidding me?" I yell, pitching a fit. "This is unacceptable! It's hotter than hell. I need to get her inside and out of the heat. What's your name, young man?" I say getting a closer look at his name tag.

"It's okay, love," Caitlin says, trying to calm me down and not make a scene.

The cast member seems distressed. "Okay, sir, I understand. Let's just get you two inside so you can cool off while we fix the issue. Please be our guest."

"Thank you!"

We enter the long blue and purple hallway. On the wall in huge letters are the words "Once upon a time . . ." I put my arm around Caitlin and lead her to the big purple couch. There's no one in the place except us.

We sit for a minute, cooling off and taking in all the large screens.

Then, the screens begin to glitch and the music stops. The room goes dark. She squeezes my hand.

"Oh no," I say. "What the hell is going on in here?"

Slowly, each screen in the room starts to flicker on and play a montage. A video for Caitlin that I cut together featuring all the "meet cutes" and falling-in-love moments in Disney animated films throughout the years. She now realizes we're not just in here to cool off.

A scene from the *Paperman*, a black-and-white short film about two people falling in love in 1940s New York. A clip of the adorable robot *Wall-E*, as well as *Bambi*, *Aladdin*, *Beauty and the Beast*, and more. It ends with an animation our talented friend Paul Briggs put together for me. As "Kiss the Girl" from *The Little Mermaid* starts to play, Sebastian holds up a sign between his pincers that reads, "Go on and ask the girl!" I get down on one knee.

I barely get the words "Will you marry me?" out before

Caitlin crumples into my arms. We're both crying happy tears on the floor as she says, "Yes." I'm still holding the engagement ring as she slips it on her finger without even looking.

I find myself being more romantic with Caitlin than with any woman I've ever been involved with. I guess that's what happens when it's real. You get starry-eyed and downright sappy.

With Billy coming in seven months, we decide to hold off on wedding planning until after he's born. But that doesn't stop Caitlin from selling me on a "babymoon."

"A what?" I ask.

"It's our last trip before the baby comes!"

She reminds me that we are already flying to Arizona for a charity event.

"There's a health and wellness spa that's close to there that I want to take you to," she says.

I'm being honored with the Childhelp Lifetime Achievement Award for my over three decades of service to abused and neglected children.

I'm preparing my speech and reflecting on all the courageous children I've met recovering from unbelievable trauma and how their stories inspire me to keep fighting child abuse with everything I have.

Almost none of them are victims of the kinds of predators you see on TV, the stranger in the trench coat with the dark van that grabs kids off the street. They are hurt by parents, relatives, neighbors, people they know.

Something I haven't thought about in years comes back to me. Flashes of memory:

When I was little, I had a babysitter who was around eighteen or nineteen. A lot of the time she's kind of fun. We play, watch sitcoms, and laze around on the couch.

But sometimes she gets weird, and it makes me feel weird,

too. Uncomfortable. She does strange stuff I don't understand. I just pretend to be sleeping when she puts my hand, or tries to put my mouth, on or near her breast. There's canned laughter on the TV in the background. My hand is heavy in hers; I'm holding my breath, I feel trapped. Then it's over, and when I "wake up" it's like nothing happened.

I learn it's a phenomenon called the freeze response. Sounds like what it is. When a child is vulnerable or can't escape, there can be a sort of playing possum effect. Don't move, don't speak, and just wait until things get normal again.

It's something that I had packed away. I won't talk about it at the gala tonight, because this event isn't about me, it's about the kids. I repack it and wait for some other time to share.

"I'm humbled to accept this award," I say, standing at the podium with my beautiful pregnant fiancée sitting in the front row, beaming.

"This recognition is a reflection of the smiles of Childhelp's children, their bravery, and their sweetness. It is a reminder of their fears, their pain, and their challenges. As I anticipate fatherhood, it is a monument of gratitude for the lessons I continue to learn about myself from these amazing boys and girls each year.

"If I can pass on one thing to my son, it will be the best part of who I've been over the years: a lifetime of service to something greater than oneself; a lifetime dedicated to the love of a child.

"And If I get this right, I'll be sitting out there one day watching the young man I've raised accept this very award."

After a night of emotion and reflection, I'm ready to shift gears and throttle back a little. Caitlin whisks me off to paradise. We end up at a gorgeous health and wellness spa called Miraval in Tucson, Arizona. It's a Zen oasis and exactly what we need.

Between pampering facials, exercise classes, fine food, and meditation rooms, it's the most relaxed I've felt in years. I come back to the room with rubber legs after a two-hour massage to find Caitlin in the doorway. She has that look on her face.

"What's that look?" I ask.

"I know you're going to think I'm crazy," she says, "but what if we get married in two weeks?"

Every relaxed fiber in my body tenses up and my eye starts twitching.

"Yes, I think you're crazy!" I say.

I thought this was settled. Still, Caitlin is nesting and wants Billy to have both of our last names. She's not looking for anything fancy.

We toss around dates and settle on February 3 in L.A., exactly two weeks away.

There's no way this can happen. We had always talked about getting married at the Little Brown Church in the Valley with Beach Boy Bruce Johnston singing "Disney Girls" as she walks down the aisle. Mike Love would officiate, and The Beach Boys would be the wedding band. There's no way we can book the church, sync everyone's schedules, hire caterers, select flowers, set up the house for an onslaught of guests, and prepare a contingency plan for rain with such short notice.

I give Caitlin an arrogant smirk. "Love, if you can get all that together in two weeks, then I'm in."

Never underestimate Caitlin McHugh, soon to be Caitlin McHugh Stamos, and her to-do list. We are married on a bright, sunny day, February 3, at the Little Brown Church, with Bruce singing "Disney Girls" as she walks down the aisle, with so many people we love witnessing our vows, exactly the way we want it.

The night before the wedding, while Caitlin is off having a

girls' night bachelorette party, I'm having my own hot, wild, sticky bachelor party, and by that I mean scrapbooking with a hot glue gun. As a wedding present, I'm making Caitlin an Up-themed adventure book chronicling our courtship. It has all our texts, pictures, plane tickets, and other memories.

I recruit my buddy Dave Coulier to help. He thinks I'm nuts to spend my last night being single stamping, cutting, and pasting instead of tramp-stamp-chasing, club-line-cutting, and grinning over some stripper's pasties. We laugh so hard. Just two wild men crafting the night away.

The phone rings. It's Caitlin.

Her voice is distressed. She's almost hyperventilating. "I need you to come to the hotel. I've been robbed. Hurry, please!"

I grab Dave and head to the Beverly Hills Hotel. When we arrive, there are cops, security guards, and hotel staff surrounding Caitlin and her friends. While the wedding party was at dinner, someone went into her room safe and cleaned it out. Our wedding bands are gone. Pricey jewelry swiped. A $175,000 necklace is missing. Great, that one was a loaner.

Poor Caitlin is exhausted from all the drama, getting her mouth swabbed, and being fingerprinted by detectives as she is preparing for her big day. I'm just happy she's safe. Before saying our vows, we are already in it for richer or poorer.

The next morning I put on my tux, straighten my bow tie, and get ready to say the two simplest and most meaningful words in the world at the Little Brown Church in Studio City. It is the perfect place for us to start our lives together, a small, humble, welcoming chapel with just enough room for family and a few friends.

Bruce Johnston sings his song "Disney Girls." It feels like it's written for Caitlin. It's all about innocence, the fantasy of finding the one, and maybe even ending up with a "forever wife and a kid someday." And here she is.

Caitlin comes down the aisle in a white strapless wedding dress with her hair cascading around her face in waves. She's holding a simple bouquet of white flowers, and a train of tulle glides behind her as she takes slow, formal steps toward me. She is stunning and completely knocks me out.

Mike Love is nodding at me like, *Good work, kid.* Mike is more than a father figure, more than a brother, and more than a dear friend. Mike Love is my hero. His unwavering support, his guidance, and his belief in me as an entertainer have touched my heart in ways I can't fully express.

Mike's invaluable contributions to The Beach Boys have regrettably been undervalued. His lyrics and hooks are etched into the annals of music history. "*Round, round, get around, I get around,*" "*I'm picking up good vibrations,*" and "*Aruba, Jamaica*" bear the unmistakable mark of Mike Love's genius. He gifted the world a sonic postcard through his lyrical imagery, painting a vivid portrait of America teeming with hope, optimism, and an infectious sense of positivity.

And by allowing me to perform with him for nearly four decades, he has granted me one of the most extraordinary gifts one can ever receive—the privilege of being a conduit for getting his timeless music out to millions. It's a gift that surpasses any material possession or fleeting fame. It is a gift that holds the power to shape lives, to bring people together, and to make their existence more meaningful. It is a privilege that I will forever cherish.

Mike's music has shaped me into the person I am today. He has shown me the true meaning of resilience, determination, and staying true to oneself. I am forever indebted to him and will continue to stand by his side, championing his legacy and witnessing the incredible impact Mike has on those who need it most, especially me. He is the right person to officiate this moment, strong and true. I've prepared my own vows and am ready to tell Caitlin what's in my heart.

"Caitlin, I proposed to you at Disneyland, the Happiest Place on Earth, because I knew that marrying you would make me the Happiest Man on Earth.

"You are every Disney princess wrapped up into one woman:

"You have Snow White's gentle compassion for others;

"Cinderella's strength to overcome hard times and emerge as the belle of the ball;

"Ariel's wit and feistiness;

"Princess Jasmine's flashing dark eyes;

"The gorgeous tumbling hair of Rapunzel;

"The adventurous spirit of Pocahontas;

"And Belle's ability to see the beauty in this Beast.

"If I could ask one wish of a Fairy Godmother, it would be to have my own mother and father here with us today. Not just because I miss them with all my heart, but because I would love to see the smiles on their faces knowing I had picked the best mother for their grandchild and a perfect partner for their own child.

"The best of who they are is now safe and warm inside of you. Our son will be a little bit of him, a little bit of her, the stellar qualities of your wonderful family, and a lot of who we are together.

"Today is a celebration of the pasts that brought us to this moment, the love we received from our families that opened our hearts to love each other, and a future filled with laughter and joy: a new wife and a baby boy.

"Our fairy tale is just beginning . . ."

36

THE HIGH CLOWN SETTLES DOWN

My therapist, Phil Stutz, puts his analysis on a three-by-five card I can carry in my pocket. Little drawings that illuminate complex concepts into simple tools for everyday use. He draws two lines on my card. One reads "Family Calm" and the other says "High Clown" with the word "Immature" beside it. Talk about telling it like it is. (I copped this move from Phil when I played physiotherapist Doctor Nicky on the hit Netflix series You.)

He knows my history and doesn't want me to relinquish the adult power I've achieved—a place of peace, connection, and creativity. When I was lonely or bored in the past, that restlessness would bring out a juvenile rebellion. I'd become childlike in my pursuit of a here-and-now kind of fun. Instead of seeking the self-created energy found in stability, I'd live for the outer world of excitement, this imaginary place of external stimulation. Stutz calls it "The Circus."

Right after the wedding, I'm definitely walking a tight wire over three rings, but I'm trying to make sure I'm taking care of business rather than slipping into clown shoes.

I'm usually hands-on in creative ventures, but this time my job of putting hands on Cailtin was my greatest contribution to the cause.

Now, I have to watch her do the literal and figurative heavy lifting. It doesn't seem fair. She gets morning sickness, fatigue, exhaustion, and pain. I just rub her feet, keep her hopped up on snacks, and duck and cover when mood swings hit. Here she is sheltering and sustaining human life while I am reaping the spoils of extra slices of pizza and tubs of ice cream. We're both eating for two.

Caitlin's water breaks on April 1 while we're watching *Jesus Christ Superstar Live in Concert.* "Guess it's Billy's first April Fool's Day joke," she says.

Her due date is in late May and she's trying to keep him in as long as possible. Dr. Crane had put her on partial bed rest since Billy dropped after the stress of the wedding robbery, but now he puts her on full-time bed rest, and I've been assigned the task of being her full-time butler.

I give her a little bell to ring whenever she needs anything, and make sure her trusty mutt, Lilo, stays loyally by her side when I can't be. Ding, ding, ding. The bell rings, and I spring into action.

I get up every morning extra early to make her Huevos RanchStamos, our take on Huevos Rancheros, consisting of four layers of tortillas filled with eggs, two kinds of beans, pico and mango de gallo, mild-enough-for-morning hot sauce, four kinds of cheese, homemade guacamole, with some jicama on the side. I love cooking for Caitlin.

Ding, ding, ding. Time for her ultimate night craving, sliced apples with peanut butter. On the morning of April 10, she starts feeling contractions. Dr. Crane checks her out and sends us home. "They're small," he assures, "but drinking a glass of wine will help." Caitlin has always been a lightweight. One glass gets her tipsy.

In the afternoon, the contractions get stronger, and Caitlin is drunk and dilated. Time to head to the hospital.

As we waddle off the elevator and into the triage area, we're greeted by the smiling hospital staff. They start checking Caitlin's vitals and ask if she needs anything. "Hello there, would you like some refreshing water or juice?" But the contractions hit hard, and Caitlin is not in the mood for any small talk. She looks at them with determination and says, "Listen up, folks. Give me all the drugs you've got and no one gets hurt!" The staff chuckle nervously, knowing better than to mess with a woman in labor.

Push, push, push. Within minutes, on Tuesday, April 10, at 8:32 P.M., Billy arrives. He's a preemie, four pounds and change. Caitlin had forbidden video or photos in the delivery room, but she is in full party mode from that glass of wine and the drugs, so she asks me to take pictures and I'm clicking away.

William Christopher Stamos has hollered his way into our hearts.

I'm so proud and excited that I announce the news on Instagram (sorry, Billy, already making you an influencer against my better judgment): "From now on, the best part of me will always be my wife and my son. Welcome Billy Stamos (named after my father). #NotJustAnUncleAnymore #Overjoyed."

I flash back to my mom's first impression of me. Stamos men don't emerge from the womb adorable, we need a little cultivation. Billy isn't super attractive on day one. He's bald, bellowing, and has a belly. He sort of looks like Don Rickles. I could deal with everything but the bald part. I start googling "Is hair hereditary? HAIReditary?" Maybe Baby Gap sells toupees?

I read it's the mother's-mother's-father's side that determines a child's follicular bounty. I'm going through the family tree fretting. ALL BALD! The online baby hair network is on fire with crap advice: too much hair in the womb gives a mother heartburn, or shave their heads and the hair will grow in thicker. I didn't expect a full mullet, but I do ask the doctor, "Now you're sure I'm the father?"

I hold my little bald boy and look into his green eyes. I'm filled with awe and amazement. Before he's said his first word, he's given me the gift of a lifetime. I've always wanted kids of my own. I would have died regretful without him.

I think what scares me the most is I suddenly understand why there are so many fucked-up people in this world. I've worked philanthropically to fight child abuse for decades and seen child actors self-destruct because of the dark elements they encountered in entertainment.

It takes a lot to be a good parent. I have no idea what I'm doing but I know it takes more than I ever imagined. A child requires love, of course, but so much time, sacrifice, patience, money, common sense, fretful nights, and constant care. It's the toughest job you'll ever love.

Caitlin bonds deeply right away. And now, the beautiful face that's always smiling at me from across the room is tucked into the crook of Billy's neck.

I just see the top of her head as they fold into a heart shape together. She coos and whispers to him as he watches her in awe. Makes sense. He's been baking in her belly for the last nine months while I've been cooling my heels on the outside, like some 1950s sitcom dad passing out cigars in the waiting room. Those two have been connected by a cord that offers food and oxygen. The cord has been cut, but it exists invisibly between them. They share essential nutrients and the breath of life. I'm on the sidelines makin' dad jokes. And by the way, who came up with the term "*dad jokes*" to describe jokes that are outdated, unfunny, or inappropriate?

I've got to be the luckiest bastard on earth, but I'm also feeling something I did not expect. I feel like an outsider. For a couple of months, I'm a protector and provider trying to figure out some foreign love language Caitlin and Billy know instinctively.

I'm showing up with a pure heart but never sure it's enough. I mean, my kid's not going to be dedicating "Cat's in the Cradle" to me, but I could use some advice right now. My dad was strong, autonomous, and his own man, but he was also there for me whenever I needed him. I wish my parents were still alive.

"Mom, did you and I curl up in a corner while dad looked on, longing to be part of our little world?

"Dad, I feel like you and I have always been connected. How did that happen? Did you do anything special? What's the secret? How can I be like you?"

I need some of that wisdom, so I call up Bob Saget. He's got three daughters. It's a weird topic and hard for dudes to talk about no matter how close they are.

"I love him so much, Bob," I say, more emotional than I thought I'd be. "But it's like I don't exist, you know? I'm not sure he's that into me."

Bob laughing at my new dad jitters puts me at ease.

"Just wait," he says seriously. "The minute he laughs at one of your jokes, you will be connected like you've never been connected with anyone before."

After that, something in me relaxes, and I start to enjoy the process. Bob is right. Billy should be starry-eyed about his mom. For now, I need to pitch in where I can, cuddle the little guy every chance I get, try to win him over with some singing and storytelling, and just be fully present so that the moment he gets curious about the hairy one at the other end of the couch, I'm ready to bring my best.

It's funny how when you stop trying to manage your emotions and just allow things to happen authentically, life falls into place. If I could tell every new parent one thing, it would be to stop worrying about how you *should* feel and just give in to how you *do* feel.

Caitlin heads out to a doctor's appointment and I'm the only semi-adult in the house. I'm on Billy duty, or as I call it "Billy Doody"'cause the kid craps like a champ.

I'm getting ready for the day and carrying him around through my morning routine so he can have a front-row seat and see how his dad does it. We park in front of the mirror and I impart upon him my patented technique of how you slow down the aging process.

I drink the blood of Lori Loughlin and Rob Lowe and live forever! Kidding. If I had any trade secrets, I'd bottle them up and make a bundle. I just use whatever soap is near the sink, and shampoo that I took from the last hotel I stayed at. Do you wanna know my true secret? I hit the genetic lotto. Thank you, Mom and Dad.

Caitlin and I give Billy some solid genes, but I'm starting to think it'll be a good thing if it takes a while for this little caterpillar kid to become a butterfly because I'd like him to make it on his personality, intelligence, kindness, and hard work.

No matter how many bits I pull, I still can't get Billy to smile. Each day as I get ready to face the world, I look at the one little face whose approval means the most to me.

I brush my forehead with the electric toothbrush. "Hey Billy, look, I thought I was taller!" Nothing. I bump my head bending down to get the hairdryer.

My Buster-Keaton-meets-Charlie-Chaplin slapstick moves are met with a little smile, but I think it might have been gas.

As I head to the fridge to get him a bottle, "Aaaaachoooo!" I sneeze loudly. I've always had an uncontrollably loud sneeze.

The cutest, tiniest little giggle I've ever heard comes from the mouth of my son. I sneeze again. Bigger giggle. It's the moment I've been waiting for.

I hold a tissue to my nose and as I honk out a massive fake sneeze, I shoot the tissue paper over his head. Now he's belly laughing. The louder the sneeze, the more he shakes with glee.

This moment is magic. This moment is therapy. It's like my shrink, Stutz, talks about, finding that "Grateful Flow," the place where obsessing and worrying give way to fulfillment and promise.

I am grateful to this child; I am connected to this child. And the crazy thing is, what brought Billy the greatest joy was inside me all along. I didn't need to try so hard, I just needed to be me, let go, and sneeze.

The High Clown of Immaturity becomes a regular ol' Dad Clown who does everything he can to make his child laugh. My top act becomes the Bonk Bit. It's a fan favorite. After bath time, Caitlin and I will take him to his room for a story. Before she starts to calm him into drifting off to sleep, I walk out of the room, intentionally bonking myself in the head. Always gets a chuckle before Mom kicks me out. If I'm on tour or in the middle of a scene on a show, I make it mandatory to slip away to FaceTime a few bonks for Billy before bedtime.

It's no surprise that Billy starts to find his footing in the world. He begins to develop his own bits. He's particularly fond of hiding, jumping out, and scaring me. I'm less fond of that bit. He inherited the move from his mom. It's like having a miniature Cato from The Pink Panther always waiting in the shadows to spring. We're a happy little household scaring the shit out of one another on a daily basis.

I get serious at times and try to steer him into astrophysics or engineering. The world needs more engineers, but I gotta say the kid has comic timing. I end up not falling in love with him because he laughs at my jokes, I fall deeper in love with him because I crack up at his jokes.

Even though I thought I was ready year after year, I was still too immature early in life to be a dad. I had the blessing and curse of looking young and feeling young. Then there is the extended adolescence that happens in Hollywood. It's like, hey, if I can still fit in skinny jeans, I don't have to worry about procreative genes.

There is often a huge gap between what you consider "fun" as a young guy and what you need to be healthy before getting married and having a child. Those two worlds sometimes meet in the middle, but most of the time they collide. If you get too worked up missing the old days, that resentment is a love killer and hurts children caught in the middle. If you look back with a little nostalgia and laugh, you're ready to build something new.

When I truly sobered up, got some good therapy, and found the right partner, making that final push to grow up wasn't hard. Holding on to some playboy past is like being the last guy at the party with ten layers of self-tanner who wears his sunglasses at night. It's not cute anymore, trust me. Hop off the treadmill in time and you maintain some dignity, age with grace, and still keep your cool.

With kids, it's all about setting aside your needs and making sure this toddler swerving around your house like a little drunk is clean, well fed, and happy.

I still set aside date nights to make sure my marriage, and Billy's family, is strong and loving. I still prioritize work so my child can see what drive, hustle, ambition, looks like. But Billy is the new axis that spins my world.

There is a conceit in corny rom-coms where the protagonist says, "You complete me." As a Disney guy, I'm down with a certain level of sentimentalism and sappiness, but I never really understood the idea of being "completed." I get it now. I still have a lot to do, but if my whole life was one sentence, Billy would be the exclamation mark at the end of it.

37

CAKE

December of 2021, Bob and I are on a double date at Nobu, Malibu, with our wives, Caitlin and Kelly. I ask Bob what he's having, reminding him that tonight's specials are cake and cock.

"And they're out of cake," I say, wearing out a favorite line of his. "They gave the last piece to that skinny old little woman over there in the corner eating all alone. Oh wait, my bad, that's David Spade." Everyone laughs.

Bob and I have had countless conversations about wanting to find true love and contentment with the one person who makes life worth living. And here we are. We did it. Sitting across from us are two of the most beautiful women, inside and out, making us look better than we had the right to. The universe decided it was our turn to experience what our parents had. Real love.

Not sure what we did to deserve this, but we're not questioning it, we just know we better respect it. We are both happily in love and talking about how grateful we are that schmucks like us ended up with girls like this.

Nobu's dimly lit Japanese restaurant has always been a celebrity haunt in L.A., but the romantic Malibu beachfront outpost that overlooks sand and sea is the current hot spot. Same menu, different view. Kind of like our lives.

Bob is in charge of ordering. He likes to do things like that: choose the meal, book flights, or hook you up with the best doctor or shrewdest lawyer. He's like a celebrity concierge.

"You gotta use my mohel for your son's circumcision, he's got the steadiest hands in the business, trust me."

I finish the joke. "By the way, I'll pass on the fried calamari! Thanks."

There is no one-upping from Bob tonight. He lets the laugh just linger in the air between us.

Bob is restrained, peaceful, quiet. In other words, not like the old Bob. He is the calmest I've ever seen him. He's not holding court or interrupting like a madman. He is fully engaged, holds eye contact, and listens.

I'm having dinner with the guy I always knew he could be. Everyone feels relaxed and connected. It's perfect. We want to commemorate the occasion with a picture, and Bob orchestrates the shot. He asks the waitress to take it, but isn't satisfied. "One more, please, hold the phone up a little higher so you don't see my 'under-neck fat.' It's fine, I'll fix it later, and post it tomorrow." For some reason his neuroses about photo-taking that normally drive me insane don't bother me tonight. If Bob is evolving, so am I. I'm learning to go easier on him; have more patience.

He posts the beautiful photo on Instagram the following day:

Loved dinner last night with my wife and brother and sister-in-law by the beach. We talked about love and life and sashimi. Lucky we are. And extremely appreciative to be with our closest of friends.

I don't think that will be the last picture I take with him, the last time I see him. I guess no one ever does.

A few weeks later I'm driving Billy around to get him to nap in the backseat. As he dozes off, I get a text from my publicist, Matt; "Call me." It's rare to hear from him on a Sunday, so I pull over into the parking lot near my home, step out of the car, and call him right back.

"Did you talk to Bob today?" he asks. He sounds worried but trying to cover it up. Great publicist, not the best actor.

"No, why?"

"Is he okay?" Matt asks.

"What do you mean 'is he okay'? Spit it out, Matt, what are you talking about?"

"I got a call from TMZ," he says. "Several sources say he's dead."

Oh, here we go again. A few weeks earlier, Matt got a call from TMZ. "Several sources say John Stamos went down in a plane crash close to San Diego." Matt immediately called me, and I answered pissed because I was taking a nap. Great sources. I live to see another day and the tabloids must go hunting for fresh accidents, breakups, overdoses, and plastic surgery misfortunes because everything is just fine at the Stamos household. Sorry to disappoint.

"Maybe Bob was in the same plane crash I died in. These clowns need to get better 'sources' or they'll be out of business soon," I shoot back. "It's probably bullshit!"

Still, I text Bob, "Baby, you around?" I called him Baby because that's how he entered himself into my phone years ago. No response.

He's probably in flight on his way home from a gig. I know he is performing in Florida, but Bob never misses a text. Even sleeping, he'll answer a text with, "I'm asleep." Planes have Wi-Fi. He'll text me back. He doesn't.

I call his wife, Kelly, and leave a message.

Candace Cameron texts me, "Hey, I got this weird DM from some girl in Florida, says Bob died."

Fuck, fuck, fuck. Too coincidental. This can't be true. I call her immediately and she reads the DM to me. "Sorry to hear about Bob dying, *Full House* was my favorite."

Candace wrote back, "This better not be a joke because it's not funny."

The girl writes, "It's not a joke. My sister is a police officer and she's on the scene at the Ritz right now. I can even take a screenshot of the police report."

As I'm trying to process what I'm hearing, Kelly is trying to call me.

"I'll call you right back, Candace. . . ."

When I switch callers over to Kelly, all I hear is a wailing scream. I hit the ground in the parking lot and my knees slam down on the asphalt.

"Nooooooooooooooooooooooo."

My son is still sound asleep in the backseat of my car. I pull myself together to drive home and start making calls. First to Caitlin, she's in disbelief. She calls her parents to come watch Billy. Then to Dave. "Dave, Bob Saget is dead." Not sure why I have to use his last name. Dave knows I'm not calling to tell him Bob Hope died. I call Lori, who's on the eighth hole of Lake View Country Club golfing with her husband. "Bob is dead, Lori." She tells me later she dropped to her knees like me.

Billy wakes up. "Daddy?"

I love you, son.

Millions mourn Bob. He's America's favorite dad to a generation of kids. Before YouTube, he was the guy that riffed on your family's grainy VHS videos. He's the filthiest comedian of all time to the aristocrats out there. He'd read the corniest copy with devilish intelligence and tells the most salacious story with purity. It's impossible to capture the spirit of a guy who belongs to everyone. I don't have exclusive rights, but the loss is personal, painful, and beyond belief.

In Bob's last Instagram post he looks too alive to die a few hours later. We all want to "die alive." No one wants to go down in some Lay-Z-Boy recliner filled with regret and remorse. No one dreams of fading into retirement discarded and forgotten. Bob felt young, energized, grateful, and appreciated. Hundreds of people came night after night to hear his storytelling. He leaves the world bright and fierce. The applause doesn't even have time to die down.

He was truly at the top of his game.

"*You created a cathedral of fucking love in this world and that was your life, Bob Saget! Cathedral of love. A cathedral of laughter. Goodness.*" Jim Carrey says it perfectly on the Netflix special I produce, "Dirty Daddy: The Bob Saget Memorial."

When you lose a best friend, you lose a piece of your history. I feel lost. That's not a good thing for me. In the past, feeling stripped of someone I loved made me want to join them. No way I'd ever try to overdose or blow my brains out, but I have a history of wanting that bad feeling of emptiness to go away fast. Not this time. No drugs, no booze, no bullshit.

I need to be here for my wife and my child. Caitlin transforms during all of this. She's beyond beautiful, intelligent, supportive, and sweet, there's something new that emerges: a grounding kind of strength that challenges me to live up to it, to be better.

I'm processing the five stages of grief in a healthy way for once:

1. Denial: Head to the shrink and make sure I don't look away. I'm not going to lie to myself about this, or dishonor Bob's memory by trying to forget his death. Not a chance. Look this in the face and be there for those who love him.

2. Anger: Don't get mad, meditate. Instead of raging and revolting, be quiet and contemplative.

3. Bargaining: The opposite of pleading for a different outcome is letting go. Bob is gone and I need to lengthen the strand that tethers our hearts and give in. His spirit is alive, and that's what counts.

4. Depression: Pray away the despair. "Hey, God, it's John, I'm hurting, bad. I need to be here for my wife, my kid, Bob's friends, and family. Keep me strong. Get us all through this."

5. Acceptance: Remember, remember, and remember with joy. Bob was life and laughter. Accept his death, embrace how the best of Uncle Bob will live on in the lessons and love I share with my son.

I'm holding it together on the surface but feeling broken, shattered, and worthless to help others. Caitlin sees me faltering, throws me in the car, and drives to Bob and Kelly's house.

We pull up to the gate in my black Tesla. A few paparazzi are across the street. They don't swarm or flash their cameras. Feels like they know the pain hidden behind tinted windows. A rare modicum of respect. Maybe these celebrity stalkers have hearts and Bob's passing means something personal to them.

Kelly comes out to meet us. Tight, tight hugs. Holding back tears. I don't know what to say to her.

I knew from the start that she really loved Bob for Bob, the way we all did. She'd listen to him rattle on about himself for a bit longer than I usually would. The first time she said to him "This isn't all about you, Bob," I knew she was the one.

He'd pout, she'd kiss him, and in a sweet tone she'd say, "You know I love you, honey."

As we hug in the driveway, I tell her, "You got ripped off. You didn't have him long enough."

That's when the paps get their pictures. They must have climbed a tree to shoot over the gate or something. We walk up the driveway and get closer to the open door. I hear crying as we walk in.

There's about ten people sitting on couches in the living room. Everyone turns to see me. Each face sadder than the next. I lose it. They hug me and hold me up.

We are in disbelief. Bob was such a big part of our lives. No one can fathom life without him. It's too soon to put that thought into words. In between the tears, there's silence. It would be easier if Bob were here filling up all the empty spaces.

This is the moment he'd turn into the celeb concierge. He'd put aside his emotions and snap into action with military precision, efficiently making all the appropriate plans and decisions so everyone else didn't have to.

Two of his daughters, Aubrey and Lara, are on their way from New York, but Jennie, his youngest, will not be at the house this evening, as she's been dealing with personal health issues. Bob loved Jennie so much and shed many tears, working tirelessly for years to make sure she had the best care in the world. I'd like to think this was an area where I was there for him. I tried to be a good listener and good hugger when it came to his daughter.

"Who's going to tell Jennie?" someone says. Once again, a sad silence falls across the room.

Then, out of nowhere, we hear this tinny version of John Mayer's "Heartbreak Warfare."

Lori and Candace dive for Candace's purse and run to the kitchen with it. It's Candace's ringtone, and she's embarrassed because John Mayer is there, grieving along with the rest of us. First real laugh of the night.

I miss Bob so much.

I slip into the backyard by myself. His last cigar is sitting in an ashtray by the Jacuzzi. It is windy and balmy. I look up to the sky and say, "Baby, please give me a sign from up there. Tell me you're all right. Tell me not to feel bad." I wait a few minutes. Nothing. Ask again. Silence.

I want to be haunted by him. The void is maddening. I'm contemplating heaven, hell, and heartbreak when a tiny hummingbird comes fluttering down from above and lands on a tree in front of me.

Hummingbirds represented my parents, and this beauty is definitely my mother, who had red hair. The bird has bright red feathers around its neck like a scarf. She assures me Bob is okay, flies up, and darts away.

Maybe his soul is at peace. The only reason to rattle the thunder and part the clouds is that you are restless in the afterlife; you have unfinished business and haven't said what you wanted to say to the ones you love. That's not Bob.

I need to stop looking for signs in the sky and accept that he's where he should be: peaceful, free, surrounded by hummingbirds of past souls at rest.

I get thousands of texts, emails, and calls that speak to our thirty-five-year friendship. People tell me how sorry they are for my loss and send me flowers like my wife died or something. We were like an old married couple: all bickering, no sex.

I lose another friend soon after Bob, Taylor Hawkins, drummer for the Foo Fighters. Heartbreaking. Just heartbreaking. When artists like this die, or any brilliant performer, it makes me so sad they're not around to influence new artists. Sure, there are tons of videos of Bob doing stand-up and Taylor ripping on the drums and singing his ass off with the Foos, but once you've seen them,

that's all, folks. Nothing new from these one-of-a-kind performers, both true originals. They reached a level most don't. And now
they're gone.

Bob had this idea that there would be a magical event making him the biggest star in the world, and at the same time,
something that would solve all the other problems he was dealing with in life. Anything less was unacceptable. His death brings
a well-deserved tsunami of love, an outpouring from all ages,
respect from his peers. What a talent. What a kind, good man.
What an icon. These are the accolades he wanted all his life. The
irony is, he already had it. His ego couldn't accept it because
the adoration didn't come in the form of having more power in
show business. I'm heartbroken he didn't think he was enough.
He was and always will be to me and the rest of the world.

The morning of the funeral, Billy was staring at a picture of
Bob and me dressed like women for a shoot in *People* magazine. We
were replicating Tony Curtis and Jack Lemmon from *Some Like It
Hot*. Billy squints his eyes and cocks his head, trying to make sense
of the picture. After a beat, he said,

"Dad, who is that?"

I say, "That's your dad and your Uncle Bobby in women's
clothing."

"Why?"

I paused. "Well, son, I did it as a tribute to a film . . . I can't
speak for Bob."

I pray that Billy will someday have a friend like I had in Bob.
And if I see a picture of the two of them in tutus, I'll know it's
brotherly love.

I grab Billy, hold him as tight as I can, and tell him how
much I love him.

Billy is turning into a real character. He knows funny and
is constantly doing bits, like his Uncle Bobby. One morning he

woke me up and started to drag me into the kitchen. I told him I had to pee first. He said, "If you have to pee and you don't go in your pants, the pee-ness goes away." His humor skews a lot closer to Bob's than mine. I just wish Bob was here to see it.

I'm still not ready to accept that he's gone. Not sure I ever will be. I try to imagine him still on the road, doing what he loves. He's standing onstage, killing. Another two-hour set in front of a couple hundred of the luckiest people on the planet. They're laughing so hard they weep. And just when they catch their breath, he grabs his guitar and slays with one of his musical closers. There's an encore, and another, and another. Everyone wants an encore with Bob.

On his drive back to the hotel after the gig, Bob calls Kelly and tells her about the show. He says he feels twenty-six again, alive, then asks her to fix up a picture he wants to post, and she says it doesn't need fixing and tells him how handsome he is. He says he loves her with every bit of his heart, and when he gets to the hotel to put his head on the pillow, he misses his daughters, his family, and his friends. God, he loves us all so much.

Bob goes to sleep dreaming of when we'll all meet again, and he's smiling. I know in my heart he's smiling, still hearing the laughter from a few hours before.

His funeral is at Mount Sinai Memorial Park Cemetery in Hollywood. He'd have been proud to join the afterlife party with notable comedians interned at his final resting place. The cemetery is haunted by the hilarious ghosts of Sid Caesar, Norman Fell, and our beloved Don Rickles.

Bob's ex-wife, Sherri, runs up to me, gives me a great big hug, and whispers in my ear, "Bob loved you so much. He also hated you. He was so jealous of you."

I wish he knew how jealous I was of him.

I join Billy one day while he's watching an old episode of

Full House. It's a special moment. Surreal. The Beach Boys are the guest stars. Bob and I are doing this beautiful scene where his character says how envious he is about my character's life: girl-chaser and rock-n-roller. Jesse turns around and tells Danny how jealous he is of his life: family man, three daughters, a dad.

I wanted to settle down and have a family. Bob had that, and I was envious. For the first time, the scene makes me cry. Hard. I think Billy understands why I'm upset. He doesn't say much, just lets me have a moment. Prescient when he wants to be, the little shit.

I reread an old social media birthday post Bob sent me:

To say we are like brothers is an understatement. We have been through so much together for 35 years. High, lows—the usual you go through with your closest of people in your life. But what I have to say here, is how damned lucky I am to have John in my life. He has always been there for me, even when I could be unbearable.

There is only one @johnstamos on this planet, and I am a better person because he's in my life. Happy Birthday, Dear John.

I may just read that every day for the rest of my life.

I think back to that last dinner at Nobu when we were all together: Bob, Kelly, Caitlin, me. I try to remember what we talked about. When you lose someone special, that final time together becomes mythic and magical. Every detail is a holy relic. You try to remember that feeling of closeness. What did we eat? Did we joke about cock and cake? Did we stay a little longer for coffee and dessert? I hope so.

If you get a chance to sit for a spell with someone you love, don't get up too quickly, stay a while, linger, indulge, savor. Order the cake.

EPILOGUE:
IF YOU WOULD HAVE TOLD ME

If you would have told me I could go back in time to avoid the grief of losing those I loved, I might have considered it because that pain remains sharp and deep. It's the kind of sorrow that sometimes makes you want to hide from the world; things you'll struggle with for the rest of your life.

If you would have told me there was a way to halt heartbreak, I had times when it would have been nice to be naturally numb. Being cheated on, lied to, and left, for lack of a better word, sucks. Imagine sheltering yourself from the jealousies and insecurities that emerge from bad love.

It's easy to be closed off, selfish, and protectively pessimistic. I could have saved myself from sleepless nights if I didn't start a new relationship with an open heart. I could have put all the energy into me, me, me.

If you would have told me I could avoid any wrong turn in my career, I would have welcomed the chance to skip a few bad moves or held out for better deals.

The picture-perfect résumé just requires the precision to

never learn from a mistake, never grow from a tough role, never sharpen a skill because you don't want to make a wrong move in the public sphere, and never experiencing the pleasure when something hard-won really hits.

The thrill of not knowing what lies ahead motivates us to take risks, try new things, and live in the present rather than constantly worrying about tomorrow. We are challenged to be adaptable, resilient, resourceful.

Life is full of unexpected moments of beauty and joy. Not knowing what the future holds opens us up to experiencing them fully.

There are so many films about time travel: *Planet of the Apes, Back to the Future, Bill and Ted's Excellent Adventure, Idiocracy.* They offer an opportunity to reimagine history and fix all the flaws of the past. It's a great fantasy because we all want to shrug off the shame of our worst moments, rewrite the scenes of our greatest humiliations, and edit the story of our lives to include only the best and brightest moments. It's human nature. But almost every movie where the protagonist seeks to alter the future defaults to an inevitable outcome: the way things happen is the way things are meant to be.

What breaks us helps rebuild us. What humiliates us can change us. Fame and fortune is as fun as it is eventually empty; the simple stuff is the best stuff. Our roots define who we will be for life, but we also break free from the family tree to become individuals. Our darkest days inform us and become our most valued teachers. Our love requires a vulnerability that is as terrifying and humbling as it is sublime and sustaining.

As I said when we began, everyone has a book in them. This was mine. There were laughs, tears, and some filler, just like life. There is a lot more life to live beyond these pages.

We flutter and fly through life at the speed of light. One day we cease to exist and become someone else's memory, someone else's misery, someone else's light.

I know I'll be back because I know those I've lost returned to me. When I am gone, Billy will look for me furiously swooping through the skies to let him know how much I miss him, how much I love him, how much everything is going to be okay.

If you would have told me I could do it all differently, I wouldn't change a thing. We're all here to hurt and heal, be ashamed and proud, live poor and rich, feel spent and rejuvenated. We are all here to honor and challenge yesterday as we tumble into tomorrow.

I'm here to live as much as I can while I've got my feet firmly planted on the ground and to return with hard-earned wings when I'm not. I'm nobody's guardian angel, but I plan to be one hell of a hummingbird.

ACKNOWLEDGMENTS

If you've made it this far and you're not looking for your name, thank you very much. For the rest of you, here you go. They're not in any order except for the most important being first.

There's only one person in the world who could write my autobiography: the person who lived it. The one who felt all the feels—good, bad, sometimes ugly, and everything in between—that's me.

And there's only one person in the world who could have helped me articulate my story as if they wore my shoes, lived my life, and understood every feeling that raced through my heart during those moments. And that's Daphne Young.

Daphne, you were able to decipher the tangled mess of my emotions and help me translate them into beautifully crafted sentences. You pushed me to defy the Hollywood pap, the generic tales of heroism and perfection, and encouraged me to share the real, unfiltered version of me in all its messy, beautiful glory. I could not have asked for a more extraordinary collaborator than you, dear Daphne. (When do we start writing the sequel?)

To my nieces, Haley, Maddy, and Jilly and my nephew, Blake. I am profoundly grateful for the support, joy, and love you've showered on me throughout the years. Being your uncle has been one of the brightest highlights of my life. Watching you all grow and mature has been an extraordinary journey, and I feel honored to have been a part of it. Your unique qualities, individual achievements, and the way you carry yourselves make me confident that Grammy and Papa are looking down on you with pride as well. Thank you for the invaluable "part-time parent practice" that has shaped me as a father to my own dear Billy boy. Your love and support have made me a better person. Keep being the incredible human beings you are. I love you, Uncle.

Dulce Rittner, writing this, I'm flooded with memories and emotions. Thirty-plus years, Dulce. A blink of an eye and a lifetime all at once. Over the years, you've been everything to me—my nanny, housekeeper, confidant, mother, sister, manager, defender, and best friend. Our relationship has been complex, vibrant, and full of life, driving each other to the brink of madness and back. Your wisdom has shaped my life. Your advice has always led me in the right direction, even when hard to hear. Thank you for every sacrifice you've made, every secret you've kept, and every piece of advice you've given. Thank you for being my truest friend and my unwavering ally. Without your guidance and love, I would not be where I am or who I am.

To Matt Polk, it's hard to put into words the gratitude I feel when I think of how you have impacted my life. You've not just been a publicist to me, Matt, but a pillar of support, a mentor, a confidant, and, above all, a dear friend. Your relentless belief in me, your meticulous attention to detail, your tireless efforts to build an image and reputation that I can be proud of; these efforts are not just professional but come from a place of personal care that is unmatched. You've stood by me when the world seemed dark and led me back into the light. You've taught me resilience and you've celebrated my victories as if they were your own. And they are. I'm infinitely grateful to have you in my life.

Roger Lodge, we moved up to Hollywood together to make our dreams come true and succeeded in every way. You've been a supportive, humble friend, cheering me on without envy. You've shown me what it means to be a true family man and father, which is a gift from you that I cherish deeply. We journeyed from the mean streets of Cypress to what we thought was the most luxurious living space in all of Hollywood, the Oakwood Apartments in Burbank—crazy times. Maybe I'll write about them in the next book. Maybe not.

Tim and Leilani (Appa and Papa to Billy), Caitlin's parents, perfectly shatter the stereotype of troublesome in-laws. Your invaluable help with Billy and the support you gave Caitlin during the countless hours I dedicated to writing this book cannot be overstated. Thank you.

Dana Walden, your support throughout the years means the world to me. I am deeply grateful for the opportunities you have generously given me and for your enduring belief in my talents. I am, in turn, in awe of you. I am lucky to call you a friend.

Marilyn Van Wagner, you held a special place in my mother's heart as one of her dearest and closest friends. Your support and assistance during her life's final stages were a godsend. I am especially grateful for your insistence that I include my mother's faith in this book, recognizing how significant it was to her. Even today, we maintain a Sunday tradition of exchanging heartfelt texts, keeping my mother's name, Loretta (or "Lily," as you fondly called her), alive in our conversations. My mother loved you so much, and I am forever thankful that she had such a genuine and loyal friend as you. God bless you.

Mikey G, my steadfast companion, you have been so much more than just security or a driver to me. You are a dear, loyal friend who has stood by my side through thick and thin. LUM, the acronym we use to express our bond, speaks volumes about my love and appreciation for you. It's a phrase that holds a deeper meaning known only to us. Mikey, you have never let me down. In moments of joy and moments of challenge, you have been there. You are more than a friend; you are family to me. Thank you for embodying the true meaning of friendship, LUM.

My sincere gratitude goes to Bob Iger, not just for being the exceptional individual you are, but also for your longtime friendship dating back to *Full House* when you were president of ABC, and your generosity in helping me realize every one of my Disney dreams and beyond.

Alan Iezman, thank you for your impact on my career. Right after my time on *General Hospital*, you served as both my agent and manager, reshaping the trajectory of my professional journey. Together, we celebrated many successes, some of which are highlighted in this book. However, I am eternally grateful to you for something even greater. I thank you for introducing me to Phil Stutz. Phil has been nothing short of lifechanging, all thanks to you. Thank you, Alan, for being pivotal in my career and leaving an indelible mark on my heart.

I absolutely must give a shout-out to the legendary Richard Weitz, who has been more than just my agent; he's been a dear friend. Now, let's talk about Richard's unparalleled talent for two things: finding me the best job opportunities and over-obsessing about getting the most envy-inducing Instagram pictures. But in all seriousness, Richard, your unwavering dedication and your enthusiasm for my life and career have been instrumental in my success over the years, and I love you for it.

Similarly, I want to express my appreciation to Brandt Joel, who was part of our team. I want to acknowledge his exceptional care in finding me the right rehabilitation center during a challenging time and connecting me with Elisa Hallerman. The impact of this support cannot be overstated, as it transcends any professional achievement. Also, my friend Aaron Olsen, and all the staff at the Cirque Lodge who were instrumental in my recovery.

To my dear and cherished Disney friend, Al Nassar, words cannot express my gratitude for the remarkable bond we share, spanning an incredible thirty-five-plus years. Not only did you play an instrumental role in crafting an unforgettable proposal to Caitlin but, more importantly, you have been an unwavering presence in my life as a true and trusted friend. Your steadfast support and unwavering loyalty have never faltered, and I hope that I have been able to reciprocate the same level of friendship and devotion. Love you, Al.

Debbie and Glen Bikerstaff, my heart overflows with emotion and gratitude as I think about the extraordinary impact you have had on my life and the lives of my family and friends. When asked, you "show up" not because you have to but because that's just who you are. I've witnessed your commitment to making a difference and your genuine care for those in need, and I'm in awe. You have celebrated alongside us in times of joy and in moments of hardship; you have been there for us in the most profound ways. Debbie and Glen, the word "gratitude" seems insufficient when I think about your role in helping me sober up and see the light. You will always hold a special place in my heart. With love and gratitude, I extend my deepest thanks to both of you.

To the Circle Flirts—Chelsea, Mike, Harold, Karen, Donny, Vanessa, Kent, and OG's Maritza, Daver, Vinnie, Lise, Annabeth, Dan, and all the side miscreants—I didn't talk about our wild adventures in the book because, well, you know why. But I want you to know that I love you all so much. We have had our fair share of fun and parties, and let's also remember our moments of responsible behavior (mostly). Our memories together are the stuff of legends, and I cherish them deeply. So, to my beloved Circle Flirts, thank you for the countless laughs, the unforgettable escapades, and the unbreakable friendship we share. Our bond is a testament to the power of genuine connections and a reminder that life is meant to be lived with love, laughter, and a little bit of mischief. #Noregrets, my friends!

To Marc "Squanto" Alexander. You've always said you wanted to write the first book on me, *Gee, Your Hair Smells Terrific*. I beat you to it. You've been my assistant, producing partner, drinking buddy, and now AA buddy, but mostly you are family to me. Marc, your friendship isn't just a joy in my life, it's a necessity. I love you so very much.

To the extraordinary members of Blackie and the Riff Riff, The Bad Boyz, Papa Doo Run Run, and The Rippers—Gary Griffin, Peter Leinheiser, Lanny Cordola, Randell Kirsch, Chris "Famer" Farmer, Richie Canata, Jimi D. Armstrong, Mark Ward, Don Zirilli, Jim Rush, Krazy Jim Shippey, Neil Morrow, Mark Vogel, John Cowsill, Teddy Andreadis, Mike Turner, Michael Campion, Rick Murphy, The Beach Boys band, Mike Kowolski, Mike Meros, Eddie Carter, Billy Hinshe, Scott Totten, Timmy Bonhomme, Keith Hubacher, Brian Eichenberger, and all the other incredible musicians I've had the privilege of playing with on TV—thank you for the countless years we have spent making music together. You are more than just bandmates; you are my musical inspiration. Your talent, dedication, and sheer brilliance have continuously pushed me to reach new heights both musically and personally. Thank you for making me look better than I am. Just knowing that I was surrounded by some of the greatest musicians in the world has given me the confidence to perform at my best. Making music alongside you is an honor.

To Gerry Beckley and Dewey Bunnell, I want to say how genuinely privileged and honored I've been to have graced stages alongside both of you throughout The Beach Boys/America tours over the years. However, it is our enduring friendship that truly holds the highest distinction in my life. So, with deep appreciation and a heart full of love, I want to thank you both. Our harmonies, laughter, and conversations have shaped me in ways I cannot fully express. In a world where true friendships are rare gems, I consider myself incredibly fortunate to call you both my friends.

To Neil Morrow: If Elvis and Bob's Big Boy had a baby . . . Not only are you incredibly talented, but your heart is as big as they come. The moments we've shared on and off the stage have been nothing short of legendary. As I often sit behind you as your drummer, I get to witness firsthand your musical charisma and your God-given ability to bring joy to anyone lucky enough to hear your voice, which has left me in awe time and time again. But beyond the music, it's your friendship that truly lights up my life. In a world that sometimes feels chaotic and uncertain, having you as a friend brings me a sense of comfort and warmth that is truly invaluable. You're an exceptional human being, and I love you.

Eric Breslow, my unlikely friend, our connection through our shared love for The Beach Boys has blossomed into a true friendship, a testament to the power of music and shared passions. Your support means the world to me.

Brigette, our friendship is one of life's most beautiful surprises; you are more than just a friend, you're an inspiration to me and Caitlin and Billy, a shining light of selflessness in a world that sometimes forgets the meaning of that word. Your willingness to always be there, not just for us, but for anyone who needs it, is a testament to the beautiful soul that you are. You give, asking for nothing in return, and it's that selflessness that makes you an extraordinary human being.

To Stacy Fike Butler, my lifelong friend: As I look back on the countless memories we've shared, from our childhood days living just a few doors down to the present, I am overwhelmed with love and gratitude for the remarkable person you are. Our dads were best friends, just as our moms were, and that has forged a friendship between us that is truly unique. Through all the ups and downs we've faced, you have remained steadfast, offering support and understanding without question. You have been a true friend—a friend who surpasses any girlfriend in my life. As we journey through life, I want you to know that I will always be here for you, just as you have been for me. Our friendship is a rare and cherished treasure I will forever hold close. Thank you, Stacy.

Daniel and Tabatha, who would have thought our casual encounters at Disney would blossom into lifelong friendships? What started as mere acquaintances quickly evolved into a genuine bond that defies time and distance. Here's to many more Disney-filled escapades, heartwarming conversations, and a friendship that will continue to grow and flourish in the most enchanting way possible.

Taylor, from the moment you joined our family, it was evident that you had a unique ability to connect with Billy on a deep level. Your genuine love, patience, and nurturing spirit have created a safe and joyful environment where he can flourish and grow. Your dedication to his well-being and development is truly remarkable. Your role extends far beyond being a nanny; you have become a role model, a mentor, and a source of inspiration for him (and for his mom and dad, too). We are truly blessed to have you as part of our family's journey. We are forever grateful for the role you play and the positive impact you have made on our family.

To Ken Hada, my rock, my Buddha, my unwavering companion—from the very first time we crossed paths in junior high, I knew there was something special about our connection. From Pup N Taco, Suds the magic clown, music, drums, Ireland, marching band, photography, Kepa, Kent, Hadulous, Gramps, Sets, Universal, and Knott's to today, your kindness, quiet yet powerful, has been a beacon of light during both the calm and stormy moments of my life. They simply don't make friends like you. The impact you have had on my life is immeasurable. Thank you, my dear friend. The bond we share is a treasure I hold dear.

Dear Ann Masterson, I knew I had found someone truly special from the first time you worked your magic on me. Through the years, you have made me look good and emphasized that inner beauty is important. You have become a trusted confidant and friend. Thank you, love you.

To my book agent, Esther Newberg, who I constantly told I would never write a book, I'm glad you made me wrong. Thank you. Also, to my newest team, Brad and Eddie. ROCK STARS!

James Melia, my first editor at Holt—thank you for getting us up and off the ground and then passing me to the head honcho: the classy, extremely bright Amy Einhorn. Amy, you allowed me to miss every single deadline and were there for me many times, talking me off the proverbial author ledge and giving me the courage to finish. (I think I finished.)

To the hardworking, talented team at Holt, especially Lori

Kusatzky, who I drove crazy with deadlines and details. Through it all, you've been positive and encouraging and worked tireless hours to make my book the best it could be. Thank you! Also, designer Meryl Levavi, who worked so hard to bring the look and style I had in my head to light. To Hannah Campbell, ace proofreader and corrector of my many, many mistakes: thank you for combing through, I know it was a lot. To the incredible publicity and marketing team, Caitlin Mulrooney-Lyski, Marian Brown, Caitlin O'Shaughnessy, Laura Flavin, and Sonja Flancher. By the time you read this, our book will be a best seller thanks to you! (It better be.)

To Tony Shepard, you are not just a "dream maker" who has gifted me with unforgettable Disney memories that my family and I will cherish for a lifetime, you are also a genuine friend, always ready to open your home, heart, and private chef, creating the most extraordinary Orlando dinners. For all that and more, I am eternally grateful. May our journey continue to be filled with magical moments, delectable meals, and a friendship that knows no bounds. Thank you, Tony, for the joy, love, and warmth you have brought into my life.

To Debbe Magnusen, I am honored to have been part of Project Cuddle and forever grateful for the incredible work we have accomplished together. Your unwavering dedication and passion have inspired me and led to the salvation of hundreds of precious babies from the heartbreaking fate of abandonment. Love you.

To The Beach Boys Crew, a profound and heartfelt thank-you goes out to each and every one of you, both now and throughout the years. As the saying goes, "You're only as good as your crew," and it is clear that our collective greatness shines brightly because of the dedication and talent you bring to each and every show.

To Steve Campeas and Tanya Benton, I am deeply grateful for your unwavering dedication and expertise in managing my finances over the years. Your expertise, professionalism, trustworthiness, and commitment to safeguarding my financial well-being have given me peace of mind, knowing that I can confidently provide for my family and friends for a lifetime. Thank you.

If I've forgotten anyone, I'll catch you on the next round. XO

ABOUT THE AUTHOR

JOHN STAMOS, a three-time Emmy nominee, has earned his reputation as a highly regarded actor and producer throughout his over forty-year career in television, film, and on Broadway. His rise to fame began with his role in *General Hospital* and he has since captivated viewers with his diverse performances in *Big Shot*, *You*, *ER*, *Grandfathered*, *Full House*, and *Fuller House* and onstage in *Cabaret*, *Bye Bye Birdie*, and Gore Vidal's *The Best Man*. Beyond acting, Stamos is a skilled musician, collaborating with The Beach Boys since 1985. He also serves as an ambassador for Childhelp.

THE KEY AND THE KEYHOLE

ANTONIO: A RICH, CREAMY SPANISH SOUP

BANG

NEGOTIATE MY BALLS

DOWN THE RABBIT HOLE

DISNEY GIRL

MERCY

CAKE

GOD ONLY KNOWS

BLUNDER DOWN UNDER

SATANS AND SAINT

THESE ARE THE GOOD OLD DAYS

THE REAL BEST MAN